Special Issue

Econophonia: Music, Value,

and Forms of Life

Edited by

Gavin Steingo and Jairo Moreno

boundary 2

an international journal

of literature and culture

Volume 43, Number 1

February 2016

Duke University Press

boundary 2

boundary 2
an international journal of literature and culture

Founding Editors Robert Kroetsch and William V. Spanos

Editor Paul A. Bové
   Abigail Lind, Assistant to the Editor

Managing Editor Margaret A. Havran

Contents

Introduction

Gavin Steingo and Jairo Moreno

The question of value might seem beyond the pale in cases of sound and music. Sound and music are objects of immense accumulation, appreciation, exploration, and investment, not just for the human species but also among other species, and indeed the world. Sound simply *is*, its existence is inexhaustible, and remarkable things happen in and through it—end of story.

Why, then, the question of value? Divesting sound and music from naive notions of intrinsic value, the essays here examine heterogeneous modalities by which sound and music produce value in and as history, politics, and ontology. In turn, the very question of what sound and music are— of what constitutes them, as well as what they constitute—is precisely what is at stake. Amy Cimini and Jairo Moreno wonder about the political forms emerging when sound and music are entrusted to do something for someone—for which they propose the term *fiduciary*—and in particular the function of aesthesis in believing *that* one senses and that *what* one senses is true. Bill Dietz and Gavin Steingo reconsider the classical political challenges of music in relation to collectivities and crowds. What are the political

boundary 2 43:1 (2016)   DOI 10.1215/01903659-3340613   © 2016 by Duke University Press

stakes of a form that toggles between contagious paroxysm and the radical privatization of aesthesis? They propose "civility" as a means for regulating extreme violence and explore the contours of a musical experimentalism that might participate in this regulative politics. Naomi Waltham-Smith adds an acoustic dimension to Giorgio Agamben's idea that there is a potentiality *of* potentiality: the potential *not to*. Against the backdrop of a notion of sound as something that resists particular identities and communal belonging, Waltham-Smith addresses two major strains in twentieth-century philosophy: the refusal of presence in French deconstruction (Jacques Derrida, Jean-Luc Nancy) and the refusal of biopolitics in recent Italian thought (Agamben, Antonio Negri, Paolo Virno).

Ana María Ochoa Gautier evaluates the ecological turn in music studies, revealing in the concern to preserve both music and the environment a pervasive inability to think nature in the plural. Proposing the notion of "acoustic multinaturalism," she makes a powerful argument to heed the call of earlier anthropological and ethnomusicological work, particularly the structuralism of Claude Lévi-Strauss and Steven Feld's acoustemology. From another perspective, Gary Tomlinson invites us to think a beginning, before the emergence of hominins, through a critique of a recently rediscovered avatar for musical power: affect. He argues that semiosis is irreducible to causal covariance between two entities and, following Charles Sanders Peirce, that semiosis begins only when a relation of "secondness" develops into a relation of "thirdness," that is, into a relation to a relation. Tomlinson then brings this insight to bear upon recent speculative realist thinking, detecting certain limitations in object-oriented ontology, and supplementing Quentin Meillassoux's mathematization of being with a Darwinian historicization of life.

Rethinking the difficult question of black music in the United States, Ronald Radano returns to Karl Marx in the company of the New South historiography to argue that black musical value derives from the anomaly of musical production within the context of slave labor. The anomalous sounding out of slaves in music and in song became an unobtainable kernel existing alongside and within the body of the slave-as-property, mysteriously "animating" the body and harboring a secret. Peter Szendy, in turn, takes us to the marketplace of pianistic technicities to find the Marx Brothers giving Karl Marx's theory of fetishism both a sound track and a theatrical staging. He posits an inherent relationship between fetishism and music, in the sense that the former names the possibility of infinite exchange that the latter presupposes. But at the same time, both music and fetish suggest the possibility of a certain coagulation: a freeze-frame or stuck key where eyes and ears grind to a halt. Rosalind Morris listens to Marx in detail, or rather to Marx as a listener and transcriber of workers. In "The Working Day" chapter of *Capital*, Morris detects a tension between dialectic and dialect, a tension between the voice of The Worker who confronts capital head-on and the voices of actual workers. A tension, yes, but also an aporia—and one, Morris suggests, that must necessarily be confronted by any political project that hopes to avoid collapsing into a mere aggregate of what already exists.

Each essay here, in its own way, reveals the profound ambivalences that any thinking of sound and music must necessarily confront. Whether the challenge is posed in terms of politics, ethics, history, epistemology, or ontology, sound and music are called upon to simultaneously complicate the problem and provide an exit route. But this route is immediately registered as a lure, and the optimism of the will flails against the pessimism of the intellect. Along this path, and through a series of turns, the value of sound and music becomes distantly audible, at once entrusting, civilizing, potentiating, relating, animating, freezing, and promising. And then: caught in these multiple snares, sound withdraws. From its completely remote place, utterly dark and utterly silent, sound severs all relations and attachments. Having done so, it begins multiplying those attachments once again.

Inexhaustible Sound and Fiduciary Aurality

Amy Cimini and Jairo Moreno

Introduction

Value, wrote Karl Marx, is content-less and simple (*inhaltlos und einfach*).[1] Then, adopting the characteristic satirical tone of the English poet Samuel Butler, he paraphrased, "'The value of a thing / Is just as much as it will bring.'"[2]

By Butler's measure, sound and music bring quite a lot, appearing to hold inherent value by virtue of their very existence and by the irrefutable fact that they suffuse the species, the world, and, to the ancients, the cosmos. Sound and music seem to be inexhaustible. Their ubiquity startles. But Marx would insist that whatever value attends to them results from a history that they help produce; the content and complexity of their value cannot be isolated from their historicity.

It should be fairly uncontroversial to observe that for humans, sense

1. Karl Marx, "Preface to the First Edition," in *Capital: A Critique of Political Economy*, vol. 1, trans. Ben Fowkes, with an intro. by Ernest Mandel (New York: Penguin, 1976), 90 (translation modified).
2. Samuel Butler, *Hudibras*, part 2, canto 1, lines 465–66, in Marx, *Capital*, 126.

boundary 2 43:1 (2016)   DOI 10.1215/01903659-3340625   © 2016 by Duke University Press

perception of sound and music historically adduces the kinds of content and complexity that constitute its value—for example, the long history of what constitutes dissonance and consonance, whether their acoustic, physio-acoustic, psycho-acoustic, and aesthetic character. Let's call this contingent, historicist notion of sound and music, and their perception, the *relational* posit. But it is also the case that the production of specific practices supported by any particular valuation requires that some fundamental kernel of human experience be grounded in the existence of sound as such. Let's call this existence as such of sound the *quasi-realist* posit.

Taking these two posits as epistemic and ontological presuppositions, we wish to consider their dynamic interaction in the production of value. On the relational side, with Barbara Herrnstein Smith, we propose that the value of sound and music is equivalent to the "experience [of it] in relation to the total economy of our existence."[3] Of particular interest is Smith's explicit recognition of a general economy. Within that general economy, we argue for the importance of *belief* and *faith* in any correlation of sound and music with the aural, understood as a general aesthesis where sound and music remain privileged but not exclusive domains.[4] The quasi-realist posit compels belief as a unidirectional commitment of the aural to the truth of sound's existence.[5] The relational posit establishes faith, a "symbolic pact" and "binding engagement" between two parties: humans, on the one hand, and sound and music, on the other.[6] Crucial to this correlation is the assumption that sound and music, as well our capacity to engage them in and as sense perception, are inexhaustible. Music studies, after all, remains generally unconcerned with the givenness of its object:

3. Barbara Herrnstein Smith, *Contingencies of Value: Alternative Perspectives for Critical Theory* (Cambridge, MA: Harvard University Press, 1988), 16. Our main object (the sonorous) goes beyond but also includes the category of the artwork anchoring her analysis.
4. For us, sound constitutes the general field of which music is a particular configuration; whatever privilege is given to this configuration comes from the authors we discuss.
5. Our use of the term *quasi realism* bears no connection to its use in moral philosophy. We refer instead to a realist presupposition (that sound is), which, in all cases analyzed here, also must be *for* us. Readers may recognize the influence here of speculative realist thought, which we do not directly engage here. The term *quasi realist* bears resemblance to the contingent correlationalism proposed by Quentin Meillassoux, *After Finitude: An Essay on the Necessity of Contingency*, trans. Ray Brassier (London: Continuum, 2008).
6. Slavoj Žižek, *On Belief* (London: Routledge, 2001), 109. Here Žižek glosses Octave Mannoni, *Clefs pur l'imaginaire* (Paris: Éditions du Seil, 1968). We borrow from Bill Dietz and Gavin Steingo's piece "Experiments in Civility," in this issue, the organization of the argument along two "posits."

"music." Inexhaustibility, we argue, finds a dynamic axis in the quasi-realist and relational posits.

We gather the dynamic interaction of belief and faith in correlating sound and music with the aural under the general name of *the fiduciary*. Emphasizing the conjunction of faith with fidelity in the shared root *fides*, the fiduciary defines an arrangement in which one party in need of something entrusts a capable other to provide, fulfill, and satisfy that need.[7] This juridical logic, we propose, is at stake in how sound, music, and sense perception function as historically important forms, figurations, and modes of mediation for politics. The fiduciary, in other words, structures the production of value, for music, sound, and sense perception, according to their capacity to faithfully work on behalf of something else.

This essay maps three distinct configurations of the fiduciary in order to query what, exactly, must be made of music, sound, and the aural to work on behalf of political claims within its protocols: first, the turn, in 1990s musicology, toward embodiment and performativity; second, a more recent, interdisciplinary "affective turn"; and, in conversation with these two, the phenomenology of Maurice Merleau-Ponty, construed broadly as "a philosophy for which the world is always 'already there' as an inalienable presence."[8] Critically, each case points toward what we might call a "radical" contradiction: if, on the one hand, music and sound and the aural appear to be inexhaustible and very much like the nonrival goods of modern economies—their use by anyone does not impinge on the use by others—on the other hand, the affordances perceived and actively pursued in and through them appear to be limited or at least to demand that they be limited to carry out a particular purpose or use. This contradiction is itself the effect of an overlap between the quasi-realist and relational posits in the shared, yet unacknowledged, realist presumption of an indefinite inexhaustibility of the sonorous.

The strong argument of this essay is that the value of sound, music, and the aural are produced and maintained by the contradictory play of the

---

7. For a concise history of the fiduciary, see John F. Mariani, Christopher W. Kammerer, and Nancy Guffey-Landers, "Understanding Fiduciary Duty," *Florida Bar Journal* 84, no. 3 (2010): 20–45. Definitions of loyalty and care are drawn from *Black's Law Dictionary*, 6th ed. (New York: Springer, 1990), 625.

8. Maurice Merleau-Ponty, *The Phenomenology of Perception*, trans. Colin Smith (Routledge: London, 2002), i; cited in Richard Schusterman, "The Silent, Limping Body of Philosophy," in *The Cambridge Companion to Merleau-Ponty*, ed. Taylor Carman and Mark B. N. Hansen (Cambridge: Cambridge University Press, 2005), 151–80, esp. 159.

quasi-realist and relational posits in the fiduciary. Assessing the fiduciary structure of what we will call the "the performative" and "the affective" thematizes variegated challenges for harnessing music, sound, and the aural in the political. Both cases (differently) participate in what David Harvey has called an "extraordinary efflorescence of interest in 'the body' as the grounding for all sorts of theoretical inquiry" over the last thirty years.[9] If, as Harvey notes, "the manner of this 'return' to the body is crucial for determining how values and meanings are to be constructed and understood," we assess how the fiduciary structures two "manners of return," in the performative and the affective, underscoring "the body," in Harvey's scare quotes, as the inscription of an ineluctable fiduciary historicity.[10] In other words, the logics of fiduciary confidence structuring our cases elucidate how the sonorous inflects the production of value and meaning for the body and, in turn, how this informs the political wagers made in the name of both.

The body's exposure to the fiduciary's "radical contradiction" comes into focus through a comparative assessment of how each case composes the givenness of its quasi-realist posit. We begin with one such posit in Maurice Merleau-Ponty's late unfinished *The Visible and the Invisible*, which finds the fiduciary at work within aesthesis itself. Nothing less than the world itself is "given" in what Merleau-Ponty calls the perceptual faith (*la foi perceptive*), a pre-reflective, somatic (though ocularcentric) certitude that we encounter an actually existing world and not some ensemble of mental representations.[11] As an introductory frame for the challenges that attend quasi-realist claims in our further cases, however, we discern contradictions in the perceptual faith that efface the very givenness it also asserts. Things correlate with but also resist the perceiving body, which Merleau-Ponty terms the "in-itself-for-us," a human-centered perspectivism in which things remain "irreducible to our perspective on them" but that, as Graham Harman remarks, stops short of a realism in which their perspective on each other matters.[12]

---

9. David Harvey, *Spaces of Hope* (Berkeley: University of California Press, 2000), 97.
10. Harvey, *Spaces of Hope*, 98.
11. Maurice Merleau-Ponty, *The Visible and the Invisible*, trans. Alphonso Lingis (1968; repr., Evanston, IL: Northwestern University Press, 2000); *Le visible et l'invisible*, ed. Claude Lefort (Paris: Éditions Gallimard, 1964). Hereafter, these works are cited parenthetically as *VI/vi*.
12. Ted Toadvine, *Merleau-Ponty's Philosophy of Nature* (Evanston, IL: Northwestern University Press, 2009), 111. Hereafter, this work is cited parenthetically as *M-PPN*. Graham Harman, *Guerilla Metaphysics: Phenomenology and the Carpentry of Things* (Chicago: Open Court, 2005), 49–53.

Not to be mistaken for "faith in the sense of decision," the perceptual faith is with us "the moment we open our eyes," asserting "in the sense of what is before any position" that "the world is what we see" (*VI*, 17/*vi*, 3). Our distinction between belief and faith, however, discerns two interlocking wagers at stake within the perceptual faith's insistence on the world's givenness: first, a belief *that we see* and, second, a trust that *we see truly.* The perceptual faith couples these wagers, in the manner of the fiduciary, but also obscures their distinction in and as perception itself. Merleau-Ponty writes,

> It is our experience, prior to every opinion, of inhabiting the world by our body . . . without there being need to choose or even to distinguish between the assurance of seeing and the assurance of seeing the true, because in principle they are one and the same thing— faith, therefore, and not knowledge, since the world is here not separated from our hold on it, since rather than affirmed, it is taken for granted, rather than disclosed, it is non-dissimulated, non-refuted. (*VI*, 48/*vi*, 28)

The perceptual faith secures the identity of belief with faith, here, at the exacting price of pre-reflective silence.[13] As "a deep-seated set of 'mute opinions' [*opinions muettes*] implicated in our lives," the perceptual faith remains constitutively unable to discern its fiduciary character even as it (silently) declares to "know itself to be beyond proof" (*VI*, 17/*vi*, 3; *VI*, 48/ *vi*, 28). At once passive and dynamic, this silence both inhabits and undermines reflection.[14] We would not have the *cogito*, for example, if the perceptual faith had not already supplied the criteria for distinguishing true from false that drive the method of doubt—a method that paradoxically reclaims pre-reflective certitude as a "product of its own analysis" without actually explaining it.[15]

By resting in silence, however, the perceptual faith dissimulates what Roberto Esposito calls, after Jacques Derrida, its immunitary aporia.[16] Perception menaces faith with "non-faith" (*la non-foi*) from within,

13. For a broader account of silence in both Merleau-Ponty and Husserl, see Schusterman, "The Silent, Limping Body of Philosophy," 151–80; and Toadvine, *M-PPN*, 128.
14. "Reflection cannot 'go beyond' this opening to the world, except by making use of the power it owes to the opening itself" (*M-PPN*, 121–22); see also Maurice Merleau-Ponty, *Signs*, trans. Richard C. McCleary (Evanston, IL: Northwestern University Press, 2009), 161.
15. Schusterman, "Silent, Limping Body," 160.
16. Roberto Esposito, *Bíos: Biopolitics and Philosophy*, trans. with intro. by Timothy

even though it is precisely as perception that faith is taken for granted. In the natural attitude, after all, perception remains duplicitous. "The natural man," Merleau-Ponty explains, "thinks at the same time that his perception enters the things and that it is formed on this side of his body."[17] We are "restricted to our perspective on the world as a perceiving individual" but remain certain that that world is "pre-reflectively real" even as it exceeds or resists us, remaining irreducible to our perspective on it (*M-PPN*, 123).[18] Seesawing between idealism and a highly attenuated realism, the perceptual faith would seem to give way to an undecidable play between "belief and incredulity so closely bound up that we always find one in the other" (*VI*, 48/*vi*, 28).

Rather than capitulate to this opposition, pre-reflective silence stubbornly propounds their coimplication in the "in-itself-for-us" (elaborated, we'll show, through the notion of *chiasm*). This paradoxical construction affirms things' necessary correlation with perceiving subjects but poses as a rejection or refusal the many perspectives that remain inaccessible within that correlation. This refusal registers, however, only as a relation to the perceiver. A bulwark against a more robust realism, the "in-itself" of Merleau-Ponty's "in-itself-for-us" cannot be for nothing and nobody. Prior to "the moment we open our eyes," that is, the "in-itself" cannot be given. In the end, the perceptual faith offers nothing more or less than evidence for a veritable empirical transcendental.

Campbell (Minneapolis: University of Minnesota Press, 2008), and *Immunitas: The Protection and Negation of Life*, trans. Zakiya Hanafi (Cambridge: Polity, 2011). See also Timothy Campbell's translator's introduction, "Bíos, Immunity, Life: The Thought of Roberto Esposito," in Esposito, *Bíos*.

17. "Natural man" refers here to the natural attitude. As Merleau-Ponty elaborates, "Everything comes to pass as though my power to reach the things and my power to entrench myself in phantasms only came one with the other; even more: as though the access to the world were only a face of a withdrawal and this retreat to the margin of the world a servitude and another expression of my natural power to enter it" (*VI*, 23/*vi*, 8).

18. As Renaud Barabas notes, Merleau-Ponty registers the importance of carving a path between realism and idealism in his early, more subject-centered work in *The Phenomenology of Perception*. "To link these perspectives," Barabas notes, "it is necessary to disclose a sense of being that is neither that of a things nor of a consciousness" (Renaud Barabas, "A Phenomenology of Life," in *The Cambridge Companion to Merleau-Ponty*, 206–30, esp. 212).

The Embodied Performative

As a framing gambit, our engagement with the perceptual faith queries what must be made of the fiduciary structure of aesthesis when the cases we call "the performative" and "the affective" broker political aspirations in and through the correlation of sound with aurality. Like the "in-itself-for-us," the givenness of 1990s musicology's quasi realism—"music"—also suppresses immunitary dynamics within its fiduciary confidence. We pick up, here, with an early moment in Harvey's efflorescent "return to the body," to trace how the body's fiduciary historicity is ramified in and through the value of sound, music, and the aural to the (self-)critical aspirations of 1990s musicology.

The fiduciary confidence of mid-1990s musicology reflects a wager that Robyn Wiegman diagnoses in fields based on identity knowledge after the New Left: "if only we find the right discourse, object of study, or analytic tool," she writes, "our critical practice will be adequate to the political commitments that inspire it."[19] Against a universalizing Western humanism, musicology would join other burgeoning identity knowledges to assert that "bodies embody knowledge and hence that different bodies would . . . liberate subordinate knowledges and restore to the province of history and culture various groups denied entry to official narration."[20] With a productive antagonist in René Descartes's notorious mind-body dualism, musicology's intervention on behalf of bodies found its (presumed) denigration congealed in normative methodological comportments: as scholarly practices detached from musical works and naturalized under divisions of gendered labor, where composers were marked masculine and performers feminine.

Reckoning the body as a medium for upturning these entrenched disciplinary values, 1990s musicology plied a narrow but forceful prescription: listening and performing bodies "know" music in a way that minds cannot, and as active, knowing agents, bodies refuse any normative social order founded on the autonomy of the *cogito*.[21] We've chosen the hybrid term *embodied performative* for this fiduciary wager in order to indicate,

---

19. Robyn Wiegman, *Object Lessons* (Durham, NC: Duke University Press, 2012), 3.
20. Wiegman, *Object Lessons*, 118.
21. The representative literature of this turn is extensive, and we do not aim at a comprehensive overview here. Outside of the historical study of music, other allied fields (e.g., ethnomusicology, music theory) are also engaged in a turn toward the body. For critical engagement with this turn across the music fields, see Amy Cimini, "Baruch Spinoza and the Matter of Music: Toward a New Practice of Theorizing Musical Bodies" (PhD diss., New York University, 2011).

first, the importance of embodied practices and knowledges and, second, the influence of Judith Butler's work on this musicological turn toward music conceptualized as bodies in action, for which we use the expression "musicking."[22] This musicological body found its locus classicus, after all, in the musical performance.

To make good on this commitment to bodies, however, musicking could not be conceptualized as an object or a thing. Rather, the strength that musicking seemed to lend the coordination of embodiment with knowledge lay with its processual, action-oriented, and temporal character. It was method, critical dispositive, and analytical tool all at once. However, this fiduciary claim harbored a number of basic tensions, suppressed in 1990s musicology, so that musicking's axiomatic value could appear under the terms of the performative. We identify four tensions, here: disidentification, political ambivalence, iterability, and dematerialization.

Butler's original formulation is fundamentally constructivist. Gender results from the repeated exercise of social rituals linked to various apparatuses. Through repetition, heteronormativity appears natural and materially grounded. She finds the possibility for the subversion of hegemonic orders in the requirement that performances of identity be constantly reiterated: no identity is ever fully and securely established. In her words,

> Gender is the repeated stabilization of the body, a set of repeated acts within a highly rigid regulatory frame that congeal over time to produce the appearance of substance, of a natural sort of being. A political genealogy of gender ontologies . . . will deconstruct the substantive appearance of gender into its constitutive acts and locate . . . those acts within the compulsory frames set by the various forces that police the social appearance of gender.[23]

Repetition is symptomatic of a constitutive gap between society and the individual psyche and between constraint and agency. This gap means that the subversion of any and all socioculturally scripted identities constitutes an ineradicable possibility.

---

22. The redundant character of our heading is strategic, reflecting a tension between performance as something corporeally bound and performativity as relationally constituted. "Musicking" was proposed by Christopher Small, *Musicking: The Meanings of Performance and Listening* (Middletown, CT: Wesleyan University Press, 1998); Judith Butler, *Gender Trouble: Feminism and the Subversion of Identity* (New York: Routledge, 1990); and Judith Butler, *Bodies that Matter: On the Discursive Limits of "Sex"* (New York: Routledge, 1993).
23. Butler, *Gender Trouble*, 43–44.

In her important 1994 "Feminist Theory, Music Theory," Suzanne Cusick inserts this subversive gap between performing bodies and formalist analysis, using her own performance of J. S. Bach's "Aus tiefer Not" at the organ as a case study.[24] The harrowing technical demands that constitute the work's audible integrity for the analyst comprise, for the performer, inaudible interpretive cues accessible exclusively to a playing body. In this dualistic economy, that is, the body's subjugation to the (analytic) mind is redeemed in and as a mode of musical meaning that exceeds it.

Retaining "musical meaning" as a measure for her success marks, in Cusick's performative, a practice of disidentification that operates firmly within the disciplinary coordinates of musicology and its more traditional components: musical works, conventions of text setting, standard historiographies of tonal complexity, and so on. An effort, more broadly, to grant positive value to the constitutive failure of all identification would have had to extend to playing bodies *and* analytic practices alike, while a genuinely antidualist critique might have to reckon analysis as a practice of bodily discipline. Instead, embodied performativity retained a dualistic core in its politics, engaging a politics of counterrepresentation within musicology, without questioning its hegemonic status in the wider area of music studies. Cusick follows Butler to the letter; Butler replaces Louis Althusser's analytic of institutional apparatuses "with a concern for the interpersonal and intrapsychic dynamics of identity conflict."[25]

In this case, musicking's value is split into two parts: the immanence of its agency and the indexical function by which, beyond that action, it works as social countersignification. This split is not only internal to the logic of the performative but also marks its political ambivalence, for no index can ever be permanently affixed: action "a" may point to nonnormative identity "b," but it may always be taken as identifying "c," "d," "e," and so on. George Yúdice remarks that the performative cuts across the wider social field of force as "the processes by which identities and the entities of social reality [were] constituted by repeated approximations of models (i.e., the normative) as well as by those remainders ('constitutive exclusions')

24. J. S. Bach, *Clavierubung*, Part III, PWV 686; Suzanne G. Cusick, "Feminist Theory, Music Theory, and the Mind/Body Problem," *Perspectives of New Music* 32, no. 1 (1994): 8–27. She writes, "For these few terrifying measures . . . , one might as well be floating in mid-air, so confused and constantly shifting is the body's center of gravity"; and yet, "neither harmonic nor contrapuntal analysis would identify this little passage as critical to the work's meaning."
25. Geoff Boucher, "The Politics of Performativity: A Critique of Judith Butler," *Parrhesia* no. 1 (2006): 112–41, esp. 114.

that fall short."[26] These "constitutive exclusions," however, encompass the political spectrum, not only those self-declared as progressive. The performative could not delimit its effectiveness to the progressive and dissensual initiatives of socially and politically marginalized sectors. Other groups claiming exclusion, such as music theorists with interests in abstract formalism, for example, could equally claim to disidentify with the philological and positivist mainstream of precritical musicology as well as with the residual historicism of embodied performativity activists.[27] Everyone, that is, always already performs.

Together, disidentification and political ambivalence ratchet up the fiduciary's "radical contradiction": the embodied performative's activist wagers, that is, must restrict an object whose value, in that wager, resides precisely with its inexhaustibility. The axiomatic value of musicking rests tendentiously on this contradiction and its iterability in the fiduciary.

Music demands insistent replay. However, in the fiduciary, trust in musicking's capacity to act on behalf of other modes of existence must be continually sustained and secured, but constant repetition without profit (affective, political, social) can as much compel belief and indeed sustain faith as it can exhaust belief and erode faith. By the same token, accumulation might well compel both belief and a slackening of the cause. Iteration, in short, threatens *fides* from within as a condition of its reliability in the fiduciary. This is the performative's immunitary aporia.

Although the embodied performative tailored its intervention to an academic discipline where some form of institutional accumulation can act as a political expedient, this demand for repetition, in the fiduciary, raises questions regarding how it can oppose an economy of accumulation that might establish a new hegemon and risk institutional co-optation.[28] Butler seeks to ward off the specters of accumulation and closure by appealing to deconstructive conceptions of emerging subjectivity and temporality. In her words,

26. George Yúdice, *The Expediency of Culture: Uses of Culture in the Global Era* (Durham, NC: Duke University Press, 2004), 31.
27. Cimini and Moreno discuss the partial subversive character of splinter groups from musicology's mainstream as "divergences," practices that, being the result of internal critique, cannot be "an origin," only "a divergence from one," as Wiegman says of queer theory. See Amy Cimini and Jairo Moreno, "On Diversity," *GAMUT* 2, no. 1 (2009): 111–96; Wiegman, *Object Lessons*, 121.
28. Compare to Harvey's elegant critique in "The Body as an Accumulation Strategy," chap. 6 of his *Spaces of Hope*.

Performativity cannot be understood outside of a process of iterability, a regularized and constrained repetition of norms. And this repetition is not performed *by* a subject; this repetition is what enables a subject and constitutes the temporal condition for the subject. This iterability implies that "performance" is not a singular "act" or event, but a ritualized production, a ritual reiterated under and through constraint, under and through the force of prohibition and taboo, with the threat of ostracism and even death controlling and compelling the shape of the production, but not, I will insist, determining it fully in advance.[29]

Butler sets constructivism and determinism dialectically here. Thus, if normativity and the law demand that subjects perform in accordance with their dictates, the constructivist position counters this demand by disclosing how its compulsory repetition signifies that subjects are constituted by the demand, not prior to it. Subjectivity is not an either/or proposition between construction and determinism but rather an emerging effect of their combination. This was Butler's brilliant insight.

If gender is materialized in and as this compulsion to repeat, then no matter how progressive the political goals, the subversion of hegemonic gender and sexuality formations remains, also, partly determined by this compulsion, opening the performative to political ambivalence. Exposing gender's apparently essential, natural inherence in bodies as a ritualized iteration of biopolitical norms also required a radical desubstantialization of the body. That is, to eliminate the metaphysics of substance that buttresses heteronormativity and "the liberal conception of the (sexed) person," the performative aimed to short-circuit any "process of materialization that stabilizes over time to produce the effect of boundary, fixity, and surface we call matter."[30]

Opposing materialization (and naturalization of gender qua essence) entailed a remarkable ontological gamble. As Elizabeth A. Povinelli puts it, "Butler's work is often presented as an exemplary case of how the critique of metaphysics of substance, intended to radically destabilize normative governance, has unintentionally led to a radical desubstantialization of the body and world" (*EA*, 106). True, as she clarifies, Butler distinguished between a traditional fixed ontology of substantial anatomy as it served

29. Butler, *Bodies that Matter*, 95.
30. Butler, *Bodies that Matter*, 9. See also Elizabeth A. Povinelli, *Economies of Abandonment: Social Belonging and Endurance in Late Capitalism* (Durham, NC: Duke University Press, 2011), 107. Hereafter, this work is cited parenthetically as *EA*.

the governance of normatively sexed persons and the qualifications of self-identical substance by gender (*EA*, 107). Nonetheless, Povinelli remarks, when resistance to biopolitical governance became coupled with decentering substance, "everything took on an almost infinite plasticity," with no clear discernment of what was susceptible to pernicious biopolitical power or "what aspects of body and matter are implicated at different levels of social, political, and cultural analysis" (*EA*, 107, 110). In her words, "to argue that there is not an immovable and unmoving substance which social and cultural discourses merely qualify is not to say that there is a strict correspondence between the forms of governance and the materialities they excrete and extrude" (*EA*, 108). No matter how efficacious its performative deployment, in other words, the "discursive construction of materiality shapes, cuts and assembles a given formation in the material world" but never does so without leaving some "unintegrated, errant aspect of materiality" that must persist as a condition of possibility for further iteration (*EA*, 109).

The musicological embodied performative thus harbors what we call a dialectic of dematerialization: though it requires music, it reduces music's materiality to the act of its performance.[31] Cusick, for example, upholds a selective materiality centered on the musicking body. In a more extreme fashion, Elisabeth LeGuin advocates a "carnal musicology" where instrumental practice constitutes not just reciprocity but a "real relationship" between composer and performer within a metaphysics of transhistorical communication, itself encumbered by Judeo-Christian concepts of fleshly incarnation.[32] Both scholars' subjectivities, more precisely, may be emergent and coexistent with their production in performances, in accordance with Butler's stipulations, but this has as a condition of possibility the existence of "music." This is why theirs must necessarily be a performance *of something*, indifferent to Butler's stipulation about performance.[33]

31. This can be read not as a reduction or replacement but as a displacement of materiality to material processes that replace the idealism of consciousness, as Butler might put it. See Rey Chow, "The Elusive Material: What the Dog Doesn't Understand," in *New Materialisms: Ontology, Agency, and Politics*, ed. Diana Coole and Samantha Frost (Durham, NC: Duke University Press, 2010), 221–33, esp. 230–31.

32. ". . . the sense of reciprocity in this process of identification is not entirely wistful or metaphorical, but functions as a real relationship." Elisabeth LeGuin, *Boccherini's Body: An Essay in Carnal Musicology* (Berkeley: University of California Press, 2006), 14. See also Tracy McMullen, "Corpo-Realities: Keepin' It Real in 'Music and Embodiment' Scholarship," *Current Musicology* no. 82 (Fall 2006): 61–83.

33. "Performativity is neither free play nor theatrical self-presentation; nor can it be equated with performance" (Butler, *Bodies that Matter*, 95).

This presumed stability, for music, produces two effects in this dialectic of dematerialization. First, there is subsumption of music's distributed materiality within solely embodied processes. And second, following Povinelli, there is confusion about how the inexhaustible perdurance of music implicates bodily expenditure at different levels of social, cultural, and political analysis. Even within the narrow sphere of European art music from the mid-eighteenth century, music's ontology is complexly distributed. It encompasses various associated modes of inscription (sketches, scores, copies), performances (imagined or not), instrumental and vocal pedagogies, instrument making, and various human networks of production and reception (composers, audiences, critics, patrons, etc.).[34] Embodied performativity privileges one form and modality out of this complex, spiriting others away just as it reduces other materialities of musical performance.

Unless one would accept the idea that "it is performativity all the way down"—and we do not—for the embodied performative to *persist* in the relentlessness of punctual performances and their endless iterations, something somehow has to *endure* materially and *subsist* temporally between those performances.[35] We believe that the very fact that music studies remained unconcerned with the givenness of its object—music—was no oversight but rather the condition of possibility for its advocacy of the performative *as* performance.

And so, in place of a *heteronomy* that might well have unsettled the centrality of "music" to musicking in order to theorize and enact a distributed agency of musical materiality (including, to be sure, that of the performer), advocates of the performative invoked instead *heterogeneity*, particularly cultural and identitarian heterogeneity, as its fundamental mode of analysis, retaining for music immanent conditions of singularity and exceptionality but circumventing undesirable legacies of musical autonomy and disinterested aesthetics. Music would remain a singular form of existence, first, on the basis of which other forms of existence (i.e., cultural, social,

---

34. For an account of the ontological dispersion of the canonic European musical work, see Lydia Goehr, *The Imaginary Museum of Musical Works: An Essay in the Philosophy of Music*, rev. ed. (New York: Oxford University Press, 2007). Recent accounts of music's ontology, which nonetheless retain for music an exceptional, albeit materially unexamined, status, appear in Georgina Born, "On Musical Mediation: Ontology, Technology, Creativity," *Twentieth-Century Music* 2, no. 1 (2005): 7–36; and Benjamin Piekut, "Actor-Networks in Music History: Clarifications and Critiques," *Twentieth-Century Music* 11, no. 2 (2014): 191–215.
35. We borrow this thought from Povinelli, *Economies of Abandonment*, 128.

political, sexual, racial, institutional) could take place, what earlier we posed as a question of indexicality. Why? Because music is taken as if it were a singular law pressed into the service of a politics of identitarian heterogeneity: such might have been the performative's ultimate musico-logical aim.

This observation finds the logic of the fiduciary at work in the embodied performative. As a singular but inexhaustible mode of existence, music is constituted and then entrusted to act on behalf of heterogeneous beneficiaries: society, the social, the political, et cetera. In the fiduciary, this is a binding but uneven relation. Music may be inexhaustible, but it is contracted to wield its power—and forbidden from withholding it—when the beneficiary's best interest is at stake.[36] In the juridical, these dual obligations form the rubric under which fiduciary responsibility is assessed: loyalty and care. Shoring up music's centrality to musicking, in the embodied performative, makes of both music and musicking something that cannot betray those for whom it is entrusted to care.

How, then, to assess musicking in its inexhaustible power, a materiality immune to scarcity on condition that it paradoxically be dematerialized? The issue here is not a return to "aesthetic autonomy" and its avatar in disinterested aesthetics; rather, it is a matter of establishing whether or not musicking has, within the purview of the performative, unrestricted power, sovereignty, and self-legislating powers—in a word, whether or not it has come to constitute an autonomous entity before it can be transfigured into a heterogeneous force across the social field. This tension—between the autonomy of musicking given in its singularity and the heterogeneity of the social effects it produces under the performative—can be accounted for historically and ontologically.

The notion that aesthetic production and art have the capacity to intervene directly in the sociopolitical arena is a relatively recent phenomenon in the modern Western history within which advocates of the performative pursue their analyses. Jacques Rancière proposes that, as the relation of art to forms of collective experience in modernity is transformed, two contradictory phenomena take place. On the one hand, around 1800, art acquires a degree of autonomy arguably unprecedented in European history; on the other hand, this autonomy allows for the identification of art with any of life's processes, social or otherwise.[37] No longer beholden

36. For a concise history of the fiduciary, see John F. Mariani, Christopher W. Kammerer, and Nancy Guffey-Landers, "Understanding Fiduciary Duty," *Florida Bar Journal* 84, no. 3 (2010): 20–45. Definitions of loyalty and care are drawn from *Black's Law Dictionary*, 625.
37. Jacques Rancière, *The Politics of Aesthetics*, trans. with an intro. by Gabriel Rockhill,

to its mimetic task of having deixis as its fundamental operation, art can, obeying its internal rules, stand outside other domains and be productive of them—the very idea of the aesthetic might be one of the most enduring of such productions. For Rancière, this duality creates "a distant analogy with a political modernity susceptible to being identified, depending on the time period, with revolutionary radicality or with the sober and disenchanted modernity of good republican government" (*POA*, 26).

Under the neologism "modernatism," Rancière identifies how forms from "this regime of the arts become identified with forms that accomplish a task or fulfill a destiny specific to modernity" (*POA*, 26–27). This is first manifested in Schiller's aesthetic state, the avatar for a true revolutionary politics that would evenly distribute across all citizens the power to attain "unconditional freedom and pure thought in common forms of life and *belief*" (*POA*, 26; emphasis added).

According to Rancière, one key challenge to modernatism's revolutionary aspiration consists in the misrecognition of its "submission to the heterogeneous powers of the sensible" (*POA*, 28). These powers, he argues, correlate to the indeterminacy of political outcomes, or what we earlier called political ambivalence. That is, the aesthetic politics of modernatism were, like the performative, a wager on possible outcomes, its disidentificatory ethos nothing more than a dissensual act delimited precisely by "the heterogeneous powers of the sensible" given a priori in musicking and axiomatically taken as "political" by its advocates. To elucidate this, we return to an earlier point. If, on the one hand, musicking could absorb any heterogeneous form that might be associated with it, on the other hand, it could not push any such form beyond itself—beyond musicking—and so could not introduce another nomos and become truly heteronomous. This too is what we mean when we say that the musicological performative turn could only be "partially subversive." And this is also why the institutional setting and discursive staging of the musicological performative might have been its greatest contradiction. The musicological regime places a non-negotiable premium on its object. So long as there is a musical object, the discipline remains in expansive mode, affirming itself in its capacity to serve as the academic institutional custodian of "music."

The aesthetic regime empties the aesthetic of exteriorities so as to

---

afterword by Slavoj Žižek (London: Continuum, 2004), 26. Hereafter, this work is cited parenthetically as *POA*. For further discussion in relation to music, see Jairo Moreno and Gavin Steingo, "Rancière's Equal Music," *Contemporary Music Review* no. 31 (2012): 487–505.

grant it an autonomy (i.e., as an exceptional domain of human experience) that affords its participation in sociocultural and political life—this is the passage from immanent power to indexical performativity. This participation, again, cannot guarantee the production of the social good and must remain what Rancière calls an "unthought" under the formulation "art *and* life." In this formulation, the conjunction *and* is both what goes without saying and what cannot be said: a matter of believing or not. Can art be trusted and entrusted? This becomes a question only within this regime, one to which embodied performativity answers with a resounding "yes!"

Interlude: The Perceptual Faith

Affirming the conjunction of "art *and* life," this celebratory "yes!" side-steps at its own risk the immunitary aporia—summarized as the "in-itself-for-us"—that pulsates within the perceptual faith. While Merleau-Ponty's aesthetics, particularly his famous analyses of painting, might wager the interimplication of subject and world against the "unthought" of modernatism, our interest in the fiduciary draws focus on how he ontologizes the perceptual faith in the dynamics of the *chiasm* of the flesh. We trace the production of a body that adduces the certainties of the perceptual faith even as it recapitulates its key contradiction. However, if the embodied performative gave us a *reduced* body, our focus on sound, music, and the aural poses the chiasmic body as a body *confused*. Confused, that is, by a correlation of sound, specifically, with the aural that troubles the fiduciary structure of aesthesis and begins to pry belief from faith in its contract.

The perceptual faith finds itself adduced in and as bodies that manifest what Merleau-Ponty calls, after Paul Valéry, the *chiasm*. In its anatomic usage, *chiasm* refers to the *x*-like crossing of the optic nerves at the back of the brain. But Valéry's adaptation transmutes the crossing of nerves into a crossing of glances, emphasizing a "reciprocal limitation" in which seeing another regrounds each seer in a body whose visibility she cannot access (*M-PPN*, 112):[38] "What I lack is the me that you see. And what you lack is

---

38. The chiasm and the flesh rely on the topology of the fold. The fold provides an ontology of spatio-temporal continuity between inside/outside, subject/object, and so on. It is Merleau-Ponty's response to Martin Heidegger's *Zwiefalt*, the folding of Being and beings, as well as a sense-perceptive complement to the formula of *"In der Welt Sein"* of Dasein and the notion that all being is a being-with (*Mitsein*). See Gilles Deleuze, *The Fold: Leibniz and the Baroque*, foreword and translation by Tom Conley (Minneapolis: University of Minnesota Press, 1993), 146n28.

the you that I see. And no matter how far we advance in our mutual understanding, as much as we reflect, so much will we be different."[39]

Chiasm describes both this dynamic crossing of the sensing into the sensible and the folding of the sensible in which we participate back into our "perceiving perspectival frame."[40] Merleau-Ponty illustrates this crisscrossing relation by analogy with the left hand touching the right. Touching induces a splitting or redoubling of each hand into a sensible and sensed "leaf" (*feuillet*), an endlessly reversible, but never coincident relation: neither hand experiences itself as sensing and sensible, simultaneously (*VI*, 175/ *vi*, 133).[41] An analogous (chiasmic) divergence structures the body; sensing projects the body into the sensible, but a necessary spacing or "spread" (*écart*) guarantees their noncoincidence.[42] Assuring that "I am always on the same side of my body, " Merleau-Ponty reframes the paradoxical structure of the perceptual faith as a reversibility that remains "imminent but never realized in fact" (*VI*, 194/*vi*, 148).

"The flesh" is the name that Merleau-Ponty gives to being's capacity to diverge from itself from within, correlating the dualisms of aesthesis as relations of (imminent) reversibility, not opposition, in a common element.[43] For Butler, the flesh is what is always "breaking apart," coordinating "relations of proximity that know no closure" or coincidence in which "the notion of substance does not and cannot hold."[44] However, as Derrida notes, there

39. Paul Valéry, *Tel Quel 1* (Paris: Gallimard, 1941); Merleau-Ponty, "Man and Adversity" (1951), in *Signs*, 224–43; see also *M-PPN*, 110–11.

40. Elizabeth Grosz, *Vital Bodies: Towards a Corporeal Feminism* (Bloomington: Indiana University Press, 1994), 102. For a further account of vision as *undergoing* in "The Intertwining," see Judith Butler, "Merleau-Ponty and the Touch of Malebranche," in *The Cambridge Companion to Merleau-Ponty*, 181–205. See also *VI*, 183/*vi*, 139.

41. "[The double sensation] can really only be doubled—can be two and not one—if there is no fusion. If there were fusion or coincidence, then either everything would be touching, fused into activity or everything would be touched, fused into passivity." Leonard Lawlor, *The Implications of Immanence: Towards a New Concept of Life* (New York: Fordham University Press, 2006), 89.

42. "If [the body] touches and touches [things] this is only because, being of their family, itself visible (*visible*) and tangible, it uses its own means to participate in theirs" (*VI*, 181/ *vi*, 137). Mauro Carbone grasps this dynamic as *compliance* with the flesh, inflecting perceptual with a juridical character in *The Thinking of the Sensible: Merleau-Ponty's A-Philosophy* (Evanston, IL: Northwestern University Press, 2004).

43. The flesh designates ". . . an in principle kinship between the sensing and sensed that can be understood, more easily, therefore through touch and Merleau-Ponty says that the palpation of the eyes is a remarkable variant of this closer palpation of the hands." Lawlor, *The Implications of Immanence*, 89. See also *VI*, 229/*vi*, 175.

44. Butler, "Merleau-Ponty and the Touch of Malebranche," 196.

remains something undecidable about this imminence: does this "ever imminent" reversibility truly "break apart," or, in the "manner of *presentiment* or
anticipation, does it hold open the possibility of a final synthesis or arrival?"[45]

Audibility, we argue, focalizes the tensions that Derrida detects in
Merleau-Ponty's ever-"imminent" reversibility. After asking himself, "what
are these adhesions compared with the voice and the hearing [*l'ouïe*]?,"
Merleau-Ponty also asserts that in the field of the audible, the flesh weaves
chiasmic relations between bodies with "incomparable agility" (*VI*, 188/*vi*,
144). While he queries a chiasmic crossing for the aural and the sonorous
analogous to that of the look or the touch, Merleau-Ponty also promises for
it an "agility" that troubles reversibility's imminence.

The flesh finds the "visible and mute" intertwined with the "invisible
and voiced" as it doubles itself, in the chiasm, into "sensible and meaningful dimensions" (*M-PPN*, 129). The silent sensible "speaks" itself in
and through its chiasmic propagation in the seer, opening onto a "linguistic sense already emergent in the silent sensible," an active, creative relation that Merleau-Ponty calls "operative language" (*M-PPN*, 129). This
doubling finds its apotheosis in music (or in the literary "little phrase" of
Marcel Proust's Vinteuil).[46] Our concern with the fiduciary structure of aesthesis, however, highlights configurations of the aural and the sonorous
that trouble reversibility and the undecidability of its imminence. Some
sounds, after all, seem entirely inadequate to the chiasm and the dynamics of crisscrossing it entails: "Among my movements there are some that
go nowhere—that do not even find in the other body their resemblance or
their archetype: these are the facial movements, many gestures and especially those strange movements of the throat and the mouth that form the
cry and the voice. These movements end in sound and I hear [*je entends*]
them" (*VI*, 190/*vi*, 144).

Although these "movements" certainly *sound*, conceding that they
also "go nowhere" in the chiasm emphasizes their failure to cross into the
sensible in the manner of the touch or the look. Without inducing a chiasmic
divergence, in the body, these "movements" provoke a simple case of self-
hearing, in which reversibility works either too well or does not work at all.

45. Butler, "Merleau-Ponty and the Touch of Malebranche," 196; Derrida, *On Touching*,
213.
46. For a detailed account of music in Merleau-Ponty's late thought, see Jessica Wiskus,
The Rhythm of Thought: Art, Literature, and Music after Merleau-Ponty (Chicago: University of Chicago Press, 2014); Mauro Carbone, "Composing Proust's Unheard Music,"
RES: Anthropology and Aesthetics, no. 48 (Autumn 2005): 163–65.

Against what he calls a generalized, "anonymous visibility" in the flesh, Merleau-Ponty tentatively concedes an audibility that crisscrosses human and nonhuman things: "Like crystal, like metal and many other substances, I am a sonorous being" (*VI*, 190/*vi*, 144).[47] Metal is a historically suggestive exemplar when it comes to operative language, but Merleau-Ponty does not account for the chiasmic dynamics of a "body that reverberates with all sounds."[48] Not only the apocryphal hammers in Pythagoras's blacksmith forge but also the bells and tongs of the late Jean-Philippe Rameau could be said to have "spoken themselves" through listeners whose musical systems would lay claim to the intertwining of "sensible and meaningful dimensions" in the sonorous. During Merleau-Ponty's lifetime, the metals of John Cage's *First Construction* (1939), Edgard Varèse's *Ionisation* (1929–31), or Karlheinz Stockhausen's *Zyklus* (1959) would parlay the "meaningful dimensions" of so-called secondary parameters, like timbre (with texture and density) toward nothing less than the future of music.

On his way to theorizing expression, Merleau-Ponty construes hearing as, above all, a relation of resemblance without reconstructing the correlation of the aural with the sonorous as a chiasmic one. Indeed, the point here is not to test Merleau-Ponty against the values of the Euro-American avant-garde but to gesture toward a few cases in which much more than resemblance is at stake in this relation. Set against Merleau-Ponty's detailed construal of vision as something we "both initiate and undergo" in the chiasm, there is no sense in which the clangorous timbres of metal can propagate themselves so as to induce the hearer to her own sonorousness (*VI*, 183/*vi*, 139). Without adducing the chiasm, a hearing based on resemblance seems to peel away from contradictions in the perceptual faith to which the chiasm responds.

Against this ambivalent acknowledgment of a sonorousness that is "like" that of crystals and metals, Merleau-Ponty indicates that we may not actually reckon our own sonorousness as a relation to the broader field of audibles at all: ". . . I hear [*entends*] my own vibration from within, as Malraux said, I hear [*entends*] myself with my throat [*avec ma gorge*]. In this,

47. This casual reference to André Malraux refers to a quotation that appears first in Malraux's novel *La condition humaine* (1934) and his later book on painting, *The Voices of Silence* (1953). In the novel, the phrase "I hear myself in my throat [*avec ma gorge*]" is associated with hearing one's voice played back over the gramophone. André Malraux, *Man's Fate* (New York: Modern Library, 1961), 73.
48. Harman, *Guerilla Metaphysics*, 43; Merleau-Ponty, *The Phenomenology of Perception*, 275.

I am incomparable, my voice is bound to the mass of my own life as is the voice of no one else" (*VI*, 190/*vi*, 144).

Finally, like seeing and touching, sounding seems to induce a dehiscence, or divergence in the body. Sounding, specifically, redoubles the ear within the throat (or, more specifically, the phonation apparatus), separating a kind of internal self-hearing, presumably, from the ear with which we hear other sounds.[49] Hearing *avec ma gorge* ensures that the speaker remains, in Merleau-Ponty's words, "always on the same side of [her] body," but not because the reversible relation of speaking and hearing remains intractably "imminent." Rather, hearing *avec ma gorge* realizes the coincidence that Derrida finds anticipated in imminence as a kind of *presentiment*. The coincidence of hearing and speaking, that is, immunizes the speaking body against the chiasmic torsion of the visible and tangible in the flesh. More than a locus only, for autoaffective self-hearing, we also register the voice of others *avec ma gorge*. So much so, in fact, that speech seems to coil like a "ribbon" connecting one throat to another, passing through the world and, perhaps, but with little consequence, reaching the ear:[50]

> But if I am close enough to the other to hear [*entendre*] his breath and feel [*sentir*] his effervescence and fatigue, I almost witness [*assister*] in him, as in myself, the awesome birth of vociferation. As there is a reflexivity of the touch, of the sight and of the touch-vision system, there is a reflexivity of the movements of phonation [*phonation*] and of hearing [*l'ouïe*]; they have their sonorous inscription, the vociferations have in me their motor echo. (*VI*, 190/*vi*, 144)

As David Krell suggests, Merleau-Ponty suppresses the sonorousness of vociferation, here, in favor of a more "transparent" intertwining

49. For a material genealogy of listening linked to Merleau-Ponty, see Peter Ablinger, "Cézanne and Music," trans. Bill Dietz, accessed July 27, 2014, earwaveevent.org/article/cezanne-and-music/. For accounts of the instrumentalization of the ear in acoustical research, see Benjamin Steege, *Helmholtz and the Modern Listener* (Cambridge: Cambridge University Press, 2012), and Jonathan Sterne, *The Audible Past: The Cultural Origins of Sound Recording* (Durham, NC: Duke University Press, 2003). By 1948, evidence of microphonic effects in the cochlea suggests a coimplication of hearing and sounding inside the inner ear. See Thomas Gold, "The Physical Basis for the Action of the Cochlea," *Proceedings of the Royal Society of London*, Series B, Biological Sciences, 135, no. 881 (December 14, 1948): 492–98.

50. David Farrell Krell, "Engorged Philosophy II," in *Postmodernism and Continental Philosophy*, ed. Hugh J. Silverman and Donn Welton (Albany: SUNY Press, 1998), 55–65, esp. 62.

of throats. After all, it is this *motor echo*—a kind of tacit activation of the phonation apparatus—that indicates that we have heard another.[51] If we "appear to ourselves turned inside out under our own eyes" when we are seen by another, it is through the throat (and not the ear) that we are turned "inside out" by another speaker (*VI*, 187/*vi*, 143).

Merleau-Ponty does admit that when it comes to hearing with the ear, we "miss" what of our voice our interlocutors hear, like the chiasmic seers of Valéry. But this chiasmic crossing is accompanied, for both speakers, with a coincident self-hearing *avec ma gorge* into which other audibles seem to never have made any incursion. In this sense, the aural both overcomes and falls short in the chiasm of the flesh. Hearing *avec ma gorge* installs within each speaker a reversibility of the sonorous and the aural that reaches coincidence each and every time she speaks. But if reversibility works too well *avec ma gorge*, that is, it also may not work at all in the ear. Some sounds, like metals, refer us to self-hearing *avec ma gorge* but do not encroach upon it. Still others may reach the ear but ultimately "go nowhere" without the relations of resemblance that Merleau-Ponty allows to stand in for reversibility in the audible.

As a dynamic fold in the flesh, the chiasmic body refuses the reduced body of the musicological performative but remains confused where the performative needs it most: in the correlation of sound with the aural in the perceptual faith. The audible's agnostic, ambivalent attitude toward the perceptual faith might be best understood historically for the questions it recapitulates and reframes for harnessing the sensible toward the political that we assess, here, under the rubric of the fiduciary. More than a proprioceptive paradox, "going nowhere" in the chiasm begins to pry belief from faith in the fiduciary. The later bookend for Harvey's efflorescence of bodies—a more recent turn to affect—distinguishes this uncoupling in a historical and political register.

The Affective Turn

In their fidelity to the power of action and of agency, intentionality, and the conscious will to engage in performative iteration, 1990s musicology might well have been affirming a radically autonomous force: affect.

51. As Steven Connor observes, much of this aural dynamic owes as much to the throat as to teeth and bones, transducers of the phonation apparatus. Steven Connor, "Edison's Teeth: Touching-Hearing," in *Hearing Cultures: Essays on Sound, Listening and Modernity*, ed. Veit Erlmann (Oxford: Berg Publishers, 2004), 153–72.

Theorists of affect posit its autonomy.[52] For Patricia Clough, for example, affect exercises "autonomy from conscious perception and language."[53] Clough also remarks how "affect and emotion point . . . to the subject's discontinuity with itself, a discontinuity of the subject's conscious experience with the non-intentionality of emotion and affect."[54] Affect precedes and exceeds the iterative demands of intentionality in the performative. At the same time, affect makes it possible to believe without doubt that musicking's deeply embodied action on behalf of political and social aims is real.

Affect has a material basis—we could in this section be speaking equally about a materialist turn. But affect is anchored by a more narrowly defined notion of materiality than the embodied performative offered in its refusal of substance. In Rosi Braidotti's words, "As a result of information and biogenetic technologies, bodily materialism is being revised in ways that challenge accepted social constructivist notions."[55] As if to realize Descartes's dream of locating the seat for modern passions, affect has a known "biological" seat—the amygdalae complex—and, according to affect theorists, it is common to the species. This scientifically validated materialism has as its corollary claims to a return to the real (and away from representation), which carries two sets of interrelated implications for analysis. First, there are epistemic-political implications for the ways we know and understand bodies in their potential to be socially present and politically pressed. Second, there are ontological implications for how we understand the fundamental constitution of bodies and the location within that constitution of this or that capacity.

The question emerges as to how this materiality might intersect or indeed affect (pun not intended) musicking's materiality, particularly in light of the importance of "resonance" as a central trope for defining affect.[56]

52. Brian Massumi, "The Autonomy of Affect," *Cultural Critique* 31 (1995): 83–109.
53. Patricia T. Clough, "The Affective Turn: Political Economy, Biomedia, and Bodies," in *The Affect Theory Reader*, ed. Melissa Gregg and Gregory J. Seigworth (Durham, NC: Duke University Press, 2010), 206–28, esp. 209.
54. Clough, "The Affective Turn," 206.
55. Rosi Braidotti, "The Politics of 'Life Itself' and New Ways of Dying," in *New Materialisms*, 201–20, esp. 201.
56. For instance, "affect is found in those intensities that pass body to body . . . in those resonances that circulate about, between, and sometimes stick to bodies and worlds, *and* in the very passages or variations between these intensities and resonances themselves." Gregory J. Seigworth and Melissa Gregg, "An Inventory of Shimmers," in *The Affect Theory Reader*, 1–25, esp. 1.

In practice, the materiality of affect and musical materiality have a pecu-liar relationship. Affect theory draws on a rich materialist philosophical lin-eage (among others, Lucretius, Baruch Spinoza, Henri Bergson, William James, Alfred North Whitehead, Gilles Deleuze and Félix Guattari, and Brian Massumi), appeals to the psychological work of Sylvan Tomkins, and invokes recent cognitive and neuroscientific research. But when affect theory calls on music, it is as a ready-made and exemplary affective power, music's complex materiality taken for granted.[57] In this sense, affect and music constitute a paradigmatic pairing, one being an alibi for the other. On this account, we remain very much on a terrain similar to embodied performativity.

Here's an example. "Music provides perhaps the clearest example of how the intensity of the impingement of sensations on the body can 'mean' more to people than meaning itself," writes Eric Shouse, who cites Jeremy Gilbert: "Music has *physical effects* which can be identified, described and discussed but which are not the same thing as it having *meanings*, and any attempt to understand how music works in culture must be able to say something about those effects without trying to collapse them into meanings."[58] Shouse adds that often "a particular piece of music" moves us more than it produces meaning. Music transmits affect more than it relays signification, often, in fact, bypassing signification altogether.[59]

But what exactly is affect—and what it is not—that it should exer-cise such power over and prior to social and cultural analysis? According to Massumi, affect is about acts, not facts.[60] Affect is a presubjective, pre-personal, a-signifying, nonconscious, and wholly corpo-material process and intensity independent and prior to intentions, meanings, reasons, and beliefs, and, *pace* Clough, it exists apart from emotions. If it is a thing, it

57. A trenchant critique of affect, its psychobiological underpinnings, and political conse-quences appears in Ruth Leys, "The Turn to Affect: A Critique," *Critical Inquiry* 37, no. 3 (Spring 2001): 434–72.

58. Eric Shouse, "Feeling, Emotion, Affect," *M/C Journal* 8 (2005), accessed February 15, 2014, journal.media-culture.org.au/0512/03-shouse.php, ¶13. Jeremy Gilbert, "Signi-fying Nothing: 'Culture,' 'Discourse' and the Sociality of Affect," *Culture Machine 6* (2004), accessed February 15, 2014, culturemachine.tees.ac.uk/.

59. Gary Tomlinson's essay in this volume approaches this question from a different per-spective [editors' note].

60. Brian Massumi, *Parables for the Virtual: Movement, Affect, Sensation* (Durham, NC: Duke University Press, 2002), 35–36; see also Lauren Berlant, *Cruel Optimism* (Durham, NC: Duke University Press, 2011), 14. Hereafter, Berlant's work is cited parenthetically as *CO*.

is something that occurs in the encounter between a human and some object in a specific situation (an object-situation, in short). Significantly, affect bypasses subjective intention toward an object, in a phenomenological sense. In a classic formulation, it is and/or partakes of a becoming.[61]

Affect theory, however, does not avoid dualisms altogether. Outside of and prior to reason and consciousness, affect operates as a bodily system immune to the labor of reason and its avatar language, as Clough, Gilbert, and Shouse all claim. "Affect cannot be fully realized in language . . . it is the body's way of preparing itself for action in a given circumstance by adding a quantitative dimension of intensity to the quality of an experience. The body has a grammar of its own that cannot be fully captured in language."[62] Unperturbed by language, affect is free from content and meaning. If the embodied performative of musicking sacrificed the "mind" at the altar of the "body," here logos is exchanged for a feelingful freedom and the imminence of action. And yet logos remains, if only as the constantly disavowed term in a dualism opposing logos to action.

Affect theory posits the idea that affect is free from belief, following the inaugural intuition of Silvan Tomkins and Paul Elkman that, as Ruth Leys puts it, "our basic emotions do not involve cognitions or *beliefs* about the objects in our world."[63] Assuming this to be formally the case, however, does not explain the relation of affect to phenomena that are part and parcel of a broader social milieu and of habitual relationships forged from and in this milieu, as in the case of art. Thus, as we saw in the privilege granted to "music" by Shouse, *form* remains close to affect as an incorporeal holdover organizing what things in the world are and how they are experienced.

61. "Affects are becoming," write Gilles Deleuze and Félix Guattari, in *A Thousand Plateaus: Capitalism and Schizophrenia*, trans. Brian Massumi (Minneapolis: University of Minnesota Press, 1987), 256. Elsewhere, in a statement such as "Man absent from but entirely within the landscape," which was said of Cézanne, Deleuze and Guattari offer a radical understanding of affect that takes place in and through art: "affects are precisely these nonhuman becomings of man." In this late theorization, art expresses the becoming independent of affect from a particular place and time. Gilles Deleuze and Félix Guattari, "Percept, Affect, Concept," in *What Is Philosophy?*, trans. Hugh Tomlinson and Graham Burchell (New York: Columbia University Press, 1994), 169. As is often the case with Deleuze, articulations of a particular concept change throughout his work. His earlier work on Hume, *Empiricism and Subjectivity*, connects habits of thought, ideas, and patterns to affect and difference; in *Bergsonism*, affect is linked to perception.
62. Shouse, "Feeling, Emotion, Affect," ¶1, ¶5; see also Leys, "The Turn to Affect," 442.
63. Leys, "The Turn to Affect," 437; emphasis added. A consideration of debates surrounding affect and free will is beyond the scope of this paper.

Affect is, then, not free from *our* belief *in* certain specified forms and genres, music and sound among them. As Lauren Berlant writes, "Affects have content and form (the repetitions—of word, lyric, music, or sound)" (*CO*, 159).[64]

In their social consolidation as genres, Berlant's forms offer something redolent of a legislative order: "genres are distinguished by the affective *contract* they promise" (*CO*, 66; emphasis added).[65] The reference is to literature, but we can displace this contractual promise to the logic of the fiduciary we explored in the performative: art can offer such a contract because it is already presumed to have expertise. And so, even though affect may be relatively free from belief, it traffics with our attachments to and need for trust, in a word, faith.

The formal agnosticism of affect theory and the social and historical embedding of form converge around music for a good reason. Thus, staying with the question of form, it warrants asking if Shouse's "music," or rather a more careful account of its ontology, might not be considered both more generally vis-à-vis "music" and more specifically as sonority (sound, noise), which is how Berlant, for example, tends to frame her case studies on the politics of affect.[66]

How, then, to reconcile the claims to affect's prelinguistic, preformal, and impersonal character with the indubitable location of affective capacities in music as forms and genres that are inextricably social before they are political? Can affect theory wager everything on the half a second that has been shown to demonstrate the belatedness of our intentionality to our

64. Berlant draws a distinction between "the structure of affect," which would include the subject's relative passivity vis-à-vis affect as biologically constituted, and "what we call affect when we encounter it," which is multiply contingent. As she describes the latter, "one assesses what affective events are according to one's education in attunement, in tracking repetition, form, and norm" (*CO*, 158).

65. Berlant follows this by asserting the mutual embedding of affects and persons as a dimension of affective historicity: "by claiming that certain affects embed the historical in persons and persons in the historical in ways that only the aesthetic situation could really capture, the cultural Marxist take on the historical novel foregrounds affect not as the sign of ahistoricism, but as the very material of historical embeddedness" (*CO*, 66).

66. An emphasis on sonority (or the sonorous, as we prefer) resonates with the status granted to music by Deleuze, whose insistence on the speed of affect is inseparably linked from an understanding of the sonorous in terms of its velocity. This link is especially strong in Deleuze's writing about Spinoza. See Gilles Deleuze and Félix Guattari, *A Thousand Plateaus: Capitalism and Schizophrenia*, trans. Brian Massumi (Minneapolis: University of Minnesota Press, 1987), 260; Gilles Deleuze, *Practical Philosophy*, trans. Robert Hurley (San Francisco: City Lights, 1988), 103.

affective body?[67] Can the postconstructivist materialism that Braidotti mentions avoid a psychophysicalism that reduces everything, music included, to a question of "biology"?

In a synthesis of recent theories of the development of human capacity for music, Gary Tomlinson does indeed suggest that the human capacity for "musicking" emerged by way of processes sufficiently independent from and prior to those that made possible higher-order mental processes associated with language and the production of symbols and forms.[68] Musicking emerged over a span of some fifty thousand years. Evolutionarily, our musical capacities reached their current stage some twenty thousand years ago without, however, crossing "a line before which all the cognitive capacities recruited in modern musicking suddenly disappear."[69] Affect might be an evolutionary result of the need to partake of sound-based information loops that allows the species to act "unconsciously" within that narrow band of 0.5 seconds. The species has retained this active and reactive capacity, as when we jump upon hearing a loud and unexpected sound, our heart pumping extra blood the better for us to flee danger, or when, according to affect theorists, the absence of any apperception within this time frame serves as precondition for action, or when, in Berlant's account of temporality, "the present is perceived, first, affectively: the present is what makes itself present to us before it becomes anything else" (CO, 4).

Still, the physicalist materialism that explains how the amygdalae—the seat of affect in the human brain—operate on such a microtemporal scale cannot explain how it may have coevolved in relation to the potentially shifting perception of materiality of the sonorous (no one knows). We do

---

67. This is known as the "half-second delay," after the experiments by Benjamin Libet measuring the timing of brain activity, a subject's intention to move, and her actual physical response. See Leys, "The Turn to Affect," 453.

68. Gary Tomlinson, "Evolutionary Studies in the Humanities: The Case of Music," *Critical Inquiry* 39, no. 4 (Summer 2013): 647–75. For a contrasting view, Tomlinson cites Terrence Deacon, who locates all art within a wider symbolic framework that makes of music less particular than Tomlinson's "musicking." See Deacon, "The Aesthetic Faculty," in *The Artful Mind: Cognitive Science and the Riddle of Human Creativity*, ed. Mark Turner (Oxford: Oxford University Press, 2006), 21–53. Tomlinson too responds to the emerging field of neuroliterature and wishes to delineate the relative autonomy of musicking vis-à-vis language, addressing implications for the wider humanities of debates pro and con "biological determinism and adaptational causality" in evolutionary studies in literature. See the essays in *Critical Inquiry* 37, no. 3 (Spring 2011).

69. Tomlinson, "Evolutionary Studies in the Humanities," 648.

know, however, that the sonorous becomes increasingly subject to formal elaboration and what we might call neurocognitive intentionality, the basic orientation of the species toward sound, first, and toward formalized and "aestheticized" sound, second. In other words, the ancestral bodily materiality and biological development behind affect ceased to evolve once it satisfied its evolutionary needs, but not so the human capacity for creative formalization out of sonorous matter, that is, "music" in the way Gilbert and Shouse deploy it, or the way Berlant posits genres. It is in the context of the emergence of this formalization that "musicking" becomes prized for its capacity to foster social comingling, a capacity easily but mistakenly interpreted as being exclusively grounded in the biological (cognitive) basis of the origins of music and considered by some as evidence of music's exceptional powers to foster human communication and sociability.[70]

At first it may seem as if biology trumps all else from an evolutionary standpoint. But drawing on the work of Terrence Deacon, Tomlinson presents a biological and sociocultural account in which musicking becomes inseparable from technological and environmental affordances. Accordingly, genes and behavior function within a feedback loop of interactions between the species and an "external world" that in turn affects the "selective pressures acting on the species."[71] This broad perspective renders moot any notion of either form or autonomy, whether biological or environmental-behavioral. Musicking is integrally biosemiotic. If biology and semiosis coexist and interact in the emergence of human "musicking" and "music," this coexistence defies chronologies. A causal series such as "first x (bio-semiosis), then y ('musicking')" would be as unproductive as its inversion.

The biosemiotic explanation subverts Gilbert's and Shouse's prescription that any cultural analysis must account for the biological basis of music. This explanation renders inseparable biological, semiotic, and sociocultural domains under the general exchange economy of biosemiosis. Similarly, biosemiosis expands the sense of "materiality" beyond merely

70. Ian Cross's work is representative. See, for example, "Music, Cultures and Meanings: Music as Communication," *Empirical Musicology Review* 7, nos. 1–2 (2012): 95–97; "Cognitive Science and the Cultural Nature of Music," *Topics in Cognitive Science* 4, no. 4 (2012): 668–77; Ian Cross and Iain Morley, "The Evolution of Music: Theories, Definitions, and the Nature of the Evidence," in *Communicative Musicality: Exploring the Basis of Human Companionship*, ed. Stephen Malloch and Colwyn Trevarthen (Oxford: Oxford University Press, 2009), 61–81.
71. Tomlinson, "Evolutionary Studies in the Humanities," 650.

the biogenetic. In fact, the expanded sense Tomlinson gives to the expression "musicking" owes to the identification of formal considerations: before it could be called "musical," musicking's capacity developed coevolutionarily through a set of three processes—entrainment, pitch discrimination, and recognition of form—themselves preceded by more basic orientations toward voice recognition, pulse, and repetition. Out of this emerges, much later, the form "music." But it would be unreasonable to ignore how language—that other significant capacity of the species (Tomlinson does not afford it the term "languaging")—retains some of these processes and orientations, and what Tomlinson, again, calls "cognitive capacities recruited for modern musicking."

Musical affect's "autonomy" from language ends up being a narrowly qualified physicalist perspective; in terms we prefer, claims to such autonomy constitute the effect of a wager. Why this wager? Can our commitment to this force of affect derail us so that we must seek extravagant psychobiological bases for it? If half a second constitutes the window for its autonomy, isn't affect fundamentally untimely, the actions it presumably compels a dramatic example of a disjointed conjunction at the heart of some of our most cherished political aspirations for art? According to Leys, affect theorists insist that the more we learn about the preconscious, prerational field of political intervention, the more able we are to understand its manipulation (if we happen to disagree politically with its uses) or resort to its force to compel action.[72]

It seems that, in part, the claim on affect's autonomy is tethered to a commitment to the production of the new and its indeterminacy as the possible enactment of the "otherwise." To mine affect is not just to explore a resource for the political; it is additionally to adopt a militant ethical attitude in the hope for, or at least the possibility of, a world otherwise. Of course, as it was in the case of the performative, this wager remains open to ambivalence and is contaminated by the fact that affect does not dwell only in the good: affect means "you never know . . ."

72. "The biological constitution of being . . . has to be taken into account," states Nigel Thrift, "if performative force is ever to be understood, and in particular, the dynamics of birth (and creativity) rather than death." Thrift, "Intensities of Feeling: Towards a Spatial Politics of Affect," *Geografiska Annaler* 86B, no. 1 (2004): 57–78, esp. 59; cited in Constantina Papoulias and Felicity Callard, "Biology's Gift: Interrogating the Turn to Affect," *Body and Society* 16, no. 1 (2010): 29–56, esp. 31. See Leys, "The Turn to Affect," 441. Leys critiques William E. Connolly's position (which resembles Thrift's) in his *Neuropolitics: Thinking, Culture, Speed* (Minneapolis: University of Minnesota Press, 2002); Massumi, *Parables for the Virtual*.

Affect theory has been critiqued for the separation of preconscious and prepersonal intensities from political intention, cognition, and meaning. First, there appears "a relative indifference to the role of ideas and *beliefs* in politics, culture, and art in favor of an 'ontological' concern with different people's corporeal-affective reactions."[73] Second—and related to the scare quotes of Leys's reference to "ontology"—this physicalist ontology trumps epistemology as well as the ontology of other materialities often called upon to do political work, for instance those of sound. What matters first and foremost is a body traversed by affect prior to individuality, personhood, and subjectivity. This leads to a third contentious issue: how affect subsists, if at all, through the passage from preindividuality to the individuality of a sentient and cogitating subject who may then act politically. For Leys, affect theory's preindividual character axiomatically posits difference among individuals as the basis for a politics. Under these politics of affect, she protests, differences among individuals replace political disagreement, and personal taste replaces normativity.[74] For Leys, the privilege given to individuality drowns out modalities of political participation other than a vacant pluralism.[75]

To our mind, the most salient issue has to do with the relation of individuality to the common and to collectivities. This marks an odd return to an old political and aesthetic problem. That is, given the important or even grounding role of aesthesis and the aesthetic for affect advocates, the individuality of experience recasts the political aporia in Kant's *Third Critique*: how to mobilize the improbable intersubjectivity of aesthetic judgment while acknowledging the power of aesthetics to move humans. Of course, for affect theorists, judgment is not at stake, at least not in its ultraexpeditious experience—judgment arrives belatedly to the constitutively autonomous affective scene.

The solution to this old Kantian quandary is equally clever and scandalous. Recall how in Rancière's analysis of "modernism" the aes-

---

73. Tomlinson, "Evolutionary Studies in the Humanities," 451; emphasis added. Leys cites Paul E. Griffiths's gloss of Elkman's view of the affects as "sources of motivation not integrated into the system of *beliefs* or desires" linked to their "involuntary triggering." See Paul E. Griffiths, *What Emotions Really Are: The Problem of Psychological Categories* (Chicago: University of Chicago Press, 1997), 243, emphasis added; cited in Leys, "The Turn to Affect," 438.

74. Leys, "The Turn to Affect," 452n32, echoing the views of Clive Barnett, "Political Affects in Public Space: Normative Blind-Spots in Non-representational Ontologies," *Transactions of the Institute of British Geographers* 33, no. 2 (2008): 186–200.

75. The target here is William E. Connolly. See his *Pluralism* (Durham, NC: Duke University Press, 2005).

thetic becomes an autonomous sphere only on the condition that it be conjoined to the wider social field. The formula "art *and* society" expressed the unthought character of aesthesis itself through the conjunction *and*. The affective turn, we suggest, provides a name for that unthought: affect. Affect, however, is immediately proclaimed to be unthinkable by the appeal to the microtemporality of its biological "materiality": it is preconscious, preindividual, and so on—in a word, autonomous. And so, affect continues to run ahead of the political ends to which its advocates wish to harness it. The politics of affect remain untimely, out of joint.

Berlant's work confronts directly the untimeliness of affect and the political. "Before it becomes anything else, such as an orchestrated collective event or an epoch on which we can look back," she writes, "the present is first perceived in the purity of affect" (*CO*, 4). The activation of this absolute present for political ends requires two sets of operations: an "affective realism" and a "psychoanalytic materialism." First, she draws on Deleuze's notion that the virtual is real (and, more precisely, that the real is on the side of the virtual and not the actual). But because affect is seemingly linked to an actual (a sound object, for instance), she must render that actual into an event (she must "eventilize" it) that capitalizes on the intensities of the virtual and makes affect emerge as an "empirical transcendental."[76] Events do not refer to happenings. Rather, events describe "diachronic emergence, or

76. Deleuze: "What is a transcendental field? It can be distinguished from experience in that it doesn't refer to an object or belong to a subject (empirical representation). It appears therefore as a pure stream of a-subjective consciousness, a pre-reflexive impersonal consciousness, a qualitative duration of consciousness without a self. It may seem curious that the transcendental be defined by such immediate givens: we will speak of a transcendental empiricism in contrast to everything that makes up the world of the subject and the object." Gilles Deleuze, "Immanence: A Life . . . ," in *Pure Immanence: Essays in Life*, with an intro. by John Rajchman, trans. Anne Boyman (New York: Zone Books, 2005), 25. It is well beyond this essay to pursue the connection between affect and the empirical transcendental in any detail—the concept is not explored by Berlant. Contemporary interest in the "event" is common to Sigmund Freud, Michel Foucault, Jean-François Lyotard, Deleuze, Jean-Luc Nancy, and Alain Badiou, who "focus on the event as an experience of radical contingency," as does Berlant's interest on the "impactive experience" of the event. "With the exception of Freud's *après-coup* [*Nachträglichkeit*] and Deleuze's perturbation," the antifoundational emphasis characterizing most of these views cast the event in terms of "nothingness, shattering, cleavage, and so on," to which Berlant adds a concern with the ordinariness of the event (*CO*, 278n17). Compare to Povinelli's Foucauldian "Eventalization": "[a] relay between mechanisms of coercion and contents of knowledge likely to induce behaviors and discourses, affective attachments and analytic tendencies" (Povinelli, *Economies of Abandonment*, 151).

creativity in the production of new patterns and thresholds of behavior . . . [a] counteractualizaton."[77] Invoking the financial-psychoanalytic keyword *investment*, Clough explains the commitment to a Deleuzian affective realism as the task to "invest objects with an affective realist . . . transformative rhythm of allusion, musicality, haptic intensity."[78] "Psychoanalytic materialism," in turn, results from particular readings of "scene" and "object." In Clough's and Ann Pellegrini's description, scene "is the encounter that produces, organizes, and disturbs affect beyond the manifest content of what's there."[79] "What's there" are objects, but these objects are "really relations anchored in a scene whose form emits the phantasm of stability."[80] In the end, there emerges what Berlant calls an "object scene" or "object scenario," in which the aesthetic encounter is cast as event and the object is rendered positively as "thing."[81]

And so we return to time. Berlant's complex conjunction of "affective realism" and "psychoanalytical materialism" allows her to avoid the miasmas of the metaphysical tradition of time (from Aristotle to Derrida). The politics of affect work because the metaphysics of temporality are no longer "a distraction," as she bluntly puts it. Also, no longer are the microtemporalities of the scientists essential to claim the primacy of affect. Instead, affective time plays out in a series of genres. Affective realism addresses a nondistracting time, "[pointing] to genres of adjustment to the immediacy of happenings in the historical present" (*CO*, 274n1). The present is central in its various figurations—chronotopical, as in the hours of the day; historical, as relates to institutions; political, as relates to "collective consciousness, activity, and desire to change a structure"; affective, as "an ongoing space of feeling things out, noticing mood's arcs and trails, and becoming habituated and alive to the intensities of a being passing through a phase that could be an impasse, or life itself" (*CO*, 62–63). In turn, habit, like

77. John Protevi, *Political Affect: Connecting the Social and the Somatic* (Minneapolis: University of Minnesota Press, 2009), 13.

78. As reported by Lauren Berlant in *"Cruel Optimism*, Becoming Event: A Response," 2, accessed July 27, 2014, bcrw.barnard.edu/wp-content/uploads/2012/Public-Feelings -Responses/Lauren-Berlant-Cruel-Optimism-Becoming-Event.pdf.

79. Berlant, *"Cruel Optimism*, Becoming Event," 2.

80. Berlant, *"Cruel Optimism*, Becoming Event," 2.

81. "One might say . . . that to eventilize an occurrence would be to force it from its status as object (use value) to thing (resistant, attractive enigma)" (*CO*, 275n13). Berlant seems unaware that any such turning into resistance and enigma constitutes use-values. For a discussion of the implication of use-value in orthodox economics and the radical dematerialization at stake here, see the editors' introduction to this issue.

ritual, provides and produces a spacing for the immediacy for affect, one might say, without overcoming affect in the form of feelingful or emotional responses to habitual and/or ritualistic practices. In Berlant's reading, habit provides a place and a time for affect to emerge and exist.

Let's see, then, how Berlant's analytic plays out in a sound genre that interests her: political speech. Whenever normative political movements attempt to communicate with their publics directly, they purport to speak without any filters (e.g., when the Right protests the liberal biases of the mainstream media in the United States). Using the example of George W. Bush, Berlant shows how regardless of political persuasion, affective politics of speech intensify noise: "the live intensities and desires that make messages affectively immediate, seductive, and binding" are felt by a public (CO, 224). More than strictly meaningful speech, the aim of this affective politics is to produce the "affect of feeling political together" (CO, 224). As a fact, this modality of listening gathers publics; but as an act, this "listening together" constitutes "an object/scene of desire" (CO, 224). This attunement, she explains, mobilizes what Charles Hirschkind calls the "ethical and therapeutic virtues of the ear."[82] These virtues are, however, on the one hand, conditions of possibility for cultivated listening, and, on the other, forces immanent to aurality. In short, they are an empirical transcendental, which is, of course, consonant with Berlant's affective realist and psycho-analytic materialist production of an "object/scene."

Something similar happens in a contrasting genre, "sonic activism" from the political left. By using noise as a sound track in a series of public video announcements protesting the Iraq War, Cynthia Madansky forbids the ear to accrete meaning (CO, 233–36). As in the case of Bush, the aim is "to provide a scene for being together in the political" (CO, 237). In a pointed theoretical intervention, Berlant swerves from a valuation of political art, or the umpteenth assertion of the temporal primacy of affect, to a demonstration of how such forms—Madansky's and Bush's—"engage the desire for the political across planes of self-idealization and paranoia" (CO, 238). Whether or not this engagement provides the means for transforming the situation becomes secondary. The critical aim of the affective turn becomes an account of how and why the fantasy of a possible transformation persists in the face of political defeats and how, even when those investments mitigate against our well-being, we continue to wager on these modalities of "cruel optimism."

82. Charles Hirschkind, *The Ethical Soundscape: Cassette Sermons and Islamic Counterpublics* (New York: Columbia University Press, 2006), 9; cited in *CO*, 224.

"The exhausting repetition of the politically depressed position that seeks repair of what may be constitutively broken," writes Berlant, "can eventually split the activity of optimism from expectation and demand" (*CO*, 227). Furthermore, there is a distinct "possibility that 'the political' as we know it in mass democracy *requires* such a splitting of attachment and expectation" (*CO*, 228).

Do we then stand now before the attenuation of the fiduciary? Perhaps. Yet, with the fiduciary in mind, we'd ask: Why not displace the argument back to a general aesthesis and claim that it is *because* we sense and perceive that political systems like democracy subsist? What if this general aesthesis is the constitutive outside of "mass democracy"?

We began with a distinction between belief and faith, one unidirectional (belief), the other bidirectional (faith), one a quasi-realist posit and the other a relational posit. That (1) there is sound and (2) that we sense and perceive truly are the foundations for quasi realism, which grounds the articulation of various fiduciary relations. Thus, it is possible to believe that there is sound (and that we sense and perceive) and yet not have faith in what sound and sense perception might offer. But it is also possible to have faith and not believe. What Slavoj Žižek would call the "Big Other," or what Berlant would simply call "democracy" (*CO*, 228), constitutes a virtual order requiring no belief but to which, nonetheless, we may "feel bounded by some symbolic commitment," or what Berlant, after Clough, might call "investment."[83] We need to distinguish, therefore, between the attenuation of the fiduciary as described by Berlant's split—which is a historical and relational, not ontological, matter—and the fiduciary as something internal to aesthesis itself: perception always already believes that *it* senses and *in* what it senses. But as Merleau-Ponty's lesson teaches us, audibles do not easily accommodate this quasi realism and its relational wager. Nonetheless, if our analysis shows anything, it is that we—somebody—insist on the fiduciary. Perhaps we perdure because of it. The temporality of such perdurance, however, is in need of final elucidation.

Bodies Fiduciary, Bodies Temporal

While our cases bookend, in a sense, a twenty-five-year interval of critical recommitment to the body, Harvey notes that this commitment was itself a return, for the body has long served as the measure of all things. Whatever else they may be, these "bodies" are fiduciary bodies. And,

---

83. Žižek, *On Belief*, 109–10. See also note 78.

indeed, each case adjudicates the body's value in and as its interimplication with political wagers made on behalf of music, sound, and the aural. But can the fiduciary stand in for this measure of all things?

The fiduciary is, of course, historically contingent, and our account registers only a relatively brief moment in its changes. While conceptualizing the body as a composite aggregate of social and political potentials, the embodied performative and the affective turns variously configure this composite as a singularity to secure a fiduciary contract with music and sound. The musicology of the 1990s inherits its fiduciary confidence, in part, from the New Left and allied identity knowledges, while the affective turn (as represented by Berlant) recalibrates this confidence in the openly affirmative paradox of "cruel optimism." Nonetheless, in the affective turn, aesthetic forms retain a singular expertise to train us in the art of scenification and eventalization, and so we entrust them even though we no longer trust their capacity to exercise political redistributions.[84]

While these cases certainly rely on the quasi-realist and relational posits, they also set into relief a set of remainders, presupposed by each fiduciary configuration: the "in-itself" of the sonorous, the "music" of musicology, or the "object" of the affective scene. These remainders, we suggest, are ramified in the kind of body each "manner of return" produces. In our analysis, the embodied performative requires a *reduced* body, and the affective produces a *diffuse* body, while the perceptual faith gives us what we might call a body *confused* by its attenuation in the audible. Sound, after all, strains the (silent) fiduciary contract that binds the body with the sensible. We close with a brief reflection on the political outcomes of these bodies.

In the performative, producing active, agential, and knowing bodies within a dualist disciplinary framework entails multiple strata of dematerialization. Selective materialisms, that is, afford few distinctions between the body as mediation for counterrepresentational practices, the body as part of a series of exchanges with the environment, and the body as a set of techniques, technologies, and socioeconomic affordances.[85] This translates into a perspective of fuzzy political scale, with little clarity regarding how an analytic of musicological bodies might work beyond and below the level of methodological individualism, or what the reach of the performative might be from the personal to the group and the public.

---

84. Berlant, "*Cruel Optimism*, Becoming Event," 2.
85. Harvey, *Spaces of Hope*, 98–99.

For this reason, as John Protevi proposes, we may better think in terms of "bodies political," bodies at once social and somatic, bodies composed personally as well as civically, bodies encompassing micro- to macrotemporalities.[86] The analytic of "bodies political" distinguishes between the somatic body, the technical body, and the representational body, but holds them in inextricable and consubstantial relation. More than mere embodied processes or things, "bodies political" are embedded in acts of "political cognition" informed by but irreducible to the categories on which the embodied performative sought to intervene—"corporeal knowl-edge," for instance, or "woman," or "formalism."[87]

The performative "manner" of returning to the body makes a wager on the power of the ongoing present tense. Its reduced body, that is, poses also a question of conjugated time. As we've argued, the embodied per-formative relies on music's presumed centrality to musicking to guaran-tee its persistence between punctual, bounded deeds of performance. The embodied performative, in other words, inserts music where questions of endurance would otherwise emerge. What is lost in this substitution, we (with Povinelli) might argue, is an analytic of tense attuned to how the per-durance of bodies is marked or produced through the temporal relationship between what is being narrated and the act of narrating it.

This substitution produces a disciplinary division of tense that con-signs to a past perfect and the future anterior not only "music" but also the ongoing expenditure of other performing musicians. This grammatical marking of the latter expenditure sits awkwardly alongside a "music" that will have already preceded, fulfilled, and exceeded the performative's punc-tual wager on the present. For Povinelli, arrangements of tense shape "how narratives of enduring . . . are socially enunciated and experienced within late liberalism" but also (differently) emphasize, occlude, or press rela-tions of consubstantiality within and between Protevi's bodies political (*EA*, 4–5). In other words, by adopting music as its "narrative" of enduring, the reduced body of the performative (inadvertently) avows an arrangement of tense that reduces other bodies political with which it remains coimplicated.

Something different takes place in Berlant's affective mapping. Not only does she expose the mechanisms by which affect's singular tempo-rality becomes transferable and distributed, but she fully embraces the distributed character of affect and of its objects (genres, habits, histories,

86. Protevi, *Political Affect*, 37.
87. Protevi, *Political Affect*, 33, 35.

techniques). "The evidence and intelligence of affect," she writes, is multiply derived from "neurological, psychoanalytic, schizoanalytic, historical, or normative" forces (*CO*, 12).[88] Rather than focus on an origin for affect, Berlant's critique derives "concepts and genres of the sensorium of the present from patterns that mediate social forces and become exemplary of a scene of sociality" (*CO*, 12). Furthermore, she openly recognizes affect's political ambivalence.

And yet, for all her attention to an irreducible materiality of bodies political, the operations of affective realism and psychoanalytical materialism at the heart of the affective object/scene are shot through with an insistence on dematerialization. Recall Clough's point about the power "beyond the manifest content of what's there," at play in the object/scene, or Berlant's suggestive words about rendering objects into things ("resistant, attractive enigma[s]"). If one could speak of a materialist phantasmagoria, this affective turn would fit perfectly, with the result that the affective body ends up being diffuse, spread (but not split) across the terrain of its interventions.

Nowhere is this diffuse character more evident than in the overtly paradoxical politics that admits—with more than a dose of refreshing realism, we may add—the dislodging of investment from expectation. The reconfiguration of the politics of aesthetics as a politics of failure does not mark a return to the moment before modernatism became consolidated, however. There is no turning back, only a turning again, a torsion of this arrangement. Here we find the autonomous force that the turn to affect names and animates: an alibi to preserve the exceptionality of the aesthetic. In yet another brilliant but troubling move, Berlant evacuates the old political of modernatism in order to make room for an ineffectual political aesthetics she calls "juxtapolitical."[89] It is not that aesthetics does not play a political role—it does, in Bush and Madansky all the same. Rather, it is the case that the aesthetic maintains an asymptotic relation to the political. This is affect's fiduciary: a contract with affect binds us to an autonomous force that we need, in some sense, but from which we expect nothing. The contract stands, however, and we thus need to scenify, over and over again. Affect, that is, marks another return: the "in-itself-for-us."

88. Berlant draws from André Green (*The Fabric of Affect in the Psychoanalytic Discourse*), who views affect as "a metapsychological cluster of activities related to the senses and emotions without originating in any particular place" (*CO*, 271n18).
89. Lauren Berlant, *The Female Complaint: The Unfinished Business of Sentimentality in American Culture* (Durham, NC: Duke University Press, 2008), 10.

The juxtapolitical renders "cruel optimism" as an ethical disposition. The resigned attitude of cruel optimism is the central modality of Berlant's political economy, which in turn renders the audible and the sonorous as an aesthetic therapy that doesn't (quite) work but may be all we are left with. In other words, "cruel optimism"—a symptom and an analytic—abdicates faith while retaining belief. This abdication recapitulates the ambivalence of the audible within the perceptual faith. From this perspective, the inexhaustibility of the audible and the sonorous is formally an illusion. The audible and the sonorous could never sustain an economy indefinitely. Or rather, it could sustain an economy that, to put it in the still-useful vocabulary of Marx, blurs the distinction between exchange-value and use-value, an economy in which *value itself* emerges as the only coin, but that, we believe, we can only trust with Marx's and Butler's satire.

Experiments in Civility

Bill Dietz and Gavin Steingo

Preface

It would seem that in many circles, music has a bad reputation. You can't trust music. One minute a piece of music is proclaiming the heights of Western civilization, the next minute the same piece is the sound track to genocide. Music is unfaithful, a slippery character. Or is it the other way around? Is it we who are slippery? Is it who or what we are in music—who or what music lets us become? There are those who would insist on using music's transformative power only for the purposes of "good"—that its value is as a partisan amplification of affect; there are others who imagine something like a music without music, a radical abdication of power—that music's value lies in its potential refusal of earthly, extant things. In both cases, music's own ambivalent "I would prefer not to" is fixed—frozen— managed into an instrument of its users. Yet in both cases, we remain vari- ably bound to music, to something insistently specific though transient, as well as to others also with us in music. What might be the value, then, of music's own inhuman, material indifference? With what exactly and how

boundary 2 43:1 (2016) DOI 10.1215/01903659-3340637 © 2016 by Duke University Press

are we bound to the identity of sonic entities, from noise to musical works (in the broadest sense of "the work"—as a framework or coherence that could encompass anything from a scored orchestral work to an indeterminate algorithm for performance or listening)? This essay is motivated by a single, polemical question: What if music's value was *precisely* its radically ambiguous nonpartisanship? Could a music committed to its own fundamental ambiguity rather than the values of specific instances for its appropriation facilitate novel forms of togetherness, of civil being?

Broadly, the instrumentalizing positions described above (amplification of affect vs. critical abdication of power) might be described as negative and affirmative poles within a normative paradigm for musical valuation in which value hinges upon the cultural work music performs. Within this paradigm, value is assessed in relation to the spectrum of prospects for identification and disidentification that a given musical instance is perceived to offer. However, in the wake of recent work in anthropology, political theory, and experimental music practice, the outlines of another accounting of musical valuation have begun to emerge. In the face of the convergence of musical modernism's apotheotic attempts to autonomize the quotidian, anthropology's so-called ontological turn, and a regulatory thinking of the political that attempts to delineate the conditions of enunciation and audition preceding vested articulation, the strategic contestation of music as identificatory metonym seems increasingly inadequate. It is within this constellation that the question of sound's "muteness," its nonanthropomorphic stubbornness, becomes significant beyond the typical disidentificatory topos of a "beyond." Following Étienne Balibar, we suggest that civility's call for the recognition of identity's intrinsic ambiguity gestures toward the emergence of a community in which "ultra-subjective violence"[1] would be reduced to an absolute minimum (and yet within which the presence of the irrational, of violence and cruelty per se, could not be reduced to absolute identity). Our aim, then, is to draw out the line between the material ambiguity—or even "autonomy"—of the sonic and musical and those "autonomous 'practices of the self' being constantly invented by [the] 'multitude,'" which Balibar describes as inseparable from the constitution of civility "from below."[2]

---

1. Étienne Balibar, "Three Concepts of Politics," in *Politics and the Other Scene* (London: Verso, 2002), 25.
2. Balibar, "Three Concepts of Politics," 33, 30.

Crowds, Music, Values

We open our inquiry with a question deeply embedded in a specific discourse, from which we quickly branch out: What differentiates the character of the bond between members of a progressive crowd from that of a reactionary crowd? Following Adorno in his calculated reading of Sigmund Freud's *Group Psychology and the Analysis of the Ego*, it is not the quality of the bond (*Bindung*) itself that characterizes the political character of a group but the intentionality preceding that bond's having been convened. This acknowledges, as Freud's earlier text does with far more radical ambiguity, that the mechanism of bonding in the formation of groups and crowds is libidinal, a relational framework applicable and adaptable to encounters from personal fantasy (being in love) to impersonal mass (constituents of a political rally).[3] Curiously enough, Adorno's text on group psychology and fascism[4] makes no mention of that particular group about which we might imagine he was most capable of speaking—that crowd of listeners known as "the audience." The simple operation of pointing Adorno's characterizations of group behavior and fascism in his text on Freud at a more particular group, the European postwar concert audience, illuminates not only the political stakes of his music philosophy but also the limits of his appropriation of the psychoanalytic vocabulary. In short, what becomes clear is that for Adorno the salient and equally ambiguous capacity of the musical work is its interpellation of the listener. He asks: What (who) is the subject of a given work? What subject position does a work offer me? Who (what) am I when I listen? And his answers are, of course, well known. It is no wonder following on the heels of World War II that art's only self-evidence, insofar as it facilitates "some gratification through identification with the existent— the focal point of fascist propaganda,"[5] could be its negative self-evidence. And it is no wonder, then, that Adorno extolls the antichoreography of postwar new music: music with which (in theory) no one could bob one's head, sing along, or march in step.

But for Adorno, the artwork's radical potential does not lie simply in

3. Sigmund Freud specifies the form of binding at work as identification, "the earliest expression of an affective bond to another person known to psychoanalysis." See his *Massenpsychologie und Ich-Analyse* (Frankfurt am Main: Fischer Verlag, 1971), 44. In this article, all translations of Freud are by Bill Dietz.
4. Theodor W. Adorno, "Freudian Theory and the Pattern of Fascist Propaganda," in *The Essential Frankfurt School Reader*, ed. Andrew Arato and Eike Gebhardt (New York: Continuum, 1982), 118–37.
5. Adorno, "Freudian Theory," 135.

its rejection of "every semblance of existing for society,"[6] since the commodity—just like the artwork—conceals the social relations of its production in the form of a fetish. The radicality of the artwork stems from its claim to nonexchangeability but not, Adorno rushes to point out, because it recovers some use-value from a world where exchange-value has triumphed. Instead, the artwork can do no more than gesture toward a lost form of use-value through the ironic gesture of uselessness: "Only what does not submit to [the principle of exchange] acts as the plenipotentiary of what is free from domination; only what is useless can stand in for the stunted use value. Artworks are plenipotentiaries of things that are no longer distorted by exchange, profit, and the false needs of a degraded humanity."[7] In other words, the "absolute artwork converges with the absolute commodity"[8] at the point at which both are fetishes, but the former short-circuits exchange-value through its complete uselessness. Only the inhuman, abstract artwork can reveal the way in which capital as "dead labor" thrives vampire-like by "sucking living labor," to use Marx's formulation.[9] As Stewart Martin surmises, "The implication [of Marx's theory of labor] for Adorno's account is that the artwork's objectivity is derived from its internalization of dead labour."[10]

In the *Grundrisse*, a young Marx had already commented that only the piano maker and *not* the pianist produces value. Stated in "mature" Marxist terms, this amounts to saying that the living labor of the pianist is not strictly speaking productive because it remains alive, while the piano maker's labor is transformed into the dead labor of the piano qua commodity. Adorno essentially agrees: that is, he does not affirm the value of living labor in the face of Marxist analysis, but instead goes on to show how the artwork flaunts its status as dead labor, unlike a chair, which pretends to hold value because it is comfortable to sit upon. It is clear, then, why Adorno rejects affirmative musical experiences—these are mere simulacra of a form of productive life no longer possible under the conditions of capitalism. And it is no wonder, then, that Adorno was particularly anxious

6. Theodor W. Adorno, *Aesthetic Theory*, trans. Robert Hullot-Kentor (Minneapolis: University of Minnesota Press, 1997), 236. Our reading of Adorno in this section is heavily indebted to Stewart Martin's article, "The Absolute Artwork Meets the Absolute Commodity," *Radical Philosophy* 146 (November/December 2007): 15–25.
7. Adorno, *Aesthetic Theory*, 227.
8. Adorno, *Aesthetic Theory*, 21.
9. Karl Marx, *Capital*, vol. 1, trans. Ben Fowkes (London: Penguin, 1976), 342.
10. Martin, "The Absolute Artwork Meets the Absolute Commodity," 20.

about the music of ecstatic crowds, which for him merely exaggerate the illusion of those simulacra.

Yet, there is also a strange reduction in Adorno's text, one with particular implications for the music he praises precisely for its rejection of the crowd. In Adorno's admission, with Freud, that the base structure and character of group bonds irrespective of political leaning are identical, Adorno names that libidinal bond itself "fascistic." As such, any potential group undertaking of "the emancipation of man from the heteronomous rule of his unconscious" is swept away with the generalization of fascism's regressive "abolition of 'psychology' . . . through the perpetuation of dependence instead of the realization of potential freedom, through expropriation of the unconscious by social control instead of making the subjects conscious of their unconscious."[11] This is, of course, the definition of Adorno's well-known claim in the same essay that fascism is "psychoanalysis in reverse." And yet, if there is something in group consciousness, in the libidinal structure of crowds itself, that points toward a potential for the "abolition of 'psychology'" *in a truly ambivalent sense*, then to label away this mechanism as such as "fascism" is also to erase the potential for an authentically progressive, emancipatory "abolition of 'psychology,'" the affirmative potential of the artwork as such, as Adorno traces it so often elsewhere in his music philosophy (for example, in listening to Beethoven: "a symphony as a whole, spontaneously experienced, can never be appropriated").[12] This throwing out of the emancipatory baby with the fascistic bathwater has had inestimable consequences, particularly in the theorization of contemporary music in Adorno's wake, and, qua Adorno's particular privileging of the emancipatory potential of the artwork's casting of subjectivity, in the political imaginary of potentials for group action.

Our contention is that reevaluating the relational framework upon which historically partisan distinctions can be drawn offers a reopening of a potential "otherwise" within the petrified domain of political group psychology. By "otherwise" we refer to the recent so-called ontological turn in the social sciences and to ontology "as the multiplicity of forms of existence enacted in concrete practices, where politics becomes the non-skeptical elicitation of this manifold of potentials for *how things could be*."[13] Insofar

11. Adorno, "Freudian Theory," 136.
12. Adorno, "On the Fetish-Character in Music and the Regression of Listening," in *Essays on Music*, ed. Richard Leppert, trans. Susan H. Gillespie (Berkeley: University of California Press, 2002), 288–317, esp. 299.
13. Martin Holbraad, Morten Axel Pedersen, and Eduardo Viveiros de Castro, "The Poli-

as the wake of Cagean "purposeful purposelessness" extended or at least threatened to extend into the composition of intersubjective constellations, contemporary music and the sonic arts, at a moment in which their raison d'être as "uselessness par excellence" threatens to devolve into stylization (a genre for a specialized, niche audience), become once again eminently relevant as fields upon which relational networks can not only be formulated but also enacted within the relative autonomy of the aesthetic domain. Practically then, to articulate this reevaluation of the collective libidinality preceding "political" appropriation requires first and foremost a rectification of Adorno's reading of Freud and his implicit characterization of group consciousness as inherently fascistic. We proceed, then, with a closer look at the makeup of Adorno's reading of Freud and Freud's original text, not only tracing the consequences of Adorno's reading via Heinz-Klaus Metzger and John Cage and more recent contemporary musics but also highlighting another reading of the Freudian text with a potential for other musical and political consequences. As the shadow of Adorno's now canonical criticality looms large—not only in the various guises of its institutionalized perpetuation but also in the negative spaces of its affirmative rejection—we then go on to examine various tropes of musical affirmation, group consciousness, and the political character thereof as articulated in the burgeoning new, critical studies of music.

The Negative Posit

Freud's text on groups offers a description of individual(ist) psychology that reads today as a remarkably prescient account of the psychology of postwar modernist music:

> Even one who does not mourn for the disappearance of religious illusions in the current cultural era must admit that as long as they were still in effect they offered those who were bound by them the strongest protection against the dangers of neurosis. . . . Left to himself, the neurotic is forced to replace the large group formations from which he is excluded with his own symptom formations. He creates his own fantasy world, his religion, his system of madness, and with them he repeats humanity's institutions with a distortion that

---

tics of Ontology: Anthropological Positions" (position paper for a roundtable discussion at the annual conference of the American Anthropological Association, Chicago, 2013), 2.

clearly testifies to the overly powerful contribution of direct sexual impulses.[14]

It is not insignificant, then, that the anarcho-individualist tendencies both embodied in the work of and espoused explicitly by Cage found their way into Adorno's later writings and came to even fuller prominence in the writings of Adorno's surrogate heir-in-music-philosophy, Metzger. After the zero hour of European modernist music's apotheosis in works such as Pierre Boulez's *Structures* (1951), works that seem to exclude the possibility of apperception by even a single listener much less a group (an audience), it is no wonder that Metzger opens his early text on Cage (which, from that point on, is to position Cage as chosen son of Music History) with Adorno's remark from *The Philosophy of New Music*: "the possibility of music itself has become uncertain. What endangers it is not, as the reactionaries accuse, that it is decadent, individualistic, or a-social. It is that it is those things too little."[15]

Cage's work is positioned to perpetuate the negative work of antifascism. Not toward the productive sublation of its listener "after" psychology, but rather prophylactically denying the listener regression into any form of the "existent" at any cost. That this conception of the Cagean project stands in distinct contrast to much of Cage's own thought and extra-German reception is largely irrelevant insofar as it functions as an inflationary placeholder for a field (New Music) that in and of itself remains to this day in various ways and to various degrees entrapped within the paradigm of negative aesthetics. The specter of Adorno looms large. His shadow stretches from the neo–high-modernist stances of a "Who cares if you listen?" Milton Babbitt in the United States and institutionalized counterparts in Europe (Helmut Lachenmann, Mathias Spahlinger, IRCAM) to the most trite "contemporary classical" confections in their presumably elevating instrumentalizations of vernacular musics. Both poles insist, indeed depend as their raison d'être, on a perpetual distinction as some form of "art music," relying upon various tropes and clichés of negativity and critique, whether those be some manner of quasi-politicized stance on culture industries or simply positing an alternative to the "speed and hecticness" of contemporary society. Even, for example, in the reception of the work of the

---

14. Freud, *Massenpsychologie*, 80.
15. Adorno, as quoted by Heinz-Klaus Metzger, "John Cage oder Die freigelassene Musik," in *Die freigelassene Musik: Schriften zu John Cage*, ed. Rainer Riehn and Florian Neuener (Vienna: Klever Verlag, 2012), 9–22, esp. 10; trans. Bill Dietz.

popular composer Arvo Pärt, whose work we can easily describe as a near dictionary definition of musical fascism (his closest musical relative being Carl Orff), one comes upon remnants of a critical vocabulary.

Here we have come full circle: that very same regressive abolition of psychology against which Adorno (perhaps over-effectively) strategically formulated his negative aesthetics (precisely the same "gratification through identification with the existent" that is the exclusive basis of composers such as Pärt's success) now itself claims to be its own cure. More fundamentally, however, the problem is not that the lingering traces of negative aesthetics in contemporary music are false or no longer ring true but rather that the fetish of negative aesthetics itself has stood for so long as the sole horizon for musical potential that its emancipatory horizon seems in the meantime all but forgotten. What is the status, however, of such claims in light of a closer look at Adorno's particular appropriation of the Freudian text? Toward the end of Adorno's text on the psychology of fascism he goes so far as to state that "fascism as such is *not* a psychological issue and that . . . [p]sychological dispositions do not actually cause fascism; rather, fascism defines a psychological area which can be successfully exploited by the forces which promote it for entirely nonpsychological reasons of self-interest . . . what might be called the appropriation of mass psychology by the oppressors."[16]

If this is indeed the case, how can this admission gel with Adorno's claim, just pages before, that "the applied group psychology discussed here [is] peculiar to fascism rather than to most other movements that seek mass support"?[17] Even if Adorno does ultimately recognize the ambivalence of the mechanisms at the base of group psychology, it is clear that his strategic aim is to highlight the fascistic potential of groups in the wake of the war and in the face of the emergence of postwar consumer capitalism.[18]

The limits of this strategy are, however, implicit in the language further linking Adorno and Freud, the language of historical teleology. The persistent contradictions between the group psychological mechanism in its ambivalent potential for appropriation and partisan distinctions between progressive and reactionary are a symptom of Adorno's inability to con-

---

16. Adorno, "Freudian Theory," 135–36.
17. Adorno, "Freudian Theory," 133.
18. Adorno writes that "there is no doubt that even the most progressive political movement can deteriorate to the level of the 'psychology of the crowd' and its manipulation, if its own rational content is shattered through the reversion to blind power." Adorno, "Freudian Theory," 135.

ceive of liberation apart from the grand telos of rational historical material-ism. His assertion that the "emancipation of man" is characterized by the emancipation from "the heteronomous rule of his unconscious" at once affirms the omnipresent parallel presence of the unconscious "through-out" history while simultaneously attempting to insert a messianic terminus of unification into a trajectory of linear development. That this posthistori-cal "level" would be irreconcilable with any form of political and/or psychic regression casts the parallelism of the unconscious, as Freud does, in the role of archaic remnant. Such temporalism of psychic topology is for both authors likewise inseparable from a vulgarly chauvinistic anthropologism pitted against primitives and savages. Indeed, Adorno's valorization of the individual against the regression of the group can be read in perfect paral-lel with Freud's account of the "Ur-horde": "The crowd appears to us as a revivification of the Ur-horde. . . . We must conclude that the psychology of the crowd is the oldest form of human psychology; what we have isolated by neglecting all traces of the crowd as individual psychology arose only little by little later and, so to speak, partially from the old group psychology."[19]

This Ur-horde is for Freud, as for Adorno, pitted against rational, modern, and insistently heteronormativized subjects. In Freud's primal ori-gin narrative of the emergence of group and individual psychologies, "the fixing of the libido on the woman" in opposition to the primal father's insis-tence on his sons' "abstinence and thereby to their affective bonding to him and to each other" is directly equated with the opening "of the exit from the conditions of group psychology."[20] Likewise, regardless of the postwar shading of Adorno's views on homosexuality, his suggestion of an equation of gayness with fascism (which, like his strategic equation of group psychol-ogy with fascism, would seem to be something he claims but also knows better than to) does indeed speak to the centrality of the monogamous, exogamous heterosexual dyad in the imaginary of his logic of historical progression.[21] The significance of this particular distribution of libidinality is inseparable from his inability and resistance to analytically conceive of a nonfascistic group psychology.

If the masses' potential for resistance is their rationality (as Adorno puts it), their existence or constitution as masses as such depends, how-ever, upon the irrationality of the libidinal bond. Further, if we would still

19. Freud, *Massenpsychologie*, 63.
20. Freud, *Massenpsychologie*, 64.
21. Adorno, "Freudian Theory," 122.

attempt to follow Adorno, what could a rationality "of the masses" actually mean—a rationality not of an individual, but an intelligence of a libidinal (and plural) body? Freud, in the writerly wildness of his commitment to tracing the asociality of the unconscious, seems almost inadvertently to come upon the beginnings of such a suggestion, of a radically other collectivity already embedded within the psychology of groups:

> Where groups made up of men and women form, sexual difference plays no role. It makes almost no sense to ask if the libido which holds the group together is of a homosexual or heterosexual nature because it is not differentiated by genders and entirely abandons the goals of genital organization. . . . It seems certain that homosexual love is particularly compatible with group bonds, even when it appears as an unrestrained sexual impulse; a strange fact, the explanation of which could lead quite far.[22]

Though certainly written as an account of deviance from the "mature" genitality of a modern heterosexual individual, taken on its own this shockingly queer paragraph seems to precisely describe that mode of homosexual becoming which Michel Foucault praised as "a historic occasion to reopen affective and relational virtualities not so much through the intrinsic qualities of the homosexual but because of the 'slantwise' position of the latter, as it were, the diagonal lines he can lay out in the social fabric allow these virtualities to come to light."[23] Or put another way, the ambivalence and indiscriminate potentiality of the group psychological mechanism (which contains within it, or rather which is characterized by, a fundamentally other relationship to the parallel terrain of the unconscious than that of enlightened, rational subjectivity) in itself already hints at the outlines of a nonfascistic collectivity, one, however, that would be fully and radically incompatible with cis-sexual libidinal distributions and chauvinisms of teleology.

Freud seems certain that the unveiling of the sexual nature of the group bond would lead to the group's dissolution, to a panic. Adorno also insists repeatedly that the condition of the smooth functioning of the fascistic group is the repression and latency of the group's sexual underpinnings. If, however, the heterosexist mores of both authors are lifted, this repres-

---

22. Freud, *Massenpsychologie*, 80.
23. Michel Foucault, "Friendship as a Way of Life," in *Ethics: Subjectivity and Truth*, vol. 1 of *The Essential Works of Foucault, 1954–1984* (New York: New Press, 1998), 135–40, esp. 138.

sion compulsion seems less and less necessary. Indeed, perhaps the very condition of a nonfascistic group psychology's formulation would be both the explicit acknowledgment of the libidinality of the group's bond *and* the decisive, conscious persistence of the group thereafter.

This brings us back to that group so conspicuously absent from Adorno's text on group psychology: the concert audience. What is an audience but a *Massenbildung* par excellence? Without the masculinist, heteronormative bias in Adorno's scene of auditory sublation, of apprehending the work in all the splendor of its liberatory potential, how might shifting the pronoun of the interpellative subject alter the promise of the work? Who are *we* when we listen "en masse"? And if in listening together we are already at least a latent nonmonogamous, queer bunch, how might a music consciously aware of and intervening into this distribution of libido help articulate the explication and exportation of such modes of being together into political actuality? How can audition be a means to something like a psychoanalysis proper (that is, not in reverse), which could lead to the "realization of potential freedom . . . making the subjects conscious of their unconscious"?

The Affirmative Posit

On the heels of our response to music's "negative" history above, how are we to respond to the ceaseless positing of music's capacity for social affirmation characterizing so much music scholarship since the 1980s? Though at times under the moniker of a return to Adorno,[24] Adorno's theorization of music as autonomous, negative, and "useless" is more often derided as Eurocentric post-Kantianism and assigned to the dustbin of history. Two major underlying factors provoked this impulse. First was a general reaction against cultural chauvinism and the Germanic, male-dominated repertoire that forms the basis of the Western canon. The second factor—which we elaborate upon in detail below—concerned the very ontological status of negation. For many "critical" scholars in the past thirty years, the

24. See the early classic anthology of the "New Musicology," *Music and Society: The Politics of Composition, Performance and Reception*, ed. Richard Leppert and Susan McClary (Cambridge: Cambridge University Press, 1987). The reception of Adorno by the so-called New Musicologists was both uneven and contradictory. For example, while McClary takes inspiration from Adorno's insistence that there exists a definite relationship between music and society, she nonetheless rejects his equally emphatic argument that this "relationship" is primarily one of negation.

idea that music can be "useless" and, therefore, a negation of the useful world of commodities and things is nothing more than ideological mystification. Music, like anything else, the argument runs, is socially useful, seamlessly connected to social constructions like gender and race (that is, it is not "autonomous"), and basically productive rather than negative. This argument is at root a critique of Western aesthetic theory *de natura*: if the central tenet of Kant's aesthetics is disinterested judgment, the scholarship of the last thirty years has never tired of repeating that everyone is always and already interested. No practice or act is ever "outside" power and material interest.[25] If such postmodern affirmations are distinct from our own (they are, as we will show), how so?

Although the pluralization of the canon was certainly a battle well worth fighting, and although from a basic positivistic standpoint critical music scholars may be correct that nothing is ever really "useless," musicology's affirmative posit came at a high price. For one thing, the allegedly "critical" theoretical work of the past thirty years has essentially affirmed the political and economic status quo. If music can only ever say "yes," as James Currie has recently pointed out, then its critical capacity is vanquished.[26] Oddly, the always contingent nature of this "yes" seems to form an unexpected link between the limits of Adorno's frail messianism and the discourses of "critical" musicology, namely the persistence of the "always-identical"[27] in both: for Adorno, the blind spot of his inability to imagine an otherwise separate from the assumptions of his own cultural and sexual identity; for "critical" musicology, the abandonment of imagining an otherwise altogether in the affirmation of multiple identities.

Our task, then, is to develop an affirmative posit that does more than affirm existing social relations. Before embarking on that task, however, it will be worthwhile to carefully examine and distinguish between several prominent intellectual trajectories of affirmation. In what follows, we describe three such trajectories in which—to anticipate later arguments—music is valorized because it:

25. As David Graeber quips, in much critical thought the "assumption is that 'objective' or 'scientific' analysis means trying to cut through to the level on which you can say people are being selfish, and that when one discovers this, one's job is done." See his *Toward an Anthropological Theory of Value: The False Coin of Our Own Dreams* (New York: Palgrave, 2001), 29–30.
26. James Currie, *Music and the Politics of Negation* (Bloomington: Indiana University Press, 2012).
27. Adorno, "On the Fetish-Character in Music," 314.

1. Recognizes and affirms the social; it admits to being always and already social
2. Makes connections and attachments with other things swiftly and flexibly
3. Deterritorializes sonic matter and social collectivities.

We address each position in turn.

1. Admitting the Social

If, for Adorno, the artwork first "converges with the commodity" as a fetish object and subsequently refuses exchangeability by virtue of its uselessness, a large body of musicological literature over the past thirty years has essentially endeavored to uncover and unmask the fetishism of absolute music without, however, accounting for the subsequent insight about music's nonexchangeability.[28] Whether directly or indirectly, music scholarship often follows Pierre Bourdieu's famous maxim that "aesthetic distinction"—that is, the assertion that *some* people value music for its own sake, outside of social and political interests—is in fact "a misrecognized form of *social* difference."[29] In other words, the very basis of Adorno's critique—namely, that artworks not only mask social relations but in fact *insist* on that masking as the foundation of their critical capacity[30]—is brushed away under the sign of "cultural capital." For Bourdieu and his heirs, "absolute" music qua fetish object serves no critical function and is instead simply a displaced form of social difference, even of social domination. From this

28. To reiterate a point made earlier, Adorno readily admits that artworks are fetishistic: "It was plausible that socially progressive critics should have accused the program of *l'art pour l'art*, which has often been in league with political reaction, of promoting a fetish with the concept of a pure, exclusively self-sufficient artwork. What is true in this accusation is that artworks, products of social labor that are subject to or produce their own law of form, seal themselves off from what they themselves are. To this extent, each artwork could be charged with false consciousness and chalked up to ideology." See Adorno, *Aesthetic Theory*, 227.
29. Pierre Bourdieu, *Distinction: A Social Critique of the Judgment of Taste*, trans. Richard Nice (Cambridge, MA: Harvard University Press, 1984), 493, our emphasis.
30. Adorno: "Artworks that do not insist fetishistically on their coherence, as if they were the absolute that they are unable to be, are worthless from the start; the survival of art becomes precarious as soon as it becomes conscious of its fetishism and, as has been the case since the middle of the nineteenth century, insists obstinately on it. Art cannot advocate delusion by insisting that otherwise art would not exist. This forces art into an aporia. All that succeeds in going even minutely beyond it is insight into the rationality of its irrationality." See Adorno, *Aesthetic Theory*, 228.

perspective, the sociological "fact" that all music is social can only result in a valorization of musical traditions that admit to their sociality and to a denigration of European "bourgeois" musics that perniciously mask those social relations.

Thus, Susan McClary writes about the "ideological basis of music's operations" that "allow[s] cultural activities to 'make sense'" whether or not people notice it.[31] For McClary, the "social" is always and already present in music—however much music aims to hide it—and the job of the analyst is to uncover those social dimensions, particularly where they are not readily admitted. Consider, for example, her seminal article, "Terminal Prestige," which begins with a series of quotes by famous modernist (male) composers expressing a deep antipathy toward an audience.[32] For Roger Sessions, Arnold Schoenberg, and Milton Babbitt, music composition is an activity that happens in the service of music itself, and an audience's reaction to it is largely irrelevant. As Schoenberg quips, the value of music is inversely proportional to a positive reaction by a crowd. Schoenberg, scion of Adorno's negative aesthetics, does not value "loneliness" in and of itself but sees it as a necessary *sacrifice* for music's historical progress.[33] McClary observes that while music is valued differently in human societies—"it may participate in ritual, facilitate the physical motions of dance or labor, serve as entertainment, provide pleasure, stand as a manifestation of ideal beauty or order, and so on"—only in the twentieth century is concert music valued precisely for its *denunciation* of social values.[34] But in every claim of musical autonomy, in every argument for a composer's withdrawal from society and for music's inherent value, McClary detects a pernicious underlying motivation. In the cases of Sessions, Schoenberg, and especially of Babbitt, the claim of purely musical value is unmasked as a power play, as a strategy for accruing cultural capital and gaining prestige.

Following McClary, much Anglophone music scholarship has largely concerned itself with uncovering what European "art" music had previously sought to cover over, to repress. If European aesthetic theory had

---

31. See Susan McClary, *Conventional Wisdom: The Content of Musical Form* (Berkeley: University of California Press, 2000), 5–6.
32. Susan McClary, "Terminal Prestige: The Case of Avant-Garde Music Composition," *Cultural Critique*, no. 12 (Spring 1989): 57–81.
33. The title of the Schoenberg essay that McClary cites is "How One Becomes Lonely."
34. McClary, "Terminal Prestige," 60. McClary interprets the twentieth-century avant-garde as a kind of apotheosis of European "absolute" music beginning in the late eighteenth century.

repressed the body, rhythm, social interaction, and sexual pleasure while valorizing the mind, harmony, and contemplative or "structural" listening, then the job of music scholars is, first, to reveal the repressed corporeal sociality within European art music and, second, to reassess low-status musics that made no excuses about their corporeal and social constitution. This explains why many musicologists in the 1990s and early twenty-first century tended to valorize musical traditions that openly celebrate the capacity for bodily pleasure and intense sociality. These musical traditions, one might say, *recognize and affirm the social*, or they *fully admit* that they are always and already social.

But there are three problems, or at least limitations, with this position. The first is political: in valorizing the always-present sociality of musical practices, theorists risk celebrating any and all "musical communities" irrespective of their outcomes, of the values driving their instrumentalizations of musically facilitated sociality. As Tracy McMullen argues, "While performing in or listening to a live musical group is often a profoundly intercorporeal experience, it is not necessarily a progressive one."[35] And as McMullen makes clear in her careful study of contemporary European orchestras, whose ranks are still heavily dominated by white men, "paeans to intercorporeality may simply put a new name on some very old phenomena: male bonding, racial segregation, heteronormativity, and the good ol' boys network."[36] This is, again, what we meant earlier when we spoke of music affirming the status quo. The second problem is epistemological: in their eager attempts to unmask what was previously repressed, musicologists often retain the very terms and binary logic that they seek to undermine. Amy Cimini detects what she calls a "crypto-dualism" in much musicological discourse: the body and the social are celebrated while the mind and contemplative listening are denigrated.[37] The "social," from this perspective, only appears against the horizon of the antisocial (mind, soul), which suggests that musicology's "affirmative posit" turns out to be awkwardly dialectical. This brings us to the third limitation, which can only be described as ontological: if music were to be completely "defetishized" into a set of social and intercorporeal relations, then it would no longer be possible to speak of "music" at all. In other words, music's very possibility requires a

---

35. Tracy McMullen, "Corpo-Realities: Keepin' It Real in 'Music and Embodiment' Scholarship," *Current Musicology*, no. 82 (Fall 2006): 61–80.
36. McMullen, "Corpo-Realities," 68.
37. Amy Cimini, "Baruch Spinoza and the Matter of Music: Toward a New Practice of Theorizing Musical Bodies" (PhD diss., New York University, 2011).

minimal level of "fetishization," requires a certain congealing of social and material relations. Here, then, the total defetishization of music qua music is impossible. This is, again, as Adorno said, precisely where the artwork converges with the commodity—even if in the twenty-first century the commodity is less a reified and "objective" artwork than a coagulation of affective relations. As Marx knew only too well, simply uncovering the social relations and necessary labor time behind commodities through analysis does not lead to the end of capitalism. Although we may "know" that the value of a commodity is not inherent within that commodity but is derived from labor time, we still act in our everyday lives *as if* the value of a commodity is based on its inherent qualities. In short, economic activities are predicated upon an essential nonrecognition (or misrecognition). This is the case with music as well: we "know" that music is really just a set of social relations and not some autonomous object or practice, but we experience music as if it is somehow something other, or more, than a set of social relations. Short of eschatology, it is therefore impossible for music to ever fully recognize or admit to its absolutely social constitution. It must always retain a certain "fetishistic" investment. Our aim, then, in contradistinction to *this* "affirmative posit," is not to dissolve (defetishize) music but to reorient (refetishize) its quasi-autonomous practices of performance and listening into a praxis of the "otherwise."[38] We return to this idea below.

2. Making Connections and Attachments

In contrast to McClary, the sociologist Tia DeNora argues that the work of critical musicology is not at all to uncover social relations embedded in musical works or performances, as this "presumes to know what [music] stands for."[39] DeNora is more interested in "articulations," that is, in the ways that musical realities "come to be articulated with social realities. to describe how music actually comes to be positioned as analogous for extra-musical activity."[40] She sums up the point succinctly: "[W]e *do things to music and do things with music*: dance and ride in the case of the bike boys,[41] but beyond this many of us may (at least occasionally), eat, fall

38. For an earlier consideration that does not yet articulate the argument in terms of an "otherwise," see Bill Dietz, "Composing Listening," *Performance Research* 16, no. 3 (2011): 56–61.
39. Tia DeNora, "The Musical Composition of Social Reality? Music, Action, and Reflexivity," *Sociological Review* 43, no. 2 (1995): 295–315, esp. 308.
40. DeNora, "The Musical Composition of Social Reality?," 308.
41. DeNora is here referring to Willis's book *Profane Culture* (1978).

asleep, dance, daydream, exercise, celebrate, commemorate, even procreate, to music."[42]

Sharpening her argument, DeNora offers a telling response to McClary's analysis of Bizet's *Carmen*. McClary's argument is that although the melodic and harmonic features in that opera are often passed off as purely musical, a critical analysis reveals that they are laden with gendered and sexual meaning. For McClary, every musical gesture is imbued with meaning: ascending melodies are analogous with sexual climax, while breaking the pitch ceiling is considered an analogue to vaginal penetration. Anyone who refutes these analogies is, to McClary's mind, misrecognizing the aesthetic for the social. DeNora's question remains: How does McClary know this? Why does an ascending scale mean sexual climax and not the rising sun or the ascending soul? DeNora argues that the musical features McClary describes are "not *necessarily* sexual . . . rather, they connote a manner of sexual energy *when we* (learn to) *hear them* as making that kind of representation, when we map a sexual activity onto music, and vice versa."[43] Where McClary attempts to decode musical meaning, DeNora looks ethnographically at how people do things with and to music. A person or group of people may learn to hear *Carmen* as sexual, but another person or group of people may plausibly eat, fall asleep, dance, daydream, exercise, procreate to it.

In a similar vein to DeNora, Lawrence Kramer emphasizes the way that music forms multiple attachments: "Verbal attributions of meaning to music have the force of constructive descriptions: they do not decode the music or reproduce a meaning already there in it but attach themselves to the music as an independent form or layer of appearance, 'its own seeming.'"[44] In Kramer's view, although meaning *seems* to derive from music, it would be more accurate to say that meanings glob on to music and only then, retroactively, appear to be qualities of the music itself.

While DeNora and Kramer both insist on music's radical *sociality*, they nonetheless do not endeavor to uncover the social relations that music attempts to conceal but instead view music as something that exists a priori and can be *used* to forge associations, connections, and attachments. From this perspective, although these scholars are interested in music's

---

42. DeNora, "The Musical Composition of Social Reality?," 300, original emphasis.
43. DeNora, "The Musical Composition of Social Reality?," 308.
44. Lawrence Kramer, "Subjectivity Rampant! Music, Hermeneutics, and History," in *The Cultural Study of Music*, ed. Martin Clayton, Trevor Herbert, and Richard Middleton (New York: Routledge, 2003), 124–35, esp. 128.

relations, they stop short of being "relationalists" in Latour's sense that an entity is constituted *by* its relations.[45] Music is valorized for its capacity to forge multiple relations and associations, but music itself is not defined by those relations. One might say that for DeNora and Kramer music is valued because it is *particularly good at making attachments.*

As was the case with McClary's position, here again we detect significant limitations. From a political perspective, the notion that music is good at forming attachments is fine, so long as we acknowledge that this capacity is completely ambiguous (an ambiguity not dissimilar from that of the libidinal bonding of groups as discussed earlier). For us, music's capacity to make connections and attachments is neither inherently progressive nor regressive, and the radicality of this ambiguity is not taken up by any of the aforementioned authors—an oversight not without political consequence, making it difficult to deny a certain parallelism between music's "flexibility" and late capitalist labor practices. From an ontological perspective, we ask: If music's value is in the connections that it facilitates, and if there is very little one can say about music "itself" in the absence of attachments, then what is the ontological status of music? DeNora and Kramer speak of music both as something that exists a priori *and* as something that does not exist in any meaningful way until it is attached. This suggests an ontological aporia that has not, to our knowledge, been addressed.

Consider *Carmen* briefly again. We have already said that for DeNora the opera is not inherently sexual but is only sexual when we have learned to hear it that way. And we have acknowledged that the opera—like all music—is open to multiple interpretations, attachments, and relations: one can eat, fall asleep, dance, daydream, exercise, procreate to it. But does this mean that one can "do" *anything* to it or with it or that one can learn to interpret it in *any* way? Does this mean that one can do anything to any music and that one can interpret any music in any way? In truth, the argument as laid out by DeNora would oblige us to answer "yes" to all of these questions, a particularly unsatisfying conclusion.[46]

45. For an excellent account of relationality in Latour's work, see Graham Harman, *The Prince of Networks: Bruno Latour and Metaphysics* (Melbourne: re.press, 2009). For a musicological account of attachments that more robustly examines the relational coconstitution of music and listening subjects, see the work of Antoine Hennion, for example "Music Lovers: Taste as Performance," *Theory, Culture, & Society* 18, no. 5 (2007): 1–22.

46. One possible solution is that every piece of music affords a large yet finite *range* of possible interpretations and attachments. One might argue, as James Johnson suggests, that the oboe melody from Haydn's "Le Poule" sounds like a hen, or even an expression

It is also worth pointing out that in both of the affirmative posits we have thus far considered, affirming music means quite precisely denying the possibility of a desire *for* music. For the critical musicologist (exemplified by McClary), a desire for music is always a desire for something else, most often some repressed tendency of normative sexuality. For DeNora and her peers, music is valued only because one can do *other* things to and with it. Such displacements of musical desire onto something else mirror the classical economic theory of commodity exchange. For economists such as Adam Smith and David Ricardo, money is conceptualized as a mechanism for the universal exchange of commodities. But in the orthodox view, money is not itself considered a commodity and is therefore not directly desirable. As the philosopher Noam Yuran points out, the desire *for* money is anathema in orthodox economics. But, he continues, this assumption actually obscures the obvious fact that money has a definite relationship to desire that is irreducible to its exchangeability.[47] Thus, if Adorno tells us that the "absolute artwork converges with the absolute commodity," this formulation works best if we understand the absolute commodity as money. And if there is a desire for money—not just for what money can buy, but for money itself—then it is not far-fetched to posit a desire for music itself, for music as an object/experience irreducible to its meanings or attachments. Disambiguating a desire for music as such vis-à-vis these musicological positions could function akin to the distinction between primary and secondary psychic processes in psychoanalysis, whereby the latent desires "revealed" in critical musicology would represent secondary articulations, those having passed through the rebus of repression. Positioned thus, music might be said to be an exemplary "queer" object of desire.[48]

3. The Deterritorialization of Sonic Matter and Social Collectivities

The third prominent intellectual trajectory that affirms music's relationship to the social is best exemplified by the work of Gilles Deleuze

---

of merriment, but *not* a funeral dirge, or the storming of the Bastille, or the promotion of slavery. Such a suggestion hinges upon various assumptions regarding mimesis and semiosis. See James Johnson, *Listening in Paris: A Cultural History* (Berkeley: University of California Press, 1995), 2; as cited in Nicholas Cook, "Rethinking Musical Meaning," *Music Theory Spectrum* 23, no. 2 (2003): 170–95, esp. 177.

47. See Noam Yuran, *What Money Wants: An Economy of Desire* (Stanford, CA: Stanford University Press, 2014).

48. The adjective *queer* might also fall short here in its colloquial tendency to refer simply to yet another constellation. Closer to our meaning would be a non- or postgenital bodily distribution of libidinality.

and Félix Guattari, who understand music as a process of deterritorialization, of becoming. For Deleuze and Guattari, musical form is rhizomatic;[49]
the "properly musical content of music is plied by becomings-woman,
becomings-child, becomings-animal."[50] From their nondialectical perspective, they wax lyrical about modern musicians who reject the "transcendent
plane" for the "immanent sound plane, which is always given along with
that to which it gives rise."[51] They associate music with assemblages and
multiplicities, but only those aimed at becomings and disidentifications. As
a process that deterritorializes sonic blocks called refrains, music ranges
wildly over different forms of life (including animals, such as birds), and precisely because of this exerts incredible force. Comparing music with painting, Deleuze and Guattari write, "Music seems to have a much stronger
deterritorializing force, at once more intense and much more collective,
and the voice seems to have a much greater power of deterritorialization."[52]
Note that the emphasis on deterritorialization and disidentification is in no
way "negative." On the contrary, these musical capacities are radically affirmative, productive, and immanent.

If McClary affirms music's social affectivity to the point of divesting
anything "musical" from music, and if DeNora and Kramer affirm music's
capacity to forge multiple attachments, rendering "music" an entity so
empty and untrammeled by the social that it can *become* social in any way
imaginable, Deleuze and Guattari, finally, explicitly affirm music's capacity
for becoming and disidentification. Of the three positions, Deleuze and
Guattari's perhaps comes closest to our own, particularly in its drawing
upon psychoanalytic discourse and rejection of the notion of desire as lack.
Although we admire their unrelenting search—via music, art, science, and
ethnography—for constructions of the "otherwise," their notion thereof is
always limited to the complete rejection or even call for the destruction of
identification per se. This complete rejection of identification is due, in part,
to the refusal of subjectivity *de natura*.

Though we wholeheartedly endorse Deleuze and Guattari's key
insight that both music and literature—music, all the more so—are "real
experimentations on the real, means of capturing, dissolving and trans-
muting existing relations of force and then reshaping them in new configu-

49. Gilles Deleuze and Félix Guattari, *A Thousand Plateaus: Capitalism and Schizophrenia*, trans. Brian Massumi (Minneapolis: University of Minnesota Press, 1987), 12.
50. Deleuze and Guattari, *A Thousand Plateaus*, 248.
51. Deleuze and Guattari, *A Thousand Plateaus*, 267.
52. Deleuze and Guattari, *A Thousand Plateaus*, 302.

rations,"[53] our agreement ends with the authors' reductive qualification of their insight—at least as it is articulated in *A Thousand Plateaus*—on music's tendency away from territorialization toward deterritorialization.[54] Instead, our interest is to explore a variety of morphogenetic processes and topological spaces, including those without "steady" states of equilibrium. Here, we come upon a repertoire for identifications inherently oscillatory and unstable, and yet distinct. Exemplary of such complex bodies with diffuse and yet determinate identities would be the periodic or chaotic attractors of dynamic systems, or something as familiar as falling snow (in Emerson's terminology, as David Grubbs and Susan Howe have recently investigated it, "frolic architecture"[55]). Deleuze himself developed a rich account of nonlinear systems, and the implications of that account for a theory of music have been outlined by his followers.[56] All too often, however, Deleuze ignores the precise ways that sound is reconfigured through music—ignores the variety of stable, unstable, and semistable states in which it might exist—and instead focuses almost exclusively on disidentification, deterritorialization, minoritarianism, and nomadism.

Returning to our initial invocation of Balibar, our investigation is not limited to seeking out mechanisms of disidentification, and is likewise not limited by an affirmation of identity that would eliminate the possibility of a social otherwise. Instead, after Balibar, our affirmative posit is one that "regulates the conflicts of identifications" in order "to *create a* (public, private) *space* for politics (emancipation, transformation)."[57] To better understand how this works, it is necessary to imagine a radical and yet *not inherently violent* framework for politics, that is, a politics of civility. If the *work* of

53. Ronald Bogue, "Minority, Territory, Music," in *An Introduction to the Philosophy of Gilles Deleuze*, ed. Jean Khalfa (London: Continuum, 2003), 114–32, esp. 130. Note that Bogue's reference to literature refers to Deleuze's single-authored work.

54. As is well known, Deleuze and Guattari also speak of "reterritorialization," but this third term does not undo the binary oscillation between the forming and unforming of a territory.

55. Grubbs and Howe's collaborative work of the same name is available on CD on the Blue Chopsticks label (2011). See also Chloë Bass's "An Architecture of Poetry and Sound," accessed June 12, 2015, hyperallergic.com/97949/an-architecture-of-poetry-and-sound/.

56. For an excellent account of Deleuze's relationship to complex system theory, see Manuel DeLanda, *Intensive Science and Virtual Philosophy* (London: Continuum, 2002), and for a suggestive attempt at constructing a Deleuzian music theory that takes full account of topology, see DeLanda, "The Virtual Breeding of Sound," in *Sound Unbound: Sampling Digital Music and Culture*, ed. Paul D. Miller (Cambridge, MA: MIT Press, 2008), 219–26.

57. Balibar, *Politics and the Other Scene*, 29–30.

art (music) is indeed that of "real experimentations on the real," our task is in large part to extract this strain of implicit "research" from its historical trajectory and to coax contemporary work into a relational "explicitness" that could be of political consequence.

Experiments in Civility (Nonfascistic Group Psychology)

To turn to civility is in a sense to turn to the question of the possibility of an authentically nonfascistic crowd: toward a form of community self-consciously convened in keeping with the libidinal character of the bond at its base, and yet also insisting upon maintaining the mobility of that bond. Civility is a form of relationality that allows for identification but refuses to equate identification with fascism. Balibar: "I shall call a politics which regulates the conflicts of identifications between the impossible (and yet, in a sense, very real) limits of total and floating identification, 'civility.' Civility in this sense is certainly not a politics which suppresses all violence; but it excludes extremes of violence, so as to *create a* (public, private) *space* for politics (emancipation, transformation), and enable violence itself to be historicized."[58]

As such, civility is neither an extension of the Adornian fantasy of a total negativity perpetually refusing and deflecting violence nor a postmodern erasure of the political's radical horizon. Instead, civility is a historicized space, a relational topology, from which a political otherwise might yet emerge. In Balibar's words, it is "a conjunctural question, a question of the art of politics—and perhaps only of art, since the only means civility has at its disposal are statements, signs and roles."[59] Our proposal, then, is to reconsider musical practices as laboratories for experiments in civility, practices ceaselessly formulating conjunctural questions.

58. Balibar, *Politics and the Other Scene*, 29–30.
59. Balibar, *Politics and the Other Scene*, 35. Elsewhere, Balibar explicitly affirms that politics is experimental. Elucidating the "proposition of equaliberty" (that is, the proposition that there is no liberty without equality and no equality without liberty), he writes that "the reasoning underlying the proposition of equaliberty ($E = F$) is not essentialist. It is not based on the intuitive discovery or revelation of an identity of the *ideas* of equality and freedom. What it is based on is the historical discovery, *which can legitimately be called experimental*, that their *extensions* are necessarily identical. To put it plainly, the situations in which both are either present or absent are necessarily the same." See Balibar, "'Rights of Man' and 'Rights of the Citizen': The Modern Dialectic of Equality and Freedom," in *Masses, Classes, Ideas: Studies in Politics and Philosophy Before and After Marx*, trans. James Swenson (New York: Routledge, 1994), 39–59, esp. 48, our emphasis.

Balibar's intervention allows us to negotiate between the negative and affirmative polarities we have thus far described. If for Adorno and Freud fascism is linked precisely to the loss of subjectivity in the crowd, and the only adequate response to fascism is the becoming "someone" of the subject (the problem being that for Adorno and Freud this "someone" is always a specific historical subject: European, hetero, and cisgendered), for Deleuze and Guattari, avoiding fascism is only possible through radical disidentification, through becoming "no one," a multitude, a crowd.[60] Balibar's argument is that modern politics is played out in the tension and oscillation between these two extremes: the reduction of subjectivity to unitary, unambiguous identities, on the one hand, and "a certain 'postmodern' utopia" that "would allow identity to float freely between roles," on the other.

Although couched in terms very different from the ones we are employing now, the various music scholars and sociologists considered above can also be understood in relation to these two poles. McClary, for example, debunks the myth of abstract or "universal" music that transcends any particular culture or historical period and shows instead that music is always produced and consumed by very specific identities. DeNora, by contrast, never advocates something like asubjectivity or pure becoming, but instead shows that multiple fixed identities swirl around and attach themselves flexibly to music. For McClary, a leap from "no one" to "someone." For DeNora, the floating of fixed identities around a radically empty mediator she terms "music." What would it mean, however, to begin to think the outlines of a musical praxis that is not reducible to becoming a "someone" (as this "someone" is always figured against the ground of hegemonic subjectivity) nor becoming "no one" (because this implies violent disidentification)? And what would it mean to think a framework for musical praxis that simultaneously goes beyond the oscillation between these two extremes?

Perhaps the latent "progressive" character of the musical crowd is that it implies neither a total loss of individual subjectivity nor the reifica-

---

60. As Deleuze and Guattari write in one famous passage, "In becoming, one is deterritorialized. Even blacks, as the Black Panthers said, must become-black. Even women must become-women. Even Jews must become-Jewish. . . . In a way, the subject in a becoming is always 'man,' but only when he enters a becoming-minoritarian that rends him from his major identity. . . . This is the opposite of macropolitics, and even of history, in which it is a question of knowing how to win or obtain a majority. As Faulkner said, to avoid ending up a fascist there was no other choice than to become-black." See *A Thousand Plateaus* (London: Athlone Press, 1988), 291–92; as cited in Balibar, *Politics and the Other Scene*, 22–23.

tion of unambiguous identities but rather regulates these extremes, opening a political space for (back to Foucault's term) "slantwise" someones. Any practice of the otherwise necessitates thinking potentiality outside the dominant paradigm of the "transcendental architecture of the horizon,"[61] that is, of a form of futurity that may be "fused" (à la Gadamer) with what is already known or at least knowable. To do so requires experimentation with the radical potentiality immanent to all people, groups, and things. As Elizabeth Povinelli observes, the Deleuzian concepts of the "fold and rhizome were meant as a politics and ethics grounded on radical immanence—the becoming community—in which 'immanence is no longer immanence to anything other than itself.'"[62] But as she goes on to suggest, Deleuze's convenient formulations leave many questions unanswered: "What if one striving potentiating meets and opposes another? Can progressive politics avoid this question—and thus the problem of extinguishment? How would the sign 'progressive' read if it were understood as always actively maintaining, producing, and *extinguishing* worlds?"[63] In brief: "How can we imagine pure immanence and radical potentiality without becoming blind to the extinguishments of forms of life that every actual world entails?"[64] Povinelli's remark recalls a point we have been making in different ways throughout this essay, namely, that immanence knows no Left or Right, has no a priori ethics or morality. Immanence, by its very definition, simply is. As a response to this, Povinelli replaces the figures of the fold and the rhizome with that of the bag and of "embagination." For her, an "anthropology of the otherwise" might profitably consider emergent social relations in terms of a bag framework that always surrounds the social but never entirely seals it.[65]

Although we find this proposal provocative, we remain nonetheless somewhat squeamish regarding the recent proliferation of "zonal ontologies,"[66] from Povinelli's bag to Sloterdijk's spheres and Latour's net-

61. Elizabeth Povinelli, "After the Last Man: Images and Ethics of Becoming Otherwise," *e-flux*, no. 35 (2012), www.e-flux.com/journal/after-the-last-man-images-and-ethics-of -becoming-otherwise/. See also her article "The Will to Be Otherwise / The Effort of Endurance," *South Atlantic Quarterly* 111, no. 3 (2012): 453–75.
62. See Povinelli, "After the Last Man." The quote "immanence is no longer immanence to anything other than itself" is from Gilles Deleuze, *Pure Immanence: Essays on a Life*, trans. Anne Boyman (New York: Zone Books, 2001), 27.
63. Povinelli, "After the Last Man," original emphasis.
64. Povinelli, "After the Last Man."
65. Povinelli, "Routes/Worlds," *e-flux*, no. 27 (2011), http://www.e-flux.com/journal/routes worlds/.
66. We borrow the term "'zonal' ontologies" from Graham Harman's blog entry, "P.S. on

works. Balibar's concept of civility is helpful here because it refers not to a zone or field of existence but rather to a practice of regulation. In other words, Balibar does not limit or foreclose what kinds of fields or zones are possible. It is not that the world is a sphere or a network or a bag but rather that it is all of these things at once and that the "art" of politics is *conjunctural*: that is to say, it creates and regulates various forms. Civility is not *only* about radical immanence but is also about the strategic control of potentiality. This means that a *civil* politics of the otherwise does not entail becoming someone else (since this someone else would still be a someone). Instead, we argue that civility is a practice of "transformation or even disfiguration,"[67] what Eduardo Viveiros de Castro calls "controlled equivocation."[68]

Holbraad, Pedersen, and Viveiros de Castro provide a striking example of how the "otherwise" might be activated:

> The relativist reports that in such-and-such an ethnographic context time is "cyclical," with "the past ever returning to become the present." It is an evocative idea, to be sure. But strictly speaking, it makes no sense. To *be* "past" is precisely *not* "to return to the present," so a past that does so is properly speaking not a past at all (in the same sense that a married bachelor is not a bachelor). By contrast, like a kind of "relativist-turbo," the ontologically-inclined anthropologist takes this form of e(qui)vocation as a starting-point for an ethnographically-controlled experiment with the concept of time itself, re-conceptualizing "past," "present," "being" etc. in ways that make "cyclical time" a real form of existence. In this subjunctive "could be" experiment, the emphasis is as much on "be" as on "could": "imagine a cyclical time!" marvels the relativist; "yes, and here is what it could *be!*," replies the ontological anthropologist.[69]

From a musical perspective, the point is not that we can ever hear *as* the other, with the ears of the other. But we can listen "vicariously" with

---

the Gabriel Video," accessed June 12, 2015, doctorzamalek2.wordpress.com/2013/11/15/p-s-on-the-gabriel-video/.

67. See Holbraad, Pedersen, and Viveiros de Castro, "The Politics of Ontology," 3.

68. See Eduardo Viveiros de Castro, "Perspectival Anthropology and the Method of Controlled Equivocation," *Tipití: Journal of the Society for the Anthropology of Lowland South America* 2, no. 1 (2004): 3–22; as cited in Holbraad, Pedersen, and Viveiros de Castro, "The Politics of Ontology," 2.

69. See Holbraad, Pedersen, and Viveiros de Castro, "The Politics of Ontology," 3.

and through others, just as we can read with them, as Lauren Berlant has recently suggested:

> When I read with theorists, with art, with a colleague or a friend, *to read with* is to cultivate a quality of attention to the disturbance of their alien epistemology, an experience of nonsovereignty that shakes my confidence in a way from which I have learned to derive pleasure, induce attachment, and maintain curiosity about the enigmas and insecurities that I also barely stand or comprehend. This is what it means to say that excitement is disturbing, not devastating; ambivalent, not shattering in the extreme. Structural consistency is a fantasy; the noise of relation's impact, inducing incompletion where it emerges, is the overwhelming condition that enables the change that, within collaborative action, can shift lived worlds.[70]

Through the "noisy impact" of relation, I do not jump out of my own skin, but I also do not come out unscathed. In basic signal processing, "noise" is defined as the interference of a transmission from Point A to Point B. Noise is that which disrupts a connection, mediation, or relation. Although never stated explicitly, in this short passage Berlant inverts this basic assumption (on which, incidentally, much media theory is predicated) by positioning noise as the result *of* "relation's impact" rather than an interference in and of a relation. In this way, connections and relations are deprioritized, since it is the relation itself—and not the break in the relation—which proves that structural consistency is a fantasy.

What if, instead of a music historical catalog of transports to being this or that (a devout subject, a national subject, a teen subject, a radicalized subject, a subject of a particular identity) or some sort of transcendent no one (a trajectory spanning mystical or sacred musics, the *Tonkunst* of the nineteenth century, and the "degree zero" of postwar modernism), we were to trace a latent history of modern music (modern in the broader sense extending back to the emergence of autonomous concert music) as what Maryanne Amacher referred to as "perceptual geography"[71]—as a trajectory of beings? Always contingent upon the maintenance of that radi-

---

70. From Lauren Berlant and Lee Edelman's *Sex, or the Unbearable* (Durham, NC: Duke University Press, 2013), 125.
71. For more on this concept, which Maryanne Amacher variably described throughout her career, see "Psychoacoustic Phenomena in Music Composition: Some Features of a 'Perceptual Geography,'" in *Arcana III: Musicians on Music*, ed. John Zorn (New York: Hips Road, 2008), 9–24.

cal ambiguity and potential mobility upon which the civil conjecture rests, perceptual geographies invite us, through identification, through entrainment, to traverse a multiplicity of beings "within" a given "work"; they are a dramaturgy of shifting affective and libidinal alignments. The willingness to be in music, the desire for music, would then be predicated on a desire for this very permeability that is the prerequisite of transformation—a desire for the shifting of lived worlds. The ethical challenge of musical civility, of being in music together, would be, then, the insistence upon building up from the nonlinear topologies, the fluid foundations of the unconscious, from the mute potential for the otherwise of materiality, and not allowing forms for sharing malleable being to be reduced to or reformed into reproductions of cultural givens.

What might a "civil" thumbnail sketch of musical modernity reconceived as a history of perceptual geographies look like—each moment imagined as a conjectural proposition? If listening together in rows in a formal concert setting was an institutional attempt to bind and freeze libidinal proliferation to a given formula (nation, identity) *and* an institutional framework equally opportune for listeners' anti-identitarian appropriations of that proliferation (swooning, the individualist moment of structural listening), the protocivil moment contained within that scene can only be made out upon the stage in a code to be observed from an outside and read, identified with. Take, for instance, a favorite historical example of social musicology: a nineteenth-century piano concerto—say, a Beethoven concerto. Here we might shift our attention away from facile dramatizations or mimings of dynamics between individual and collective and instead win a newfound entry to the development and orchestration of musical material itself in the permeability and transference of motives and forms not only between the two "entities" but throughout the assembled body on stage. Here, tracing the path of note-to-note procedure would not be a means to trace some manner of identificatory or rational coherence but to vicariously move through another subject's combinatorial, transformational play within yet another code: Beethovenian development as a bracketed, horizontal space of perceptual geography.

This same read, still upon the stage, though at its edge, could show us an Anton Webern whose work consciously begins to propose our apperception of coherence as such, where the procedure of material distribution vies for the foreground of attention with any given material instance (pitch): here, a vertical, three-dimensional perceptual geography, modulating shifts of attention between the grid of representation and the constituents of that grid. The unresolved break with representation initiated by Cage that shifts the relationality, which up until *4'33"* was something to be read between pitches, to something between human (and nonhuman) beings might most effectively be traced in a work such as Christian Wolff's 1964 *For 1, 2 or 3 People*. Here, the vicarious mental work of perceptual geography is mapped into real space in an embodied geography of performance but at the expense of excluding the meaningful participation of an outside, observing body. Here, the work becomes a space for rehearsing a relational virtuosity by means of musical instruments. Within the performing collective, the literal relations between musicians, their perception of each others' cues and coordinations, describe an indeterminate geography in which sound becomes secondary to the intersubjective, collective execution of it. In such works, the break with representative space might be said to simply bisect the proscenium scene to the exclusion of the audience, leaving only the stage activated. Parallel and opposite to this tendency in Wolff's early work, one can also describe a breaking down of representation that privileges and expands the space of the audience to the total exclusion of the virtuoso and the stage. Likewise transferring the relational play that was so long restricted to the interaction of discrete frequencies to the interactions of human subjects, some of the work of the English Scratch Orchestra or Pauline Oliveros's *Sonic Meditations* (1974) represents a sort of sonic commune approach in which deskilling allows participants to engage with the relational geography of given works without the mediating code of musical performance history. Particularly in Oliveros's early work, the works' reduced material means come drastically close to the facticity of the bodies engaged in them. Finally, hints of a tendency away from either representational polemic are legible in the work of those few composers (Amacher most prominently, and some of the work of Robert Ashley, for example) who actively begin to conceive of their works as some manner of disfigured or nonnormative sensible distribution in time, explicitly as the composition of transformative trajectories of identification.

The challenge to contemporary music is not to insist upon or bring into being any particular mode to be privileged but rather to maintain and articulate the very radicality of potentiality upon which any given mode is afloat. Beginning from and holding on to a potential otherwise in any elaborated form (be that an ordering of sounds or a composition of listening) must be of necessity conjectural. That maintenance of definite, specific instability embodied in material form is perhaps the primary work experimental music might offer.

Such experimentation is crucial in light of contemporary politics, particularly when considering post-2010 movements like the Arab Spring and Occupy Wall Street. What these movements have illustrated is not that politics is foreclosed in our neoliberal situation after the "end of history" but rather that radical politics *has nowhere to go* after its initial disruptive or dissensual moment. From Tahrir Square to Zuccotti "Freedom" Park, contemporary politics seems to literalize the Marquis de Sade's proposal that "insurrection should be the permanent state of the republic." But if indeed these movements can meaningfully be described as insurrectional, it is also the case that they meet their own reified (and commodified) image at every turn. As Rosalind Morris observes, contemporary protest movements

> assume force (to influence events) not through a dialectic of recognition but through an anonymous circuiting of their (digital) image through the global media. This circuiting permits the gathering sense of a mass whose enormity is materialized iconically and rendered effective by virtue of its approach to an impossible totality. In the return of its image to itself (in a circle but not a dialectic), the rallying crowd assumes its possible identity as a collective subject.[72]

Music, we submit, and experimental music in particular (that is, music committed to the explicit navigation of relational potentiality in the wake of representation), might usefully be employed as a means to organize and regulate this collective subject outside the topography of a monadic immanentism, the dialectic, or the circle by affording novel configurations, new perceptual geographies. As Morris writes elsewhere,

> Every once in a while I am convinced that what antiwar [or, we add, antiviolence] movements need, more than anything, is music: a sound and an anonymous lyrical form for antiwar sentiment, such as was produced in the 1960s. That music would be one that could possess people. It would fill their mouths with words that come from elsewhere, but that nonetheless seem to express their deepest sentiments. It would precipitate crowds and even masses, and without giving them an image, it would let them assume collective force.[73]

72. Rosalind Morris, "Thesis on the New Öffentlichkeit," *Grey Room* 51 (Spring 2013): 94–111, esp. 106.
73. Rosalind Morris, "Witchcraft," *Social Text* 26, no. 2 (2008): 113–33, esp. 131. Note that this article is about pre-2010 antiwar movements and not post-2010 movements like the Arab Spring and the Occupy movement.

Though the evocation of 1960s antiwar music recalls many of the problematics of identification and disidentification that we have been tracing, such an experimentally resituated sonic practice without image or transcendental horizon would come from an "extimate" elsewhere immanent to the musical assemblage itself. The value of such musics would derive not from the bodies that make it or from the structural features of its harmonies and sounds, but rather from the experimentation with "anonymous" forms and energies that lie below the level of partisan distinctions. As Jairo Moreno observes in his account of 2006 immigrant demonstrations in Los Angeles and throughout the United States, "The organizers themselves remained largely indifferent to the sonorous aesthetic of the demonstrations."[74] By engaging in an "ethics of indifference," the organizers avoided the reduction of sonic politics to the articulation of particular identities, and during the protests "no single statement is known to have articulated even that old trope of the 'people's voice' to the music making of the multitudes." By simultaneously avoiding identitarian modalities of expression and floating identification, these demontrations' sonic negotiation of what Moreno refers to as "interdiction"[75] perhaps evinced an incipient form of truly civil politics.

As an experimental and underdetermined practice, civility does not entail the dissolution of subjects into disidentified and yet normatively

74. Jairo Moreno, "On the Ethics of the Unspeakable," in *Speaking of Music: Addressing the Sonorous*, ed. Keith Chapin and Andrew H. Clark (New York: Fordham University Press, 2013), 212–41, esp. 238. The demonstrations in question "were in response to H.R. 4437 (the Border, Protection, Antiterrorism, and Illegal Immigration Control Act of 2005, commonly known as 'Proposition 4437'), passed by the U.S. House of Representatives in December 2005." Moreno then recounts some of the events that unfolded: "On March 7, an estimated 20,000–40,000 people gathered in Washington, D.C.; three days later, 300,000 marched in Chicago, with organizers putting the number at 500,000. . . . Downtown Los Angeles was the scene for the single largest demonstration, known as 'La Gran Marcha,' with at least 500,000 people participating, on 25 March. . . . [On April 10], over 170 events took place across the country, with rallies of 5,000–10,000 people in states such as Iowa, Kansas, Tennessee, and Wisconsin. . . . Sporadic marches were reported as late as July 2006" (228–29).
75. "I wish, then, to think of the *unspeakable* not as a limit but as an *interdiction*, which in a fictional etymology (*inter*, between; and *dicere*, to speak) hosts a double movement. On the one hand, it commonly implies a prohibition or forbidding by decree, a speech act that silences. On the other hand, an interdiction is a speaking-across, an act of translation. In both these movements, there is no positive content to the interdiction outside the political investment each makes and the force each mobilizes in the interest of that investment." See Moreno, "On the Ethics of the Unspeakable," 237.

repressed crowds or masses, nor does it propose a singular subjectivation of "the people." For, as Balibar reminds us, "*subjectivation* keeps involving *subjection*."[76] There is no exit from this contradiction, which is not merely "a gap between the ideal and the real" but is rather inherent in all politics, affecting it "from inside."[77] Following Balibar, we do not therefore suggest civility as a new form of politics per se but rather as a "necessary dimension of politics as such."[78]

To render civility sensible does not entail—or at least, does not only entail—the subjectivation, the becoming visible and audible, of previously silenced subjects. It does not only entail, in other words, "the emancipatory breakthrough that sets a new stage for the political by giving a new visibility to the discourses and the bodies that were barred from public expression."[79] Instead, civility requires a recognition of and allusion to the "*hidden* side of the scene,"[80] which in our analysis would be a material-libidinal infrastructure undergirding sense perception but which itself is never directly perceived. Music is one particular way of approaching this "other scene," of alluding to but never directly capturing those same "anonymous" material forces that constitute the infrastructure of politics' own infrastructure. In this light, then, the significance and weight of an "experimental" aesthetic practice such as we have suggested vis-à-vis contemporary music cannot be understated. At its best, experimental music provokes and enacts that experience of "nonsovereignty" to which Berlant refers, the ambivalent and risky experience of other people, other entities, and other scenes, as they make their presences felt by withdrawing.

Thus, if there is a politics *of* art, this is only because politics is itself an "art," that is, an equivocal category encompassing both *techne* ("technique") and *poiesis* ("creation"). Balibar again:

> To see politics as an art means, on the one hand, that it is neither an ethical discipline, governed by the categorical imperative of moral or religious values (which is not to say that values and ethical choices

76. Étienne Balibar, "Civic Universalism and Its Internal Exclusions: The Issue of Anthropological Difference," *boundary 2* 39, no. 1 (Spring 2012): 207–29, esp. 208.

77. Balibar, "Civic Universalism," 208.

78. "Interview with Étienne Balibar," in *Communities of Sense: Rethinking Aesthetics and Politics*, ed. Beth Hinderliter, William Kaizen, Vered Maimon, Jaleh Mansoor, and Seth McCormick (Durham, NC: Duke University Press, 2009).

79. "Interview with Étienne Balibar," 322. This is Balibar's characteriziation of Jacques Rancière's position.

80. "Interview with Étienne Balibar," original emphasis.

are not involved in the goals and means of political action), nor a mere application of scientific knowledge, as the positivist tradition has repeatedly maintained (which is not to say that knowledge of facts and structures is irrelevant to politics). Rather, it is a discipline of action, combining forces and changing their relationship.[81]

To inversely and yet likewise begin from an understanding of art as politics—as the prospect of renegotiating of our relations to material being—would intimate the necessity of a profound reorientation in and to artistic practice, one having little or nothing to do with the doxa of so-called critical art, and one which yet seems as necessary and significant as it does arduous.

81. "Interview with Étienne Balibar," 319.

The Sound of the Outside

Naomi Waltham-Smith

1

A provocative question takes hold of Jacques Derrida at the beginning of the text that grapples most directly with—or, given the book's
theme, one might say, that touches most immediately upon—the thought of
his friend and fellow thinker of exteriority, Jean-Luc Nancy. This supposedly
uninvited question seizes hold of Derrida: "When our eyes touch, is it day
or is it night?" "Let's see," he begins, with a determination to show "a limit-
less patience": "can eyes manage to touch, first of all, to press together
like lips?"[1]

Caught in the grip of a perplexing question that appears to eschew
the ear entirely, Derrida's thought nonetheless begins to takes shape as a
twofold meditation on sensation without which the contact between sound
and ontology in recent Continental thought would be unthinkable. This is

1. Jacques Derrida, *On Touching—Jean-Luc Nancy*, trans. Christine Irizarry (Stanford,
CA: Stanford University Press, 2005), 2. Hereafter, this work is cited parenthetically as
OT. Originally published as *Le toucher, Jean-Luc Nancy* (Paris: Éditions Galilée, 2000).

boundary 2 43:1 (2016)   DOI 10.1215/01903659-3340649   © 2016 by Duke University Press

because the question leads Derrida to propose a sensing that is at once inside and outside itself. Derrida's initial preoccupation is an Aristotelian dilemma that concerns sensation in its interiority: specifically, is sensation capable of sensing its own sensing, capable of sensing itself? Derrida selects the comparison with the touching together of lips so as to press the question of what it is exactly that comes into contact when two eyes are said to be touching. Starting from a deconstruction of touch that finds an interruption in every moment of contact, Derrida elevates this interruption between sensation and its object into a higher-order noncoincidence that fractures sensation itself. Derrida rehearses this dislocation in a rapid displacement from the eye to the gaze: "If two gazes look into each other's eyes, can one then say that they are touching?" But then later, feigning to catch himself in this (deliberate) slippage, he writes, "This presupposes that these eyes see *each other.*—These eyes or these gazes? You're going from one to the other" (*OT*, 2). As if to suggest the ungraspability of this difficulty, Derrida permits himself a brief digression on the question's reference to darkness that allows him to reframe the question in even more explicitly Aristotelian terms: the problem of sensation's self-reflexivity is recast as a choice between potentiality (figured here as darkness) and actuality (or day).[2]

> Don't we have to make a choice between looking or exchanging glances or meeting gazes, and seeing, very simply seeing? And first between seeing the seeing and seeing the visible? For if our eyes see what is *seeing* [the other person's act of looking] rather than *visible* [things in the world that are capable of being seen, including the other's eye], if they believe that they are seeing a gaze rather than eyes, at least to that extent, to that extent as such, they are seeing nothing, then, nothing that can be seen, nothing *visible*. Away from all visibility, they founder in the night. They blind themselves so as to see a gaze; they avoid seeing the visibility of the other's eyes so as to address themselves only to his or her gaze, to his or her sight that is merely seeing, to his or her vision. (*OT*, 2)

Derrida thus fractures sensation into, on the one hand, a sensing that senses its own proper object of sensation (that is, an object that is capable of being sensed), and, on the other hand, a sensing that directs

2. See the discussion in book 2, part 5, of Aristotle, "On the Soul," in *The Complete Works of Aristotle: The Revised Oxford Translation*, vol. 1, ed. Jonathan Barnes (Princeton, NJ: Princeton University Press, 1984).

itself to sensation itself, that is, to something that, at least in this present analysis, is incapable of being sensed. In this way, Derrida follows Aristotle in exposing a moment of privation at the heart of all sensation, a blind spot, if you will, that takes place precisely as sensation turns back on itself, refers to itself and seeks to touch itself. Insofar as sensation cannot sense itself, sensation thus encounters itself precisely as a *capacity not to* sense.

It is via this figure of a groundlessness and privation (Derrida's night and, as we shall see later, Giorgio Agamben's presupposition) that sound, in its turn, comes to occupy a decisive place in a body of European thought that evolves in the wake of Derridean deconstruction. It is perhaps at once surprising and appropriate, then, that sound should be conspicuous in its absence from one of the clearest accounts of this figure of sensation in relation to its own privation. Only because aurality takes place as an unheard audibility can it become the presupposed ground of being and of community.

To advance this claim requires stitching together a number of claims made by a pair of philosophers whose field of contact could be loosely characterized as a response to Derrida's critique of presence but whose thought also becomes interwoven at a few more specific points of inter-section (self-reference, exemplarity, singularity, community without condi-tion). I work along this seam, leaping forward from an ontological thread toward a political one and backward toward the sonic. In what seems like a cross between a tightrope walk and a cat's cradle, I bring alongside one another the refusal of presence and the refusal of biopolitics so as to tease out an idea that remains audible and yet unheard in this body of thought. This idea only gets off the ground with a provocative claim: that sound is recruited in post-Derridean thought as a means of deconstructing the moment of self-identity in metaphysics, but, precisely in becoming the exemplary mode through which to do so, sound risks reinstating itself as a quasi-transcendental. The ontological and political gesture that sound authorizes is one of indetermination, of finitude, and of an existence with condition or property, and yet sound risks becoming the obstacle to the unraveling and indetermination that it precipitates. This risk is a reflection of the significance that aurality holds for a rethinking of ontology and com-munity in recent Continental philosophy. This is not to say that any single philosopher makes such a grand claim, although each of those discussed in their own way lends an attentive ear to the claims of the sonorous if not an especially powerful voice. Rather, it is my endeavor to make resonate an idea that becomes audible only when elements of these philosophies are brought alongside one another in a certain configuration. This demands a thinking that is only inside the texts insofar as it is always-already straining beyond—outside—them. It means tracing the limits and folds within, against, away from each text and among them as a community of texts.

Sound, too, must be thought among its community. Before the measure can be taken of aurality's ramifications first for philosophy and then politics, it is necessary to situate its significance within the context of the second central theme that Derrida announces in the above passage. At issue here is the exterior limit of sense, not in the direction of its object but in the form of the contact that each sense has with each of the other senses. The question proposes a juxtaposition of the senses of sight and touch and thereby opens up an inquiry into the relation between them, seeking to explain both what joins them in unity and separates them from one another. At first blush, the question foregrounds sight and touch so prominently that hearing seems to withdraw from thought or remains merely presupposed in the dialogue that Derrida stages between "himself" and the question. Nonetheless, sound and hearing insinuate themselves into Derrida's thought in this text in a way that is perhaps not immediately intelligible. Behind the image of the lips pressed together can be discerned a muted voice, silenced in the auto-affection of a seeing that sees seeing itself.

Hearing, then, makes its return just before the peroration of Derrida's monologue. Just before he ponders the boldness of touching his friend's eyes ("I could precisely touch them, with my finger, lips or even eyes, lashes and lids, by approaching you—if I dared come near to you in this way, if I one day dared" [*OT*, 3]), Derrida explicitly invokes hearing. He has just reached the provisional conclusion that, if it is night when our eyes touch, then surely this must mean that eyes touch *blindly*—that is, that they touch without seeing, that sight sees itself only insofar as it suspends its capacity to see. He then goes on to resolve this aporia with an appeal to the ear: "Unless this is precisely how they begin to hear and understand each other" (*OT*, 3). Rather than read this as a banality according to which hearing achieves greater acuity when the eyes are closed, I argue that one should instead discern here a much more provocative claim: that aurality finds its origin ("they *begin* to hear") and its force in the figure of self-relationality that Derrida problematizes in this passage. And, what is more, it is precisely because aurality is nothing other than the (im)possibility of this self-relation that it becomes the condition of possibility for rethinking every figure of relation and of community. Hence, I will argue that aurality is ontology, and that, because the coming politics can no longer afford to be thought on the basis of ethics, morality, action, or agency, but only from the fundamental structure of relationality at the level of being, aurality provides a paradigm for politics. For this reason, aurality does not merely open out onto or point toward what lies outside the philosophy of sensation: *if aurality is the (im)possibility of relation, it is always-already ontology and politics.*

2

For now, this thought is left as if unheard, however, and in the account of the community of the senses that follows in *On Touching*, Derrida accords a privileged position not to hearing but to touch. Derrida's claim that touch enjoys an exorbitant privilege not only in the history of metaphysics but also in Nancy's thought merits close attention, because it is both an obstacle to and a template for the alternative claim advanced here that aurality provides the fundamental structure for Nancy's analysis of the sensorium and, further, for his engagement with ontological questions. If hearing is modeled upon and ultimately subordinated to touch insofar as it finds its origin in self-touching, then any argument falls away in support of sound's privileged status in motivating Nancy's rethinking of being and community. By contrast, if it can be shown that hearing is what exposes itself in the impossibility of self-touching, if hearing is what intervenes in and interrupts every contact, this would suggest that the deconstruction of touch is advanced on the basis of a presupposed aurality, albeit one characterized by its suspension and privation. If this can be demonstrated, then many of the arguments that Derrida marshals around touch can be made apropos of hearing.

It is first helpful to situate Derrida's analysis of metaphysical haptocentrism in *On Touching* within the wider context of his critique of presence and in particular alongside the originary scene of phonocentrism that stands elsewhere as a prime example of this mode of thinking. In his first sustained engagement with phenomenologist Edmund Husserl in *La voix et le phénomène*, Derrida comes to center his attention on the voice and on the experience of hearing-oneself-speak.[3] He notes that, for Husserl, the distinctive phenomenological power of the voice lies in its capacity for pure

3. Jacques Derrida, "The Voice that Keeps Silence," in *Speech and Phenomena and Other Essays on Husserl's Theory of Signs*, trans. David B. Allison (Evanston, IL: Northwestern University Press, 1973), 70–87. Hereafter, cited parenthetically as TV. Originally published as *La voix et le Phénomène* (Paris: Presses Universitaires de France, 1967).

auto-affection: in hearing itself speak, the phenomenological subject is able to relate to itself without any passage through exteriority. Derrida explicitly contrasts this situation with that of sight and touch, where that which is outside the sphere of the proper (an external view of a part of the body, the image in the mirror) always-already intervenes within the field of auto-affection. In an argument that he will repeat in his engagement with Husserl in *On Touching*, Derrida contends that the experience of touching and of being-touched is never an experience of immediate self-presence because the surface of the body, as something exterior and exposed to the world, always interrupts the supposed simultaneity and continuity of the contact between touching and touched. The operation of hearing-oneself-speak, by contrast, "seems to reduce even the inward surface of one's own body" and "seems capable of dispensing with this exteriority within interiority" to give rise to a seemingly absolute proximity of the self to the self and of the signifier to the signified (TV, 79).

Derrida famously deconstructs this scene of self-presence by rejecting the idea that Husserl's transcendental reduction is capable of an absolute reduction of space. What distinguishes speech from other modes of signification is its "purely temporal" character (TV, 83). And yet, if writing and gesture openly attest to the spatiality of all signification, it is precisely through its temporalization that speech "introduces into self-presence from the beginning all the impurity putatively excluded from it" (TV, 85). As Martin Hägglund succinctly explains, the present can never be present to itself because it is always related to a constitutive outside; hence self-presence is always-already undone from the outset by the folding in of an exteriority: "Given that the now can appear only by disappearing, it must be inscribed as a trace in order to be at all. This is the becoming-space of time. The trace is necessarily spatial, since spatiality is characterized by the ability to remain in spite of temporal succession. Spatiality is thus the condition for synthesis, since it enables the tracing of relations between past and future."[4]

In this way, the theme of "the pure inwardness of speech" is "contradicted by 'time' itself" because the auto-affection of temporalization is always-already marked by the externality of space: time can only relate to itself in being "outside-itself" (TV, 86).

Whence, then, the privilege accorded to touch by Derrida on his

---

4. Martin Hägglund, "The Necessity of Discrimination: Disjoining Derrida and Levinas," *diacritics* 34, no. 1 (2004): 40–71, esp. 43.

book on Nancy? If aurality, even in its seemingly most pure form of hearing-oneself-speak, reveals the fundamental deconstructive gesture that destroys all claims to self-presence, why must Nancy's insistence on exteriority in the form of spacing come hand-in-hand with a privileging of touch instead (see *OT*, 199)? Derrida argues in this text not so much for a phonologism in the history of metaphysics but for a quasi-transcendentalism of touch according to which this sense becomes paradigmatic not only for the operation of the other senses but moreover also for the way in which the senses relate to one another.

The "quasi-transcendental privilege of the tactile—of spacing, in truth" that Derrida discerns in Nancy's thought obtains, though, only once touch is disassociated from those qualities that the philosophical tradition has repeatedly attributed to it, namely immediacy and continuity. That is, touch acquires its privileged status among the senses to the extent that it becomes a touching that is at once a not-touching. True to the deconstruction of presence, according to which all purported immediacy is marked by exteriority and discontinuity, Nancy defines touch by the fact that it withdraws from touch even as it touches: it is a contact that interrupts itself, that always-already inserts an interval in its supposed immediacy. Touch spaces itself.

There is no disputing the significant role that the thought and language of touch play across Nancy's writings, but it is equally the case that he finds in sound and listening this very same structure of spacing and arguably the privileged example of spacing. In the essay "À l'écoute," whose first version predates Derrida's *On Touching*, Nancy conceives of sound and of listening itself as resonance and repeatedly develops the theme of its spacing: all sounding is a "re-sounding"[5] and hence "sound . . . spreads in space" (*LG*, 7). Later Nancy elaborates: "The sonorous present . . . spreads through space, or rather it opens a space that is its own, the very spreading out of its resonance, its expansion and its reverberation" (*LG*, 13). Furthermore, the folding in of exteriority that Derrida discerns in Nancy's deconstruction of touch is identified as a fundamental character of sound's structure: "to sound is to vibrate . . . not only for the sonorous body to emit a sound, but . . . also to stretch out . . . to resolve into vibrations that . . . place it outside of itself" (*LG*, 8).

---

5. Jean-Luc Nancy, *Listening*, trans. Charlotte Mandell (New York: Fordham University Press, 2007), 8. Hereafter, this work is cited parenthetically as *LG*. Originally published as *À l'écoute* (Paris: Éditions Galilée, 2002).

At several places in the notes, Nancy directly addresses the issue of the sonic's quasi-transcendental status. He studiously resists a hierarchy of the senses: even as he demonstrates that it is possible to think each of the other senses of the basis of hearing, he insists upon a spacing both between and internal to each of the senses such that each sense exposes an aspect of those that make up the interior differentiation of the other senses. In its internal inconsistency, each sense exhibits itself and its others. While conceding a certain exemplarity for the sense of touch, Nancy nonetheless insists that the senses are "together [in] touching themselves while still distinguishing themselves"; "every perceptible mode or register exposes one of the aspects of 'touching (itself),' separation or conjunction, presence or absence, penetration or retraction, etc." (*LG*, 71n13). Similarly, "nothing is said of the sonorous that must not also be true 'for' the other registers," provided that one adheres to the deconstructive caveat and insists upon the heterogeneity of the senses in and between them, so that everything that is said of the sonorous holds not only "for" but also "'against' them, 'next to' as well as in opposition, in a complementarity and in an incompatibility that are inextricable from each other." Each sense is an example, and in the context of a meditation on listening, the sonorous becomes *the* example through which to think each of the senses and their relation to one another: thus, if "each perceptible system makes a different model and *resonance* for all the others[,] each sense is both an *example* and a differencing in such a '*vibrating* (itself),' and all senses *vibrate* among themselves, some against others and some with others" (*LG*, 70–71n12, my emphasis).

The danger that Nancy comes up against here is inherent in the category of the example. Nancy is later at pains once more to defend against any suggestion of transcendental aurality: "Not, once again, that this reverberation is absent from other perceptible systems: on the contrary, it comprises them all (a color or a texture also 'resounds,' one might say). But sonority, ultimately, is *nothing but* its reverberation" (*LG*, 76–77n71, original emphasis). In this "nothing but" that Nancy reserves for aurality, he appears to risk the teleological impulse through which examples (that are replaceable, substitutable, and hence dispensable) morph into a transcendental exemplar. Derrida warns that this logic of exemplarity sets in the moment that one identifies even one aspect that is incomparable in the model. Compare here Nancy's insistence that "nothing" be said of the sonorous that "must not also" be said of the other senses with Pierre Maine de Biran's claim that "we can apply to sight *almost* all that we have said of touch."[6] Observing that an analogical logic of the "just as" commands the logic of the community of the senses that Nancy puts forth, Derrida discerns in the difference between *as* and *almost* the interval that he "earlier risked nick-naming 'transcendental'" and on account of which "touch is not quite a touch—not a sense *as* or *like* the others" (*OT*, 147).

In the tension between Nancy's "nothing . . . not also" and his "noth-ing but," I propose to hear a secret temptation to fall into a logic of exem-plarity. If there were truly "nothing" that could be said of any of the senses that must "not also" be said of all the others, then the aurality could not attain any particularity by virtue of its being "nothing" but reverberation because the same would have to be said of the other senses. Even if Nancy rejects the "almost all" of haptocentrism, the spacing of the senses that he describes, however, demands that, while aurality is "nothing but" rever-beration, the other senses are "something besides" resonance. To which one could only add that aurality is "nothing but" resonance to the extent that resonance is always-already "something besides" itself, but in this way aurality becomes exemplary for the community of the senses.

At the same time, though, I insist that there is nothing to shy away from in this exposure, for the logic of exemplarity contains within itself the undoing of the teleological impulse that is the condition of possibility of exemplarity. In becoming more than just one of a series, the exemplary example locates itself both inside and outside the series at one and the same time ("one may include it in the list of the sense or just as well exclude it" [*OT*, 154]) and in this way reproduces the logic of spacing and of folding that Nancy discerns in resonance. If sound is always-already outside itself as resonance, then sound is always-already exemplary: inside only to the extent that it is already outside. This then shifts the question onto a second-order interrogation of the relation between the sonorous and exemplarity: it is less a question of whether aurality is exemplary (of sensation in gen-eral) than of whether it is exemplarily exemplary because all sensation is

6. Pierre Maine de Biran, *The Influence of Habit on the Faculty of Thinking*, trans. Mar-garet Donaldson Boehm (Baltimore: Williams and Wilkins, 1929), 63, as cited in Derrida, *On Touching*, 147, Derrida's emphasis. Maine de Biran (1766–1824) was a French thinker who, alongside the nineteenth-century French philosopher Jean-Gaspard-Félix Lacher Ravaisson-Mollien, marks the beginnings, for Derrida, of a metaphysical haptocentrism and forms something of a prehistory to the phenomenological tradition represented by Husserl and Merleau-Ponty.

exemplary. Put another way, can it be said, for Nancy, that aurality is exemplary of exemplarity, that sound is where exemplarity touches itself, vibrates against itself, re-sounds itself, that sound is how this outside-inside comes to itself, relates to itself?

Nancy does indeed claim something of an exemplary status for aurality in relation to this structure of self-reflexivity: "Indeed, as we have known since Aristotle, sensing [*sentir*] (*aesthesis*) is always a perception [*ressentir*], that is, a sensing-oneself-sense [*se-sentir-sentir*]: or, if you prefer, sensing is a subject, or it does not sense. But it is perhaps in the sonorous register that this reflected structure is most obviously manifest" (*LG*, 8, translation slightly modified).

This claim must nonetheless contend with the objection that, of the senses, touch is most capable of sensing itself. Notwithstanding his analysis of Husserl's phonocentrism, Derrida tracks the phenomenologist's argument for according a special status to touch.

Husserl squarely attributes touch's privilege to the sense's purported auto-affection. Specifically, Husserl takes the scene of the hand touching the hand and attempts to demonstrate that, through the hand's capacity to affect itself with its own sensation, the sense of touch has privileged access to the possibility of self-relation. Husserl discerns in this touching of the hand by the hand a "double apprehension" that is missing from the other senses: "We do not have a kind of extended occularity such that, but moving, one eye could rub past the other and produce the phenomenon of double sensation. . . . I do not see myself, my Body, the way I could myself. What I call the seen Body is not something seeing which is seen, the way my Body as touched Body is something touching which is touched."[7]

While identifying the objectal structure of apprehension (the perception of the external thing), Husserl is determined to specify the reflexive moment of self-touching. "The same touch-sensation," he proposes, "is apprehended as a feature of the 'external' Object and is apprehended as a sensation of the Body as Object."[8] In other words, the hand feels itself touching such that the feeling-itself-touch*ing* of the hand is immediately also a feeling-itself-touch*ed* of the hand, and this happens not only when one hand touches the other but also whenever my hand touches an external object.

7. Edmund Husserl, *Ideas Pertaining to a Pure Phenomenology and to a Phenomenological Philosophy*, vol. 2, trans. Richard Rojecewicz and André Schuwer (Dordrecht: Kluwer, 1989), 155–56.
8. Husserl, *Ideas Pertaining to a Pure Phenomenology*, 155–56.

This double apprehension distinguishes touch from sight and from hearing for Husserl: the eye does not see itself seeing—at least not directly. This returns us to Derrida's initial question and the aporia it presents in its choice between seeing the visible (the eye that sees) and seeing the invisible (the seeing itself). Similarly, when I hear myself speak, the hearing and the heard do not coincide, for I hear what is audible but do not hear hearing itself insofar as it is inaudible. Touch is, by contrast, privileged at the heart of Husserlian intuition because it is supposedly immediate and spontaneous, requiring no analogical mirror effect, but instead consists in the coincidence of the touching and the touched, of the tangible and the intangible.

Of course, if Nancy were to privilege touch, as Derrida claims, it would not be because of its supposed immediacy. In fact, Derrida goes on to demonstrate an incipient deconstruction of touch within Husserl's own analysis. Despite his insistence on the pure immediacy of self-touching, Husserl himself is forced to concede the necessity of a minimal passage through exteriority: "The touch-sensing is not a *state* of the material thing, hand, but is precisely the *hand itself*, which for us is more than a material thing, and the way in which it is mine entails that I, the 'subject of the Body,' can say that what belongs to the material thing is its, not mine."[9]

Thus, even the double apprehension must partake of this detour via something foreign, something outside the touching and the touched, in order that I might distinguish between "me" and "not me" and to be able to say, "This is my body." Unless the heterogeneity of the external material thing insinuates itself between the touching and the touched, there can be no "*double* apprehension" but only the single sensation of one thing only (of touching collapsed into touched or touched collapsed into touching). Husserl explores an alternative possibility of touching that he calls *Herzgefühl*, or heart sensation: here he dare not speak of double apprehension because there appears to be an absolute union of touching and touched and the absence of any tactile surface, so he reaches for an intermediate experience of touch whereby the heart can be felt when I press firmly into the flesh to feel through the surface of the skin and internal organs. Beyond this exteriority of the surface, Husserl finds the exteriority in the generic situation of touching as double apprehension in the *visibility* of the hand: "there is visually a certain image of my touching hand."[10]

9. Husserl, *Ideas Pertaining to a Pure Phenomenology*, 157–58.
10. Husserl, *Ideas Pertaining to a Pure Phenomenology*, 174.

It is possible to discern such exteriority in aurality, however, without such a coercive reading. Aurality can then become the exemplary self-relation of sensation, not because it exhibits a pure self-reference, in which the audible and the inaudible coincide, but because the sonorous is always-already outside itself, and its self-relation is therefore nothing other than resonance and spacing. "Sound is . . . made of referrals." It resounds in space "while still resounding 'in me'" (*LG*, 7). Sounding is already "'re-sounding' since that's nothing else but referring back to itself." But resonance always exceeds any itself: its vibrations "return it to itself and place it outside itself" (*LG*, 8). It is also on account of this capacity for reference that Nancy is able, in an initial gesture to which we shall return, to carve out a shared space of sonority and signification. Insofar as both sound and meaning consist in referrals, they not only refer to one another but share a space of referral.

In a second, more decisive move, however, aurality's capacity for (self)-reference permits Nancy to pass over from a theory of the senses via a notion of subjectivity to a theory of being: "this space can be defined as the space of a *self*, a subject" (*LG*, 8). This passage from ontology is possible precisely because the exemplary sense already has the structure of being. Sonority shares the structure of being: "a *self* is nothing other than a form or function of referral: a *self* is made of a relationship to self, or of a presence *to* self," or "'self' is precisely nothing available (substantial or subsistent) to which one can be 'present,' but precisely the resonance of a return" (*LG*, 12). Rephrased in a way that seeks to take the measure of sound's value for ontology and for politics, we can say that Nancy thinks ontology on the basis of aurality, or that his thought is a phono-ontology. This relation between sound and being can also be expressed according to the logic of exemplarity: sound is an example of being because, among the senses, it is the exemplary form of ("nothing but") the resonance that is being. Nancy also imagines that sense is Being as its own circulation,[11] so we might even say that being circulates exemplarily as sound. It is also the case, though, that, as resonance, the sonorous, even as it turns back on itself, carries being alongside itself outside itself. Sound is being only because both aurality and being are always-already outside themselves and each other. Thus we can say that *sound exemplifies being*.

11. Jean-Luc Nancy, *Being Singular Plural*, trans. Robert D. Richardson and Anne E. O'Byrne (Stanford, CA: Stanford University Press, 2000), 2. Hereafter, this work is cited parenthetically as *BSP*. Originally published as *Être singulier pluriel* (Paris: Éditions Galilée, 1996).

3

Nancy's philosophy attests to the value of sound in deconstruction's refusal of presence because it thinks from the fundamental structure of resonance in order to propose an alternative account of being that undoes the fiction of self-presence at its very origin because being-as-resonance is both inside and outside itself.

> Sound has no hidden face; it is all in front, in black and outside inside, *inside-out* in relation to the most logic of presence as appearance. . . . To listen is to enter that spatiality by which, *at the same time*, I am penetrated, for it opens up in me as well as around me, and from me as well as toward me: it opens me inside me as well as outside. . . . To be listening is to be *at the same time* outside and inside, to be open *from* without and *from* within, hence from one to the other and from one in the other. Listening thus forms the perceptible singularity that bears in the most ostensive way the perceptible or sensitive (*aisthetic*) condition as such: the sharing of an inside/outside: division and participation, de-connection and contagion. (*LG*, 13–14)

Hence Nancy argues that sonorous presence takes place "next to itself." Sound is how we encounter being. It is "co-presence," or "the presence of presence"—that is, the way in which presence is present if not exactly *to* itself, then *with* itself, *alongside* itself (see *LG*, 16). Listening is thus not a relation to a "self" (to "me" or to an "other") but a relation to a relation (to the "to itself" that is referral) at which the self takes place. In what amounts perhaps to the highest estimation of the sonorous, Nancy insists that listening, as an opening onto the sonorous, is not a "metaphor" for access to self but "the reality of this access." While denying that this access wins for hearing and the sonorous "a privilege in the strict sense," he concedes that it amounts to a "remarkable particularity." Even if "all perceptible registers make up this approach to 'self,'" the very fact that there are many approaches to self without any possible totalization attests to an "internal diffraction, which perhaps in turn lets itself be analysed in terms of repeats, echoes, resonances, and also rhythms" (*LG*, 73n23). In this way, the sonorous again exhibits a certain exemplary status insofar as it shares with being the same structure of relation not only at the local level of the self's self-referral *but also* at the second-order level of the relations between the various perceptible registers that share the same underlying structure. Aurality provides the structure of being in its interiority and its exteriority.

Even if it can be established that sound offers an exemplary mode of thinking, of accessing, the subject after phenomenology, it remains to consider what is at stake in incorporating aurality into this project. That Nancy lends so attentive an ear to sound does not merely mobilize the sonorous to advance a seemingly arcane dispute with Husserl and Derrida but puts aurality in the thick of a recent renewed interest in using ontology to rethink politics and community. The same structure of copresence that Nancy discerns in his analysis of being-as-resonance is fleshed out in one of Nancy's most significant contributions to the field of ontology. The result here is that, in granting access to being, listening itself in turn gains access to a philosophical and political potential from which it was otherwise barred: by incorporating sound into ontology, its body opening up like a resonance chamber, sound's power is amplified. In *Being Singular Plural*, Nancy's self-confessed ambition is nothing less than a complete redoing of the whole of first philosophy: in a radicalization of the Heideggerian notion of *Mitsein*, Nancy argues that being, at its origin and foundation, is fundamentally *plural* (*BSP*, 26). Society or community is not an addition to some preexisting solipsistic Being, but rather, there can be no philosophy of the subject as such. Before "me," "the Other," or "the world," there is simply a being-*with*. Although Nancy makes no reference of the sphere of the sound in this text, but instead prefers to use the language of touch, being-with shares with listening the distinctive relation between inside and outside described earlier: "The 'outside' of the origin is 'inside'—in an inside more interior than the extreme interior, that is, more interior than the *intimacy* of the world and the intimacy that belongs to each 'me.' If intimacy must be defined as the extremity of coincidence with oneself, then what exceeds intimacy in interiority is the distancing of coincidence itself" (*BSP*, 11–12).

It is precisely because sound bears, in its very form, an alterity that is not secondary but originary—because sound is therefore spacing—that sound always exceeds itself. It is not that sound plays a part in ontology or that sound is recruited by a certain philosophical project to which it is subservient or merely instrument. Rather, sound is never mere sound but always-already stretches itself out, spaces itself such that sound is already sensation, ontology, politics, relationality. My hypothesis, then, is that because sound is always-already unraveling at its limit—because sound is always-already its outside—sound's own spacing precipitates displacement within an ontology of sound. There is a movement from the being of sound, the nature of sound's existence, toward the specific character of being-in-the-world and of relationality that finds its condition of possibility in the sonorous. To this extent, aurality participates in the political stakes that are raised by Nancy's radical reversal of first philosophy. Observing that political philosophy, represented here by Jean-Jacques Rousseau and Karl Marx, regularly "run[s] aground on the essence of community," Nancy proposes a shift from the notion of community that finds its definition in a shared or common property (race, gender, nationality, and so on) toward conceiving of Being exclusively and originarily as coexistence (*BSP*, 24). In a striking move that evacuates community of all substance, Nancy proposes the idea of a community that has nothing in common besides its coexisting. There is no substance, no essence, no work that could be shared: what is shared is nothing but sharing itself. In other words, this community has nothing in common besides its being as being-with, and this being-with is nothing other than the sharing out of being. Insofar as sound-as-resonance is precisely this being-alongside and this sharing out, what Nancy elsewhere calls "the inoperative community"[12] is bound together solely by its shared sonorousness: a community in listening.

4

Nancy's passage through sound en route toward a rethinking of ontology and politics on the basis of community is surprising enough on its own, but what makes this incorporation all the more striking is the exemplary status that Nancy claims for the sonorous in this spreading out of thought and, moreover, the very exemplarity of this exemplarity insofar as Nancy is not *alone* in his attempt to implicate sound at the very foundation of politics. Even if Nancy is the most vocal in his engagement with the sonorous, it is possible to discern a foundational sonority in a number of recent bids to think what we might describe, after Alain Badiou, as a community without condition.[13] Music scholars may have observed for some time

12. Jean-Luc Nancy, *The Inoperative Community*, trans. Peter Connor, Lisa Garbus, Michael Holland, and Simona Sawhney (Minneapolis: University of Minnesota Press, 1991). Originally published as *La communauté désœuvrée* (Paris: C. Bourgois, 1986).
13. See Alain Badiou, *Conditions*, trans. Steve Corcoran (New York: Continuum, 2009), 148, where he cites Nancy and Agamben alongside Maurice Blanchot. Badiou, though, insists on distinguishing his own position because the cumulative effect of this strain in recent Continental thought is to keep in force an imperative that Badiou cannot accept. To the extent that it exists under various conditions of impossibility, the name of "community"

sound's capacity to transcend political or ethnic boundaries. To suggest, however, that aurality—not its use, but in its very fundamental structure—somehow makes possible the thinking of a politics beyond any criterion of belonging remains a radical hypothesis. Just as sound exposes the structure of sensation and of being in general and the relation between these registers within Nancy's thought, so too does it constitute both the structure of relationality within and between the thinking of a body of philosophers who try to think community on the basis of sound. The ontology of sound functions as both contagion and disconnection among this body of thought. Between Nancy's thought and that of Italian philosopher Giorgio Agamben, for example (and we can only speak of examples, in that sound begets only that which is already outside-itself), there emerge widening gulfs as well as points of contact.

The greatest obstacle to relating Agamben's politics to the structure of resonance that Nancy exposes is Agamben's almost total silence on this theme. Unlike Nancy, who devotes himself to an exploration of listening, Agamben rarely if at all engages with the sonic, and never as his central theme. While another Italian thinker, Paulo Virno, may use virtuosic performance as a means to think through his own version of the Italian resuscitation of Aristotelian potentiality, the sonorous only ever appears at the margins of Agamben's thought. It becomes possible to begin to discern the echoes of this peripheral resonance when one turns to those themes that Agamben shares with Nancy. In fact, Agamben's work stands out amid this philosophical landscape precisely because it gives a decisive political potential to the logic of exemplarity we have examined through Derrida and Nancy, and, moreover, the category of the example is used to implicate the purely sonorous component of speech (before or underneath its signifying force) in the analysis of community and of political power. Agamben is perhaps most renowned in the Anglophone world for his political writings and in particular for his engagement with the Foucauldian theme of biopolitics, but he is widely regarded by other Italian thinkers who contend with this

---

loses its power as a catalyst for emancipatory politics. Beyond this, Badiou also doubts whether this notion of community would actually consist in a presentation of collectivity without transcendence: insofar as community represents the truth of the collective as the exposition of a sense, it involves the exposition of something beyond or before the collective in which it finds its significance. There are, furthermore, a number of other communities without condition (among them, Michael Hardt and Antonio Negri's multitude and Jacques Rancière's part that has no part) that share with Badiou's conception of the generic a debt to Marx's idea of the proletariat as a class that is not a class.

theme as an apolitical thinker whose commitment to ontology has left him uninterested in developing any concept of political agency. The closest he comes to advancing anything like a politics is perhaps in his reflections on community. A sketch of what he calls "the coming community" is confined to a short, fragmented, and rather poetic text of the same title. He shares not only with Nancy but also with Blanchot and arguably Badiou as well an attack on any substantive notion of communal bond. Agamben repeats Nancy's insistence on the coupling of singularity and plurality at the foundation of being, together with a transcendental indetermination. "The coming being is whatever being," he writes, before subtracting every property from being: "such-and-such being is reclaimed from its having this or that property, which identifies it as being to this or that set . . . and it is reclaimed for the simple generic absence of any belonging."[14] Because the singularity exposed as such comes not with indifference but with all its predicates, there is never the intelligence of a thing, a quality, or an essence, but the "intelligence of an intelligibility" (*TCC*, 2).

This exposure of intelligibility resonates with certain aspects of Nancy's conception of listening, to which we shall turn momentarily, but first it is worth noting that it is only fitting that aurality should intervene in the thinking of singularity. The purely sonorous, as that which exceeds the meaning in every utterance, has been repeatedly invoked as a figure that deconstructs the antinomy of universal and particular.[15] As Nancy explains, the singular distinguishes itself from both the individual and the particular: if the individual is an immanent totality without externality, and the particular presupposes the whole of which it comprises a part, the singular disrupts the opposition universal/particular and with it that of same/other and instead appears as a punctual indivisibility that shows its plurality in saying "*each* one" and hence "with" (*BSP*, 32).

Agamben likewise targets the presupposition of a dialectical relation between universal and particular: the universal is present not only in particular embodiments and the particular is not only the embodiment of the universal, but the universal exceeds the particular just as the particular is always more particular than any particular embodiment. Universal

14. Giorgio Agamben, *The Coming Community*, trans. Michael Hardt (Minneapolis: University of Minnesota Press, 1993), 1–2. Hereafter, this work is cited parenthetically as *TCC*. Originally published as *La comunità che viene* (Torino: Einaudi, 1990).
15. Adorno is perhaps a classic case here: while he has many names for that which in the object exceeds its concept, he frequently identifies this excess with sensory perception and specifically with music in its relation to philosophy.

and particular can neither coincide nor be held in a dialectical relationship because neither category is self-identical. Neither particular nor universal coincides with itself, but is always-already outside itself. Just as the singularity of Nancy's being immediately opens out onto its plurality ("*singuli* already says the plural, because it designates the 'one' as belonging to 'one by one'" [*BSP*, 32]), so too does Agamben's whatever-being already take place outside itself. Both partake of an alterity that is not secondary or supplementary, but originary. "Whatever" is not a property that can be added to being. If it adds anything at all, it adds a threshold, an empty space. "But a singularity plus an empty space can only be a pure exteriority" (*TCC*, 67). This allows us to advance the analysis of sound's exemplarity: if, for Agamben, the singular example is the "face" of being, the coincidence of a singularity with its "pure exposure" or the experience of "being-*within* an *outside*" (*TCC*, 67–68), Nancy makes sound exemplary of this exemplarity: sound is an entirely "visible face," a being "*inside-out*" (*LG*, 13). Sound's com-pli-city (its folding together) with singularity thus stems from the structure of resonance as a movement outside of itself even as it vibrates in itself.

5

There is, however, a further, more specific way in which Agamben and Nancy's conceptions of singularity implicate the sonorous in the political: both refer the question to sense, and in so doing, insofar as sense is referral, they revive the figure of self-relation once again. But that is to anticipate an argument that must contend with the aporias of self-reference. The link that Nancy, in a first step, forges between singularity and sense is more intuitive. He begins with the identification of meaning and being: it is not that we *have* meaning but that we *are* meaning insofar as "we" is where the circulation and production of meaning takes place. Neither does Being have meaning; rather, it is given as meaning, and that meaning in turn is the circulation, the spacing that we are. "*Meaning is itself the sharing of Being*" (*BSP*, 2). Because being and sound share a structure of spacing and referring, Nancy can then speak of a shared space of meaning and sound. It is here, perhaps, that one can also speak with greater justification of a quasi-transcendentalism of aurality, for it is by means of sound that Nancy is able to cut across the mind-body dualism to bring together sense and sensation. In this, Nancy is able to establish a point of contact between being and meaning, and between community and communication, without reimposing a teleological structure. Among the sensory registers,

Nancy contends that "the auditive pair [of hearing and listening] has a special relationship with *sense* in the intellectual and intelligible acceptance of the work (with 'perceived meaning' [*sens sensé*], if you like, as opposed to 'perceiving sense' [*sens sensible*])" (*LG*, 5–6).

Agamben, for his part, brings out the intimacy between singularity and sense by identifying whatever-being with "purely linguistic being" (*TCC*, 10). In a thought indebted to both Foucault and Derrida, Agamben proposes that being be grasped properly by means of the paradigm, or the example. As has already been suggested above, the example straddles the distinction between inclusion and exclusion, but what is most intriguing about Agamben's project is its claim that being shares this topology of the example with the structure of language itself—and, at the risk of anticipating the argument ahead, it is with this gesture that Agamben captures sound within ontology. An example must first be subtracted from its ordinary use in order to become an example: it is only insofar as the example is at the same time excluded from the class that it can stand for all the objects of that class. Following Aristotle, Agamben contends that the example opens up a new analogical context that exceeds both deduction and induction. The example does not provide a universal "rule" that could be applied a priori to particular instances, nor can the example be rendered intelligible through the gathering together of all the particular cases. Instead of moving from universal to particular or from particular to universal, the example moves from singularity to singularity. The generality that this movement effects derives from the comparison between the singular example and the class that the example, by means of its exclusion, makes intelligible. The example, or para-digm, is hence a showing-alongside (*TCC*, 10).

One might argue at this point that sound is the exemplary example of the example since it has the structure of an intelligibility exhibited only as the effect of a spacing outside, but Agamben does not incorporate sound into his ontology, at least not directly. The focus instead is on language. The primary claim is that exemplary being is linguistic being. Exemplary being is not defined by any property except its being-called, or we might term its being-intelligible. In this way, being is not defined by its being-red, for example, but simply by its being-*called*-red. Proposing the case of the grammatical example, Agamben is at pains to point out that as soon as the word is taken as an example of an element of speech, its immediate denotative character is withdrawn. In order to exemplify the class, the grammatical example steps outside of the class and thereby ceases to function linguistically as any other member of that class would do. The grammatical example becomes intelligible as a being-in-language only on account of the spacing that opens up between the example and the linguistic elements it exemplifies; this gap means that the example is not *in* language but at its limit. The intelligibility of the example is the outside of language. This leads Agamben to argue that linguistic being is "a class that both belongs and does not belong to itself" (*TCC*, 9). Even as it exhibits its belonging to a class, it steps outside of that class to do so.

Agamben takes this further and generalizes this structure of the example for language as a whole. The new analogical dimension beyond the dialectic of universal and particular can be grasped when (in a gesture similar to Nancy's move from the analysis of sensation as resonance to the diffraction among the community of the senses) one considers not just the structure of the example itself but the relations *between* examples. Think of the difficulty in giving an example of the example: because the example shares with other examples nothing beyond the fact that it is excluded from the class for which it stands and which it constitutes, what is there to determine the membership of the set of examples? Any example generalizes the community of examples given thus far because there can be no final example. If the example is defined only by the possibility of its exclusion, by its potential not to be inside, it necessarily blocks the arrival at any telos or totalization.

In theory, then, the logic of exemplarity would know no limit or end. However, the very character of exemplarity means that the possibility of exemplarity becomes its presupposed transcendental condition of possibility. Because there is no criterion or property that would permit or restrict the addition of further examples to the community of examples, the community as a whole presents the pure possibility of belonging as such, which is also to say the very possibility of being-in-language. This reference by the community of examples to the possibility of exemplarity depends upon the moment of privation within the structure of exemplarity. Recall that Agamben stressed how the example becomes an example only in the suspension of its signifying power. If language is exemplarity all the way down, this moment of privation determines that the movement of exemplarity finds its limit when it is ceases to be an example of anything but itself. Exemplifying the example means showing the example alongside its own intelligibility as an example, that is, the very possibility of its being an example.

My analysis of Agamben's thought of the example aims to elucidate how the logic of exemplarity is motivated by a certain suspension or privation: the movement of the "as not," which thinks the example "as" the other members of the class it exemplifies, provided that, in its status as example, it is also "not as" any other member of the set. Moreover, my analysis seeks to demonstrate that the logic of exemplarity terminates in a figure of self-relationality. This idea that privation is at its limit self-reference brings us back to Derrida's question: "When our eyes touch, is it day or is it night?" Derrida speculates that it is only with a certain privation that it becomes possible to sense not the object of sensation (the eye) but the sensing itself (the gaze). To see seeing itself, seeing must lose sight of what can be seen. Sight must withdraw its reference from what is visible and instead paradoxically "see" what is invisible. Seeing itself, however, is not merely invisible in that it is incapable of being seen, but it is also what permits objects to be seen; it is that "without which" objects remain not only unseen but also incapable of being seen. At its limit, withdrawn from its object, sight displaces its gaze from the merely visible to the very possibility of visibility itself. By contrast, in the usual course of seeing, whereby what is seen is not the gaze but the visible (here the eye), the gaze goes unseen; or, we might say that sight sees *through* the gaze, as though it were transparent. Sight forgets itself. Unless there is nothing left to see.

If at this point, with Derrida, we are on the point of hearing and understanding, Agamben's thought dares to approach this ear. Just as Derrida's eyes only see sight in their blindness, a central hypothesis of Agamben's philosophical enterprise is that language forgets itself. Language's structure of exemplarity that is language comes up against its limit in a topological structure directly symmetrical to that of the example. Agamben contends that, in order to signify, language forgets its own condition of possibility: it presupposes (meaning that it cannot "say" but instead "forgets") that *there is language*. While this has been a theme of Agamben's work since his earliest writings, more recently he has made an explicit connection between this presuppositional structure of language and the paradigm of biopolitics that he sees as determining all forms of government and power in Western modernity. I recall his now famous and highly condensed maxim: *"The sovereign exception . . . is the presupposition of . . . reference in the form of its suspension."*[16] There are two components to this definition that merit explanation. First, by comparison with the example—which is excluded from the set insofar as it is included in it—Agamben defines the

16. Giorgio Agamben, *Homo Sacer: Sovereign Power and Bare Life*, trans. Daniel Heller-Roazen (Stanford, CA: Stanford University Press, 1998), 21. Originally published as *Homo Sacer* (Torino: G. Einaudi, 1995).

exception as that which is included only to the extent that it is excluded; it is something that comes within the sovereign's power only because it is excluded from the law's protection and thus becomes exposed to its full, extralegal force. Second, when Agamben speaks of "reference in the form of its suspension," he means a reference that contracts in a withdrawal from its external referent back toward itself. A reference that applies in not applying is one that relates only to itself. Like the sensing of sensing itself, like the sight of the gaze, a referral that suspends itself is a self-reference: it is not an example *of* but exemplarity itself. Thus, Agamben proposes that language, insofar as it is exemplarity, can only encounter what is most interior (the fact that there are examples) as outside itself. Language forgets its own condition of possibility (the pure fact of being-in-language) and instead imagines that what ought to be most intimate is in fact beyond.

6

Throughout his writings, Agamben has identified guises under which this supposed outside-of-language manifests itself, but there is perhaps no figure more exemplary of the nonlinguistic than pure sound. This distinction between sound and sense orients Nancy's initial thoughts on aurality, leading him to propose two forms of aural perception: hearing (*entendre*) and listening (*écouter*). Hearing has an intimate connection to sense because *entendre* also means "to understand," "as if 'hearing' were above all 'hearing say' (rather than 'hearing sound'), or rather, as if in all 'hearing' there had to be a 'hearing say,' regardless of whether the sound perceived was a word or not" (*LG*, 6).

Nancy prefers a reversal: "in all saying . . . there is hearing, and in hearing itself . . . a listening." Speculating that sense might not exhaust itself in making sense but may "want also to resound," he founds his entire proposal on the idea of resonance as a foundation of "sense." But what is the nature of this foundation? What is the topological relation of this fundamental sound to signification? Nancy appears to suggest that that which sits at the limit of sense (sound without sense) is the very foundation of sense. If hearing is about understanding sense, listening is about straining for a possible, yet not immediately accessible, meaning; listening is the very edge or margin of sense. "Listening is listening to something other than sense in its signifying sense" (*LG*, 32).

Moreover, Nancy makes an explicit reference to the dimension within speech that Agamben isolates in his analysis of the presuppositional structure of language: "a 'voice': we have to understand what sounds from a human throat without being language, which emerges from an animal gullet . . . the rustling toward which we strain or lend an ear" (*LG*, 22).

Nancy's footnote reference here is to a text that appeared in parallel French and Italian, but it also appears as an epilogue to the English translation of *Il linguaggio e la morte*.[17] In that book, Agamben sets out the argument that what appears as mere sound, as the dark margin around language, turns out to be nothing other than language itself in its very possibility. Agamben is interested in exposing that Voice that would be "no longer the experience of a mere sound, and not yet the experience of meaning" (*LAD*, 34). This Voice is no longer the mere animal cry but a pure intention to signify without yet actually saying anything. It is "a pure indication that language is taking place." Like the Derridean blind touching that discloses the taking place of seeing (not yet seeing any *thing* beyond the taking place of sight), the Voice refers to the taking place of sense before any actual reference. Agamben turns to examples of denotation's withdrawal or suspension to expose this otherwise presupposed dimension of language. It is when words fail that one suddenly encounters the possibility of sense in the form of its suspension. Agamben also cites the example of shifters, words characterized by their inherent deixis: words such as *I*, *this*, or *now* refer not to any concrete substance but to something determined only in the instance of discourse (this speaker who appropriates language here, this object that is referred to now, this moment that takes place in language, and so on).

> The voice—which is assumed by the shifters as a taking place of language—is not simply the *phonē*, the mere sonorous flux emitted by the phonic apparatus, just as the *I*, the speaker, is not simply the psychosomatic individual from whom the sound projects. A voice as mere sound (an *animal* voice) could certainly be the index of the individual who emits it, but in no way can it refer to the instance of discourse as such, nor open the sphere of utterance. The voice, the animal *phonē*, is indeed presupposed by the shifters, but as that which must necessarily be removed in order for meaningful discourse to take place. (*LAD*, 35)

17. Giorgio Agamben, *Language and Death: The Place of Negativity*, trans. Karen E. Pinkus (Minneapolis: University of Minnesota Press, 1991), 107–8. Hereafter, this work is cited as *LAD*. Originally published as *Il linguaggio e la morte: un seminario sul luogo della negatività* (Torino: G. Einaudi, 1982).

The Voice is "the taking place of language between the removal of the voice and the event of meaning" (*LAD*, 35).

If Voice is the taking place of language, it points to the very fact that *there is language*: that it is possible to speak and to signify. If Voice is therefore the experience of the very possibility of sense, and the structure of referral is what makes signification as a network of referrals possible, this would suggest that *Voice is nothing other than resonance*.

Two readings of sound's relation to sense are thus presented. The first identifies the sonorous with what comes before and underneath sense; it is what must be removed or negated in order that sense take place. The second reading, by contrast, proposes that resonance takes place *in between* sense itself, in its referring to itself. It is possible to read Nancy's text as straining toward this second interpretation. In fact, it is what permits him to claim a shared space between meaning and sound. He suggests that listening is attuned not so much to that which exceeds, precedes, or lies beyond sense (resonance as mere sound without significance, what Agamben calls the "mere voice") as it is to the very structure of referral that sense is (resonance as the pure possibility of sense).

Nancy argues that listening is in tension with or in relation to self, where "self" is understood not as a substantial "I" or "another" but as a referral back toward and beyond itself (*LG*, 12). The suggestion here is that listening is a relation to a self-relation, provided that this self-relation is understood as a spacing-itself-out that never fully coincides with itself. For Agamben, Voice has the form of a self-relation: of language's power of reference turned back upon itself as it withdraws from any external object of signification. When Nancy folds Agamben into his deconstruction of sense, however, he does so in a way that seems to privilege the first interpretation. He speaks of an indistinct "transcendental murmuring" that takes place "previous to the voice" (*LG*, 25). He refers to the sound that emerges from the animal gullet, but, crucially, the reference here is to a passage that makes clear that the "rustling" to which Nancy's ear strains is not the animal cry itself but already its removal in the advent of human language: "When we . . . hear the rustle of invisible animals . . . what matters is the indistinct pattern that we sometimes hear moving to the side, the sound of an animal in flight" (*LAD*, 107). This dissipating of mere sound is what makes the emergence of sense possible, and yet this resonance is always-already spreading itself out and removing itself from itself.

This is perhaps why Nancy says that "sense opens up in silence" (*LG*, 26). This line of thought leads Nancy to adopt a series of formulations from Bernard Bass's reading of Lacan that closely approximate Agamben's own. Nancy first speaks of a "meaning to say [*vouloir-dire*]" that is "beyond a saying," echoing Agamben's reference to "a pure meaning to say without saying [*puro voler-dire senza dire*]."[18] Nancy then recuperates Bass's definition of the Lacanian voice as "an enunciation without utterance" (*LG*, 28). Nancy's ear listens for the Lacanian voice as "'the alterity of what is said': what, in the saying, is other than what is said, in a sense the non-said or silence, but still the saying itself . . . in fact less that of a non-said than of a non-saying in saying or of saying itself." Nancy continues this quest for precision in a footnote here: "Hence, in a sense, the 'saying [*le dire*],' but the 'saying' as non-said [*non-dit*] *and also* as non-saying [*non-disant*]" (*LG*, 28–29). Thus, the voice *is* saying itself insofar as saying remains un-said and does not actually say anything. In this way, Nancy draws close to Agamben's isolation of the dimension of Voice and, with it, the notion of community without condition: the very possibility of being-in-language is not outside, beyond, or before language but *is* language itself in the moment that it suspends its power of reference (it is non-saying)—*and also* this moment remains forgotten and transparent (that is un- or non-said) in any actual operation of language. This un-saying un-said in saying is the very condition of possibility of speech; or, in Nancy's words, "This pure resonance is a nonperceptible transcendental of signifying sonority." A silent, unheard resonance is therefore the transcendental condition of possibility of sense—and, in turn, of being and community.

There is, then, a striking intimacy between Nancy's and Agamben's thought. So perfectly attuned are the symmetrical logics of speaking and of listening that one could that say Agamben's Voice resounds in Nancy's ear. To the extent, though, that every con-tact hesitates in tact—that all touching is always-already a withdrawal from touch—the contiguity between the Agambenian Voice and the Nancean ear spaces itself out, separates itself even as it joins them together. For Agamben, this fracture is an inevitable consequence of grounding sense in the negative foundation of a Voice—doubly negative in that it consists in the erasure of mere sound and its own disappearance in actual speech (*LAD*, 85). This means that language comes to be divided into planes: one that corresponds to the taking place of language, and one that corresponds to what is said in this taking place. Language divides into meaningful discourse, on the one hand, and its con-

18. My translation. Compare Agamben, *Language and Death*, 61, where the translation somewhat condenses the sense of the Italian.

dition of possibility, on the other. This is to demonstrate again that sense has the structure of exemplarity: it exists as a form of self-relation, as the relation or referral between sense (as meaning) and its taking place (as pure resonance). As argued above, however, the structure of exemplarity finds its end in the division that is the state of exception: the taking place of sense is included in sense only to the extent that it is excluded.

Agamben contends that this leads to a series of manifestations of this scission, chief among them, perhaps, the one thematicized in both Nancy's essay on listening and in Agamben's meditation on the relation between language and negativity: the division between (mere) sound and (meaningful) sense. This in turn spawns the division between hearing (a meaning) and listening (to resonance) and, through analogy with the other senses, between each sensory register and its "tense, attentive, or anxious state" (seeing/looking, tasting/savoring, smelling/sniffing, touching/palpating) (*LG*, 5). This distinction between a sense and its intensification replicates the relation between sense and its taking place. The question is whether the relation is one of exclusive inclusion (listening *exemplifies* hearing) or inclusive exclusion (listening is an exception to the rule of hearing).

7

In the con-tact between Agamben's Voice and Nancy's ear, a further division intervenes. The division that differentiates each of the senses from themselves, denying them internal consistency, comes between them as a community. While Agamben is concerned with a pure possibility or intention of *saying* in sense, Nancy is drawn to an alternative proposition, that "sense consists first of all, not in a signifying intention but rather in a *listening*, where only resonance comes to resound" (*LG*, 30, my emphasis). Nancy at times ponders the coincidence of ear and voice, wondering, "Is even listening itself sonorous?" (*LG*, 5). At one point, he suggests that a transcendental sonority is a shared condition of possibility between the voice and the ear because this resonance "animates the auditory apparatus as much as the phonatory apparatus" (*LG*, 29).

A number of topologies beyond straightforward coincidence suggest themselves for the relation between ear and voice. First, one could say (and at times this appears to be Nancy's claim) that voice *is* listening in the same way that listening *is* sense because they share the structure of a resonance—or, better (drawing upon the analysis in *Being Singular Plural*), voice, listening, sense, being, community all share a common form only to the extent that they are nothing other than this sharing. Just as the various senses differ from one another even as they share a certain structure such that the perceptible realm is immediately plural, so too does this same structure of spacing produce diffraction and proliferation: voice *and* ear *and* sense *and* being *and* community, all "singular plural" like the community of senses.

Second, another kind of isomorphism between voice and ear may be detectable that speaks in some way to their perceived reciprocity. Perhaps, if Agamben's Voice takes the form of the exception, listening is its inversion into the logic of the example. Nancy, it could be argued, proposes such a transvaluation of presupposition into exemplary exposure when he reverses the idea that all hearing is a "hearing say." First, "in all saying . . . there is hearing," which shows that the ear is presupposed in the form of an exception in the speaking voice. But then there is "in hearing itself, at the very bottom of it, a listening," which means that when the ear goes to the ground (when the possibility of being-intelligible is forgotten in the movement of the Voice), it is in the form of a self-relation in which it exemplifies itself as a resonant listening. If sonority, as the condition of possibility of sense, is what is presupposed in the exercise of saying (as its inclusive exclusion), the ear stands in a relation of exception to the speaking voice. But then hearing shows itself (alongside itself) as listening. If listening is a hearing that strains beyond sense as the object of hearing toward its condition of possibility, listening is a hearing that hears hearing itself—it hears the very possibility of being heard, which is to say its capacity to be understood. On this point, it is possible to connect Nancy's idea of the resonance as the condition of possibility of sense and understanding with Agamben's idea that the grammatical example becomes intelligible only by standing outside the class, by resonating, if you like. Listening thus consists in the relation between the ear and its intelligibility. Listening is the resonance of sound with, against, alongside its audibility.

This is to suppose, however, that audibility, in giving itself to itself in its self-relation, can in fact resound and that, unlike the eyes that touch blindly, listening is audibility *heard*. And why should it not? If the condition of possibility of sense is a referral that is outside itself in being inside itself (that is, a resonance), then it follows that listening is a referral to resonance (which is exactly what Nancy maintains), which means a referral to a referral to a referral, where each referral always refers outside of itself in referring to itself. The difficulty is whether this relation is essentially a resonance of resonance, which would mean that listening is an example of an example of an example, or, if the movement of exemplarity from singularity to singularity can only ever find its end in the exceptional logic of presupposition, in which case listening would be an unheard audibility as much as the Voice is an unsaid sayability.

8

Agamben, though, seeks to overturn the presuppositional structure that he sees at the heart of metaphysics by insisting on exemplarity at the level of the very possibility for speech and for aurality. To understand Agamben's endeavor, it is helpful to note another fracture that is symptomatic of the Voice. Modern linguistics recognizes that language divides itself into speech and its possibility in the form of the opposition between actual discourse (*parole*) and the set of possible utterances (*langue*). This distinction ties the notion of Voice to the engagement with Aristotelian potentiality that has become a major theme of Agamben's project. As he sees it, metaphysics consists in the attempt to shoehorn the relation between potentiality and actuality into the dialectic of universal and particular. If actuality is simply the actual realization of a universal potentiality, then the entire series of actualized particulars would be nothing but the fully realized universal potentiality from which they stemmed. This would make the universal potential the condition of possibility of the actual particular and hence a transcendental in the same way that Voice, as the potentiality for speech, is the condition of possibility of actual discourse. The same risk exists in making aurality into a transcendental—especially if listening, conceived as pure resonance, becomes the condition for every actual instance of hearing.

Only by following Aristotle's argument with great precision in order to reveal that all potentiality must always-already be impotentiality does Agamben hope to challenge the presuppositional structure of language and being in metaphysics.[19] Only if a potential is at the same time also a potential-not-to-be is it possible to speak of a genuine potentiality rather than the realization of a possibility in waiting. This means that potentiality might always exemplify itself: it cannot be a pure auto-affection of the same

19. Finding a notion of impotentiality in Aristotle's *Metaphysics* that has been overlooked by the entire history of Western thought has been a cornerstone of Agamben's philosophical project. The clearest elaboration of his argument can be found in "On Potentiality," in *Potentialities: Collected Essays in Philosophy*, trans. Daniel Heller-Roazen (Stanford, CA: Stanford University Press, 1999), 177–84.

but must always-already be outside itself as the simultaneous potential to be and not to be (in language). If humanity is not to be determined by its linguistic being, it is not enough to expose the dimension of potentiality that remains presupposed in speech. To illustrate the move that needs to be made, Agamben draws upon Foucault's notion of the archive.[20] As Agamben reads this notion, it names the plane of enunciation in which the speaking being appropriates language so as to effect the passage from mere voice (potential) to signifying discourse (actual). The archive is the relation between the unsaid set of possibilities of speaking that make up *langue* and the set of said utterances that comprise *parole*. Agamben then proposes to repeat Foucault's operation, but slides it in the direction of *langue* so as to relocate it from the gap between *langue* and *parole* to the gap between *langue* and the archive. Whereas the archive is the relation between actual speech and its taking place (its potentiality), Agamben gives the name "testimony" to the relation between language-as-possibility and its own potentiality. The potentiality of potentiality—that which in potentiality makes it potential rather than merely actualizable—is the potential *not to*. Hence, while the archive is the reference of the unsaid to the said, Agamben's testimony is the reference of the unsayable to the sayable. Thus, testimony is the relation of potentiality to itself, provided that it always-already moves outside of itself, becomes other than itself in turning back on itself. Testimony is the resonance of impotentiality; it is the sound of impotentiality and hence attests to an originary indetermination, to an irreparable finitude and hence to an originary being-with.

It is on this point that Agamben's refusal of biopolitics takes its distance from the Derridean refusal of presence.[21] The biopolitical capture of the essential inoperosity of human life finds its most succinct expression in the conversion of the experience of saying in the form of its privation into the fundamental determination of humankind as a pure potentiality to speak. It is not just a matter of being un-said, or even of being un-saying, but of being fundamentally unsayable. So, if Voice is an unsaid sayability

20. Giorgio Agamben, *Remnants of Auschwitz: The Witness and the Archive*, trans. Daniel Heller-Roazen (New York: Zone Books, 2002), 143–45. Originally published as *Quel che resta di Auschwitz* (Torino: Bollati Boringhieri, 1998).
21. One of the paradigmatic instances in which Agamben announces the interval between his own project and that of deconstruction comes in an essay on self-referentiality and language, the English translation of which is published in *Potentialities*: "The trace is from the beginning the name of this self-affection [of potentiality]. The aporias of self-reference thus do not find their resolution here" (217).

(a potentiality of speaking that goes unsaid in speech), Agamben gives the name "infancy" to the experience of a particular unsayability (a potentiality not to speak). This impotentiality of saying reveals itself in the fact that humanity does not immediately have its own voice. Agamben's project of thinking being and community on the basis of a fundamental capacity not to speak, on the basis of humanity's originary disconnection from language, traverses even his more overtly political and theological writings, but announces itself as early as *Linguaggio e la morte*. There he observes that humanity is defined in the Western tradition as the speaking being insofar as he possesses the faculty for language. The task he sets himself is to consider "what if humankind were [not] *speaking* . . . yet continued to speak?" (*LAD*, xii). He maintains that thought and (later in *Infancia e storia*) history[22] are possible only if language "is not *our* voice" (if it is not immediately proper to us), only if it is possible that we are capable of not speaking (*LAD*, 107). If humanity were immediately in language and had no need to first appropriate it, humankind would be determined by that condition, and that would contravene the aim that Agamben shares with Nancy to think community without condition, as a community of singularities that have nothing but their indetermination in common.

With the idea of aurality as a fundamental indetermination, it is difficult to resolve the paradoxical danger of reinstating sound as a transcendental in order that the sonorous may challenge transcendentalism in general. The risk here is that sound is mobilized to produce a reification of indetermination and in so doing effectively reimposes a condition in which to ground the community. Thinking ontology and community on the basis of sound-as-impotentiality would reproduce a determination of indeterminacy insofar as it becomes necessary to have a privation, to have the potential *not to*. "This is why it is so hard," Agamben concedes, "to think . . . a 'constitution of potentiality' entirely freed from the principle of sovereignty."

> Instead one must think the existence of potentiality without any relation to Being in the form of actuality—not even in the extreme form of . . . the potentiality not to be, and of actuality as the fulfilment and manifestation of potentiality—and think the existence of potentiality even without any relation to being in the form of the gift of the self

22. Giorgio Agamben, *Infancy and History: The Destruction of Experience*, trans. Liz Heron (London: Verso, 2007), 59. Originally published as *Infanzia e storia* (Torino: Einaudi, 1978).

[to the self]. . . . This, however, implies nothing less than thinking ontology and politics beyond every figure of relation.[23]

So, let us return to (and at the same time move outside of) the question that comes to Derrida's ear: "When the ear and the voice touch, is it day or is it night?" It is not enough to discern here, at the origin of hearing and understanding, an audibility or inaudibility. If listening is a relation to a relation, it withdraws its ear from the possibility of relationship even as it stretches out toward itself. To listen is to be at once inside and outside relationality. Resonance is the sound of an outside, and sound the outside that we always-already are.

23. Agamben, *Homo Sacer*, 47.

Acoustic Multinaturalism, the Value of Nature, and the Nature of Music in Ecomusicology

Ana María Ochoa Gautier

In recent years, questions regarding music, sound, and nature have intensified. This intensification is visible in various domains of musical practice, such as the increased audibility of composers involved in acoustic ecology as both practitioners within and theorizers of the field; the global presence of sound collectives employing audio recordings and music scholarship for the purpose of denouncing environmental problems; and the emergence of what are considered "new fields" of study, such as ecomusicology, biomusic, and zoomusicology. This coincides with a growing interest in listening and in sound as phenomena and the institutionalization of sound studies as a disciplinary field.[1] Finally, it coincides with a renewed

I thank Julio Ramos, Jairo Moreno, and Gavin Steingo for helpful critical and generous conversations and comments, and Margaret Havran for her editorial work on this essay. I would also like to thank Arturo Escobar and Enrique Leff for their help and encouragement, even though a deeper engagement with the specific elements of their work has inevitably been left for another moment. The responsibility of the content of this essay is, of course, mine. Unless otherwise noted, all translations are my own.
1. Jonathan Sterne, ed., *The Sound Studies Reader* (Durham, NC: Duke University Press, 2012); Michael Bull, ed., *Sound Studies* (London: Routledge, 2013).

boundary 2 43:1 (2016)   DOI 10.1215/01903659-3340661   © 2016 by Duke University Press

questioning of the relative merits of "cultural" versus "musical" analysis in the Anglo-American musicological tradition, reflecting the increasing difficulty of keeping apart the colonially inflected disciplinary divisions of music studies in terms of both musical object and method (musicology, ethnomusicology, music theory, etc.).[2]

The concatenation of questions about sound, music, and nature, the emergence of sound studies, and the renewed debate on the analytic paradigms of musical disciplines point to a shifting conceptual ground of the acoustic in the humanities. And the musical disciplines are not alone. As Eduardo Viveiros de Castro remarks, the present moment is one in which "the terrifying communication of the geopolitical and the geophysical, everything, contributes to the crumbling of the foundational distinction of the social sciences—that between the cosmological and anthropological orders, forever separated, that is, at least since the seventeenth century (recall the air pump and the Leviathan), by a double discontinuity of scale and essence: evolution of species and history of capitalism, thermodynamics and stock market, nuclear physics and parliamentary politics, climatology and sociology, in two words: nature and culture."[3] In the case of music, this "separation between the cosmological and anthropological orders" takes the form of rekindling the long historical debate in the West about sound and music as phenomena that lie between nature and culture,[4] but one moved by an urgency that it did not have in earlier periods, now posed by "the intrusion of Gaia" into the affairs of humans.[5] This is not so much a "crisis" of thinking as it is a radical transformation of the conditions for posing questions regarding what historically in the West have been considered the differential fields of nature and culture (*ATDC*, 49).

In what follows, I explore how ecomusicology has articulated the

2. Kofi V. Agawu, *Representing African Music: Postcolonial Notes, Queries, Positions* (New York: Routledge, 1991). Hereafter, this work is cited parenthetically as *RA*. See also Olivia Bloechl, *Native American Song at the Frontiers of Early Modern Music* (New York: Cambridge University Press, 2008).
3. Eduardo Viveiros de Castro, "Transformação na antropologia, transformação da antropologia," *Sopro*, no. 58 (2011): 4–15, esp. 4.
4. Jonathan Sterne, *The Audible Past: Cultural Origins of Sound Reproduction* (Durham, NC: Duke University Press, 2003); and *Music Theory and Natural Order from the Renaissance to the Early Twentieth Century*, ed. Suzannah Clark and Alexander Rehding (Cambridge: Cambridge University Press, 2001).
5. Isabelle Stengers, *Au temps des catastrophes: Résister à la barbarie qui vient* (Paris: La Découverte, 2009), 49. Hereafter, this work is cited as *ATDC*.

question of sound/music and nature, and the values that coalesce around the emergence of this discipline. I find it is significant that while the problem of the environment in many of the fields of the social sciences and the humanities has questioned the idea of nature and the implications of this for recasting the politics of critique within the disciplines themselves (as is the case with philosophy and anthropology, for example), ecomusicology, to the contrary, announces its emergence as a new encompassing musical field fueled by recourse to the notion of nature. Rather than assume the collapse of the distinction between "the cosmological and anthropological orders," ecomusicology, until now, has tended to reaffirm such a distinction, even while it critiques the separation between "Man and Nature."

I will argue that this peculiar affirmation largely rests on the values ascribed to sound/music and to different musicological disciplinary practices that are inherited from the genealogy of musical disciplines. In this essay, then, I explore values by closely analyzing the literature in ecomusicology and then go on to propose a contrast with Feldian acoustemology as a tradition that—through its links to sound studies, acoustic practices, and structuralism—suggests a different entry point into the problematics of sound/music, the anthropological, and the cosmological. This alternate entry point is central to articulating what I am here calling acoustic multinaturalism.

The Operational Implications of Naming the Field

In this essay, the question of value in the emergence of ecomusicology as a discipline is understood less as a problem of recognizing the relative merit of different approaches to ecomusicology by specific authors than of exploring the mode through which the discipline has framed the problematics that it seeks to articulate. According to Isabelle Stengers, if the act of "naming is operating and not defining—that is, appropriating—the name cannot be arbitrary" (*ATDC*, 50). So rather than defining ecomusicology, what I seek to do in the following sections is to explore how the emergence of the field operationalizes a series of problematics through the modality of naming. A "problematic space is characterized always by a polemic that emerges with the nomination of the problem itself" (*ATDC*, 50). So we return to the classic question: What's in a name? What does ecomusicology seek to operationalize?

According to Aaron S. Allen, the term *ecomusicology* "gained currency in the 2000s in American and Scandinavian academic circles."[6] In his definition, ecomusicology, "or ecocritical musicology[,] is the study of music, nature and culture in all the complexities of those terms" (EC). For Denise Von Glahn, "ecomusicology explores relationships to the natural world and questions how those relationships imprint themselves on music and scholarship; who gets to articulate the relationships; and . . . how select composers understand the essential dynamic between humanity and the rest of nature."[7] Thus, what initially seems to position the discipline is a mode of thinking about nature framed by a specific body of literary critique.[8]

This framing is accompanied by a "holistic" impulse that seeks to bring the diverse musical disciplines, as well as the different approaches to questions of acoustics, music, and the environment, under the discipline's purview. Allen conceives of ecomusicology as a mixture of literary ecocriticism studies with Charles Seeger's "holistic sense of musicology," that is, "including what today are historical musicology, ethnomusicology, and other related interdisciplinary fields" (EC). It is also meant to function as an "umbrella term that may bring together fields that do not usually interact [in order to] encompass a broadness [that] allows scholars considerable flexibility to combine diverse disciplines in ecocritical studies of music," a crucial issue because "'nature' is one of the most complex words in the English language, and the study of it, as with the similarly contested words 'music' and 'culture,' can take many approaches" (EC). The term *ecomusicology* is also "applied to a diverse array of musical and artistic endeavors including soundscape studies, acoustic ecology and biomusic" (EC). In 2007, the American Musicological Society established the Ecocriticism Study Group (ESG), and in 2011, the Society for Ethnomusicology established the Ecomusicology Special Interest Group in response to increasing interest.

In its effort to encompass diverse approaches to the question of

---

6. *Grove Music Online*, s.v. "Ecomusicology," by Aaron S. Allen, accessed July 21, 2014, www.oxfordmusiconline.com/. Hereafter, this work is cited parenthetically as EC.

7. Denise Von Glahn, "American Women and the Nature of Identity," *Journal of the American Musicological Society* 64, no. 3 (2011): 399–403, esp. 403.

8. Within literary studies, ecocriticism is just one mode of framing the question of literature and the environment. The debate is increasingly engaged with the broader theoretical impulse that questions an ontology that affirms the separation of nature and culture. For a discussion of Anglo-American literary studies and the questions of nature, see Timothy Morton, *Ecology without Nature: Rethinking Environmental Aesthetics* (Cambridge, MA: Harvard University Press, 2007).

sound/music and the environment, and through its particular articulation of music, nature, and culture, ecomusicology has tended to reaffirm a multi-culturalist ethos—that is to say, an ethos that accounts for all forms of diversity under a single epistemological umbrella, the concepts of "nature" and "culture." Rather than unsettling the division between the cosmological and anthropological orders, that is, unsettling the very ontological grounds of "nature" and "culture," it seeks to establish a musicological holism on a disciplinary foundation that take such terms for granted. What emerges is a mode of naming that sets the terms of the polemic a priori and, in doing so, erases different histories of framing the problematic of "nature" in music. But a brief look at different trajectories of thinking about sound/music, nature, and culture shows us that these have not necessarily been uncontested terms.

As Allen himself recognizes, "interest in ecomusicology has paral-leled increasing environmental concern in North America since 1970, a period of greening in academia when environmental studies developed in the physical, natural and social sciences as well as in the humanities" (EC). The 1970s was the moment of formal emergence, for example, of the term *acoustic ecology*. In the initial editorial of *Soundscape: The Journal of Acoustic Ecology*, launched in the year 2000, composer Hildegard Wester-kamp cautiously stated that "the term acoustic ecology first appeared in the mid-seventies, to our knowledge, when the World Soundscape Project (WSP) at Simon Fraser University in Vancouver, Canada published *The Handbook for Acoustic Ecology* and describes it, despite its earlier ante-cedents, as 'a relatively new field of study . . . in the process of defining itself.'"[9] This handbook "attempted to bring together 'most of the major terms dealing with sound from the areas of phonetics, acoustics, psycho-acoustics, psychology, electro-acoustics, communications and noise con-trol, together with those from music which seemed appropriate for an environmental handbook, and several soundscape terms which we have invented and adapted.'"[10] Acoustic ecology, then, was initially framed by

9. Hildegard Westerkamp, "Editorial," *Soundscape: The Journal of Acoustic Ecology* 1, no. 1 (2000): 4. It is beyond the scope of this essay to analyze the debates within acoustic ecology. One need only look at the different issues of the journal *Soundscape* to note the types of polemics and activities that the field has articulated. For some of the polemics and diversity of approaches that it has sought to encompass around the issues of sound experimentalism and the environment, see David Rothenberg and Marta Ulvaeus, eds., *The Book of Music and Nature* (Middletown, CT: Wesleyan University Press, 2001).
10. Westerkamp, citing R. Murray Schaefer's preface to Barry Truax, *Handbook for*

an experimental history of sound composition that generated a repertoire of sonic terminology along with different modes of experimentation with sound. Through its forty-year history, such experimental work has generated intense debate not only about notions of sound and the implications of recording the sounds of "nature" but also, more recently, about an increasing set of polemics on the nature of acoustic representation and the question of the real.

The 1970s was also the decade when scholars such as Steven Feld and Anthony Seeger began a series of studies on indigeneity, music, and nature that called for a transformation of the anthropological and musicological grounds on which ethnomusicology had been constructed. These two scholars in particular began a crucial discussion that articulated the relation between myth (or the cosmological), sociocultural anthropology (or questions about human sociality and what today we call affect), and understandings of sound/music and their relation to questions of "nature." This discussion began to question the *conceptual* ground of the terms discussed (music, animals, sounds, nature, culture, persons), thus initiating a movement away from questions of social anthropology (i.e., how musical sociality and performance is articulated) toward an inquiry into acoustic ontology that began to unsettle the very division between culture, nature, and sound/music.[11]

Any attempt to encompass these tendencies under the single umbrella of musical diversity and an affirmation of nature leaves untouched the polemical questions surrounding the very ideas of sound and nature that Feld and Seeger placed on the agenda. Rather than holistically encompassing the *simultaneity* of these different genealogical trajectories, we need to explore what "organize[s] their common space of possibility."[12]

Acoustic Ecology (Burnaby, BC: Aesthetic Research Center, 1978). In Westerkamp, "Editorial," 4.

11. As I explore below, in the case of Steven Feld, this leads directly to the emergence of what he has termed "acoustemology." In the case of Anthony Seeger, it is important to note his seminal and crucial participation, due to his research and early activities in Brazil as a teacher, in the early and today seminal Brazilian anthropological debate on "nature" and "culture." Seeger's first book is significantly titled *Nature and Culture in Central Brazil: The Suya Indians of Mato Grosso* (Cambridge, MA: Harvard University Press, 1981). See also Anthony Seeger, Roberto da Matta, and Eduardo Viveiros de Castro, "A Construção da pessoa nas sociedades indigenas brasileiras," *Boletim do Museu Nacional*, no. 32 (1979): 2–19.

12. Patrice Maniglier, *Le moment philosophique des années 1960 en France* (Paris: PUF, 2011), 7.

This common space of possibility is shaped by the fact that the 1970s is also the moment of "emergence of a varied constellation of environmental disciplines in the irruption of the ecological era"[13] as well as a moment of transformation of the possibilities of portable sound technologies due to increased access to digital technology. That is, the ecological question began to unsettle the taken-for-granted conceptual and methodological ground upon which questions of "nature," music, and sound had been historically articulated at a moment of experimentation with sound recording and circulation. While the fields briefly mentioned here operate mostly within a Euro-American disciplinary and compositional context, I would like to suggest also that the coincidence of this moment with different "liberationist" movements, however articulated in different parts of the world, was simultaneously unsettling the relation between territory and knowledge that eventually led to postcolonial or decolonial critique.[14] Instead of a "holistic" multicultural approach, we find that the *conceptual ground* for issues of domination-territory, culture, nature, music, and sound began to be radically interrogated. Questions of sound/music, ecology, and culture started to be deterritorialized by the simultaneity of avant-garde experimentalism, anthropological inquiry, changing sound technologies, and the consequent reorganization of musical modes of production and association that articulated an emergent, on-the-ground postcolonial critique. In proposing a new discipline, ecomusicology ultimately appropriates the sense of urgency that the topic of sound/music and nature has acquired today. To be sure, this creates a much-needed network of interaction between musical scholars concerned with these issues. But the *terms* through which networks are operationalized are also crucial in defining how the network itself actually works.

As repeatedly noted by scholars in ecomusicology, questions regarding nature and music are not new and have been central to the development of Western music theory, to the emergence of sound studies, and to ethnomusicology. So what is new, rather than a topic, is the sense of urgency it acquires today. Alexander Rehding even posits the turn to environmental issues as the central question of twenty-first-century musicology, in contrast to the question of psychoanalysis, which, for him, arguably guided

13. Enrique Leff, "Sustentabilidad y racionalidad ambiental: hacia 'otro' programa de sociología ambiental," *Revista Mexicana de Sociología* 73, no. 1 (2011): 5–46, esp. 14.
14. Ana María Ochoa, "Plotting Musical Territories: A Comparative Study in Recontextualization of Andean Folk Musics in Colombia" (PhD diss., Indiana University, 1997).

twentieth-century scholarship.[15] Environmental issues emerge, then, as central to the field in relation to a sense of crisis; this in turn provokes questions about the political purposes of music scholarship and how it is undertaken in the context of a broader transformation of the type of analytical labor that has prevailed in the humanities, in particular in music studies, over the last decades. As a result, it is posited that ecomusicology "might represent a genuine departure from general musicological practice: while themes and methodologies are still in flux, the field derives much of its relevance and topicality from a sense of urgency and from an inherent bent toward awareness-raising, praxis (in the Marxian sense), and activism" as "distinguishing marks in a discipline that is often reluctant to make political commitments" (EAN, 410). For Rehding, "the critical issue that ecomusicology will have to wrestle with is how to implement this sense of crisis," and "the task of the immediate future is for ecomusicology not only to hone its guiding questions but work out its political leanings and define the nature of the tasks that it seeks to pursue" (EAN, 410). Rehding is correct: the political emerges as the key issue here. But the political is not only a form of "activism." Narrowly framed as such, it has the potential to emerge as an "outside" of theory. This is actually a fundamental issue, since understanding "the political" as an outside of theory that only returns through appeals to activism depends in good measure on how sound/music–nature/culture relations are themselves conceived. It is to this issue that I now turn my attention.

The Irruption of Gaia into Musical
Disciplines and the Humanities

According to Rehding, one of the central means of addressing ecological questions in musicology has been "the use of conceptions of nature as epistemological or musical wellspring" (EAN, 410). He explains how "the various deconstructive movements of the 1990s have . . . shown exhaustively how concepts of nature have been employed to exercise argumentative or rhetorical authority" in modes of understanding music (EAN, 410).

---

15. Alexander Rehding, "Ecomusicology between Apocalypse and Nostalgia," *Journal of the American Musicological Society* 64, no. 2 (2011): 409–13. Hereafter, this work is cited parenthetically as EAN. It is important to note here how critical thinking emerged in different parts of the modern world, taking different historical trajectories. The trajectory from psychoanalysis (or a linguistic turn) to nature (or an ontological turn) does not necessarily depict a global trajectory.

Yet "the deconstructive approach may enter into contradiction with the very real urgency of the issues expressed by the ecological movement" because what is at stake is not the way nature is used to harness musical authority through discursive means. As Rehding pointedly states, citing Kate Soper, "'it is not language that has a hole in the ozone layer'" (EAN, 411). So, what seems to be the problem here, according to Rehding, are the limitations of the existing musical disciplines, because the urgent issue (climate change) is not addressed through discourse analysis.

For historian Dipesh Chakrabarty, in contrast, what is at stake is the idea of the political and its effect on critique, particularly as it has been articulated by postcolonial historical studies, due to the political challenges posed to a humanist-centered discipline by the nonhuman temporalities and entities.[16] There is no question for him that the rise of postcolonialism has been a crucial move within the politics of culture and the cultures of politics throughout the twentieth century, refracted by and to many scholars and activists around the world as an indispensible critique of power.[17] But the issue for the field of history is the impossibility of framing power inequalities as solely a problem of capital:

> The critique that sees humanity as an effect of power is, of course, valuable for all the hermeneutics of suspicion that it has taught postcolonial scholarship. It is an effective tool for dealing with national and global formations of domination. But I do not find it adequate in dealing with the crisis of global warming. . . . Climate change, refracted through global capital, will no doubt accentuate the logic of inequality that runs through the rule of capital; some people will no doubt gain temporarily at the expense of others. But the whole crisis cannot be reduced to a story of capitalism.[18]

Idelber Avelar frames a related problematic for literary studies, one that itself builds on Chakrabarty's own mode of positing the limits of the notion of critique for the field of history:

16. Dipesh Chakrabarty, "The Climate of History: Four Theses," *Critical Inquiry* 35, no. 2 (2009): 197–222.
17. It is in this sense interesting to note that the "crisis of the humanities" provoked by the intrusion of Gaia into human affairs coincides with an increased production of books articulated as knowledge "from the South." This is precisely the result of the multiplication of knowledges "otherwise" that emerges from the deconstruction of mainstream disciplinary formations "in the North."
18. Chakrabarty, "The Climate of History," 221.

The unveiling as cultural of traits assumed or mistaken as natural has been the bread and butter of our fields for many decades. . . . Throughout the twentieth century nature has been a constant presence in the humanities, but only negatively, as the object of an operation of denaturalization. The renewed inseparability of natural history and human history experienced today challenges the humanities to understand nature in ways other than simply through the lens of a culturalist critique of naturalization. It is no longer enough to unveil the cultural ground of concepts, notions, and habits hitherto taken to be natural. In the urgency of the ecological crisis we live today we can no longer afford not to face the question of a nature as positivity.[19]

To rephrase Avelar's statement: we can no longer afford a particular Western ontology and its relation to academic knowledge, that is, the "persistent anthropocentric effort of 'constructing' the human as the not given, as the being itself of the not given, as observed in all of Western philosophy, even the most radical."[20] Avelar, moreover, links Chakrabarty's critique of capital to a critique of the anthropocentrism of human rights where the only juridical subjects endowed with rights are human. So, bringing Chakrabarty's and Avelar's critique together, we see what is at stake once we recognize the sense of urgency provoked by climate change: first, a radical transformation of the sense of the political, by centrally acknowledging the history of the global techno-industrial complex[21] that gives rise to the current crisis; second, the implications of the current crisis for questioning the ontological grounding of the concepts that have given us our notions of the political, including power, rights, nature, and culture; and third, the consequent need to recast our modes of thinking.

19. Idelber Avelar, "Amerindian Perspectivism and Non-human Rights," *Alter/nativas*, no. 1 (2013): 1–21, esp. 8, accessed July 21, 2014, alternativas.osu.edu.
20. Eduardo Viveiros de Castro, *Metafísicas caníbales: Líneas de antropología postestructural* (Buenos Aires: Katz, 2011), 44. Hereafter, this work is cited parenthetically as *MC*. See also Bruno Latour, *We Have Never Been Modern* (Cambridge, MA: Harvard University Press, 1991); Isabelle Stengers, *The Invention of Modern Science* (Minneapolis: University of Minnesota Press, 2000); and Marilyn Strathern, *After Nature: English Kinship in the Late Twentieth Century* (Cambridge: Cambridge University Press, 1992).·
21. Such a techno-industrial complex developed under different political regimes globally in the twentieth century and so involves a complex history of capital and power that also includes noncapitalistic regimes. See Clive Hamilton, *Requiem for a Species: Why We Resist the Truth about Climate Change* (New York: Routledge, 2010).

What is also at stake, then, is ultimately that the problem of difference cannot continue to be understood solely in terms of *cultural* difference as the basis for exposing the history of power inequalities and of constituting notions of human and cultural rights. Within the anthropocentric Western tradition, notions of nature as a negatively constituted operation have corresponded to the operationalization of positively constituted notions of cultural diversity and epistemic relativism. This is why questioning the positivity of the terms *nature* and *culture* has become central to the transformations of critique itself and to the conceptions of rights and capital associated with them. For us to understand the implications of this for musical disciplines, it is important to briefly recall the turn to culture in musical disciplines in the last decades and its implications for understanding the current turn to nature.

On the Positivities of Musical Disciplines:
Music Analysis and Cultural Relativism

The central problematic in the history of ethnomusicology has been a division between the methods and truth value in the study of cultural dimensions of music (understood here as the anthropological dimension of the field), and the methods and truth value of the study of what used to be called "musicological" characteristics, by which was usually meant the theoretico-analytical dimensions of music qua hard scientific musical data: scales, pitches, rhythmic structure, and so on. Due to the rise of cultural studies since the 1980s, with its emphasis on different forms of critique of power and the recent history of social constructivism in anthropology, this history took different turns.

The "reflexive turn" in Anglo-American ethnomusicology in the 1980s and 1990s, derived largely from the critique on "writing cultures" in anthropology, coincided with transformations in the music industry and the consequent rise of world music as both an analytical term in the discipline and a category of the music industry. This conjunction brought to the foreground strategic questions regarding the political-epistemological operations of writing, archiving, producing, and circulating music, as well as a reorganization of the questions of musical production, economic distribution, and the politics of representation that took precedence in those decades. Such questioning of the historical and epistemological strategies of production in ethnomusicology had very different outcomes in the work of different scholars, and it is not possible to summarize them here.[22] Questions of production (both of ethnographic writing, of the musicological archive, and of the recording industry) became central for critical thinking in this period, a terrain of thought largely operationalized by the critique of the concept of world music. Simultaneously, critical, or "new," musicology in feminism and queer studies emerged. This "began to reshape the scope of Western musicology toward a dehegemonized pluralism."[23] Also, the field of popular music studies consolidated as a different but interrelated mode of affirmation of cultural relativity and diversity, under the aegis of cultural studies.

All this operated an incipient denaturalization of the *canonic center* of the different musical disciplines along with an affirmative politics of cultural diversity. Because of this, today it is widely assumed that the tenets of the Western music canon have been destabilized, since the musical disciplines are no longer absolutely defined by a division of the field between the West (musicology and music theory) and the rest (ethnomusicology), which makes "cultural" analysis a requirement for all. Thus, Nicholas Cook can proclaim, "We are all ethnomusicologists."[24] Even though such destabilization of canonic repertoires is relative, as noted by both Philip Tagg and Mark Pedelty recently,[25] the idea that "cultural" or "contextual" analysis is important for understanding music history, ethnomusicology, or the history of ideas in music theory has recently become a keystone of all musical disciplines. All this comes with an affirmation of the need to recognize cultural difference. Thus, all musical disciplines become "cultural" and acknowledge the importance of cultural diversity. By the same token, what used to be the central problem for ethnomusicology becomes the problem for everyone else: the tension between the modes of establishing the truth value of "cultural" analysis and the truth value of analytical methods framed by the scientific disciplines for musical studies.

22. Suffice it to say, for now, that while for some, in terms of ethnographic writing, such a turn was deeply embedded in a more profound relation to anthropology, for many such a turn with the coincidence of the rise of popular music studies resulted in a distance from the dialogue with anthropology via the emergence of cultural studies.
23. Regula Burckhardt Qureshi, "Other Musicologies: Exploring Issues and Confronting Practice in India," in *Rethinking Music*, ed. Nicholas Cook and Mark Everist (Oxford: Oxford University Press, 1999), 311–35, esp. 311.
24. Nicholas Cook, "We Are All (Ethno)musicologists Now," in *The New (Ethno)musicologies*, ed. Henry Stobart (Lanham, MD: Scarecrow Press, 2008), 48–70.
25. See Philip Tagg, "Caught on the Back Foot: Epistemic Inertia and Visible Music," *IASPM Journal* 2, nos. 1–2 (2011): 3–18; Mark Pedelty, "Ecomusicology, Music Studies, and IASPM: Beyond 'Epistemic Inertia,'" *IASPM Journal* 3, no. 2 (2013): 33–47.

Within Anglo-American musical disciplines, one of the reactions against the self-proclaimed excesses of this culturalist turn has been to reinstate the need for music analysis as central to understanding non-Western musical cultures, thus recasting the historical disciplinary debate and the problem of ethnomusicology anew. This is perhaps most clearly voiced by Kofi Agawu initially, who states that an excessive culturalization diluted the musical object and operated as a new form of colonialism by invoking "the culture" or the "metaphysics" of those researched as grounds for establishing the truth value of musical cultures. According to Agawu, this invalidated historical Western modes of musicological analysis, frequently invoked as politically and analytically relevant by local researchers themselves, researchers who needed methods such as transcription or music theory analysis to carry on their own decolonizing projects. Thus, if cultural analysis is problematic, a proper reaction to it may be to reinstate proper music theory methods—that is, the more proper scientific, analytical dimension of music (thereby supposedly affirmative of local musics)—in order to "empower" communities by providing the valid analytical tools.

Agawu bases his critique of "ethnotheory" on a critique on "ethnophilosophy" by African philosophers, particularly Paulin Hountondji. According to Hountondji, and through a proposal adopted by Agawu for the critique of ethnomusicology, ethnophilosophy diminishes the significance of African philosophy, particularly its potential for a speculative ground through oversimplification of the local. He therefore calls for "imaginative elements of our [African] past," along with "philosophy as a scientific discourse of universal standing" (RA, 182).[26] Agawu states that all theory ultimately is ethnotheory since, after all, it is all locally produced, and he sees in the metropolitans' efforts to find a local music theory a denial of musical change and of adoption of different musical terminologies throughout history by different people. He proposes acknowledging such changing terminologies in the name of a project that affirms the positive dimensions of translatability as a mode of decentering metropolitan power. He then pursues this proposal as a postcolonial critique of the excessive culturalist localisms of metropolitan ethnomusicology: "to accept the translatability of all indigenous produced knowledge is to accept the existence of a crucial level of nondifference between the conceptual worlds of any two cultures" (RA, 143). For him,

26. For a different reading of Hountondji's work, see Gregory Schrempp, *Magical Arrows: The Maori, the Greeks and the Folklore of the Universe* (Madison: University of Wisconsin Press, 1992).

"gone are the days when African music was either reduced to a functional status or endowed with a magical metaphysical essence that put it beyond analysis" (*RA*, 183). Although he does not directly define what analysis is, it is evident by the examples he provides in the pages that follow this critique that it is the analysis of "hard" facts of music—pitch, tonality, rhythmic structures, and so on—in the name of a "compatibility between conceptual worlds . . . [that] can facilitate a more even-handed traffic in intellectual capital between musical cultures" (*RA*, 188). This will produce an "unhierarchized network" in which "Eurocentric cross-culturalism will be replaced by a dense network of exchanges in which origins and destinations change regularly and swiftly and are accessible to, and at the same time enriching for, all actors" (*RA*, 188).

However, on the one hand, "dehierarchizing the network" is not only a conceptual problem but also a problem of the economics of academic production and circulation. On the other hand, the paradoxical move Agawu makes here is to affirm a new mode of cosmopolitanism in the name of Western understandings of epistemology. As such, Agawu's critique does not necessarily undo the geopolitics of knowledge that have privileged the methods and analytical values of the center but casts them under the guise of a new cosmopolitan diplomacy of translation with no apparent hierarchies.

On the one hand, Agawu reaffirms the researcher (no matter where he or she is located) as the transcendental subject of knowledge (and by fiat of capital's relation to knowledge), thus importing a Western metaphysics of knowledge as the mode of universal (now understood as cosmopolitan) knowledge production. A central tenet of scientific transcendence is the excision of the political from its operations of truth making.[27] Scientific facts (and, by implication, those that are considered the "hard facts" of musical analysis) acquire their truth value precisely because they claim not to be political or influenced by political choices, because they are "natural," by which is generally meant, in a vague way in music studies, that they constitute the object itself.[28] As such, a mode of knowing or an epistemology (the

---

27. For an analysis of how this is done in the formulation of Western notions of knowledge and epistemology, see Latour, *We Have Never Been Modern*; Marilyn Strathern, *Partial Connections* (Lanham, MD: Rowman and Littlefield, 1991); and Isabelle Stengers, *Power and Invention: Situating Science* (Minneapolis: University of Minnesota Press, 1997).
28. For a history of the complex philosophical entanglement between ontology, epistemology, science, and the emergence of a notion of a transcendental subject in Western

subject's scientific understanding of the nature of an object) is confused with an ontology—one that supposedly counts for all cultures. Differently located modes of musical thought count as thought precisely because they are "reduced to a dispositive of recognition" (*MC*, 18), since such cosmopolitanism eminently depends on forming networks based on the mutuality, or "translatability," of concepts. By linking this cultural relativism to a mode of cosmopolitanism that affirms the transcendental values of Western epistemologies, what we have is, in the name of a postcolonial decentered cosmopolitanism, the affirmation of notions of knowledge, culture, and science deeply entrenched in the last few centuries of Western thought. The reduction of others to "magical" assumptions is critiqued, but instead of invoking the need for different ontologies to move away from magical conceptions to differently positioned ontologies, what is invoked is the historical need for a decentered notion of recognizable conceptualizations that enable a global mutuality of recognition upon the Same proposed by the West. Paraphrasing Viveiros de Castro, the Other is recognizable as Other only as long as it remains the Same (*MC*, 15).

To summarize: if in the name of musicological critique and of social constructivism musical disciplines extend the notion of culture by naturalizing culture as something all peoples "have" and of musical analysis as something all peoples "do," in the name of a "proper" postcolonial analysis, what is extended is Western epistemology's notion of scientific transcendence as the transcendence of the researcher, no matter his or her location. Here the main function of acknowledging different musical systems seems to be "the repressive recontextualization of the existential practice of all the collectives of the world in terms of the 'thought collective' of the analyst," as Viveiros de Castro puts it (*MC*, 16). This reinstates an internal Mobius strip that feeds back on the distribution between the truth value of Western epistemic methods (which has "truth-claims" that are not socioculturally contingent)[29] and the truth value of cultural relativism. So, ultimately, the recent history of critical discourse in musical disciplines has tended to deploy a positivity of Western scientific methods as well as a positivity of the idea of cultural diversity, that is, of nature (as the scientifically given) and culture (as the humanly made but scientifically studied). While the cri-

---

philosophy and politics, see, for example, Latour, *We Have Never Been Modern*, and Stengers, *Power and Invention*.
29. Martin Holbraad, *Truth in Motion: The Recursive Anthropology of Cuban Divination* (Chicago: University of Chicago Press, 2012), 29.

tique of so-called cultural analysis as pertinent to all fields begins to unveil the limits of culturalism, it leaves intact that distinction between nature and culture upon which the simultaneously competing and complementary truth value of cultural relativism and the truth value of the scientific-mathematical and philosophical legacy of music theory analysis are based.

This becomes even denser if we consider the fact that the idea that all peoples "have" cultures is itself modeled on a notion of science. Martin Holbraad has traced how, in the transformation of evolutionary theories of culture into theories of cultural diffusionism in nineteenth-century anthropology, the idea developed that "what we all share by nature is the capacity to be socially and culturally different from each other—our unique nature, so to speak, is to be cultural."[30] In this transformation, the natural sciences provided the model for analysis and definition of a proper scientific object for the social sciences through the naturalization of the notion that all peoples "have" cultures: "Treating social and cultural orders as a part of nature meant that they could still be studied in the same sense, if not necessarily in the same way as other natural phenomena. . . . According to this image, people of all societies make sense of the natural world around them, including themselves as part of that world, by means of their own cultural repertoires and according to their own social arrangements."[31] Thus, the idea that all peoples have cultures becomes naturalized as a scientific model of study in a feedback between the scientific expectations of studies of culture and the natural sciences.

I do not doubt that different analytical methods in music are valuable tools that potentially could be deployed to empower communities who need to use them. But the problem with deconstructing the geopolitics of knowledge without unsettling the ontological implications of the distinction between nature and culture is that it ultimately leaves intact the geopolitics of knowledge, this time not by relativizing the culture of the other but by extending the assignation of truth value through the way that questions of ontology in Western metaphysics are entangled with the truth value of science in epistemology. None of this unsettles the philosophical ground for formation of concepts in musical disciplines.

If what the ecological crisis names are the limits of the positivity

---

30. Holbraad, *Truth in Motion*, 27. On how this transformation takes place in the relation between language and culture, see Richard Bauman and Charles Briggs, *Voices of Modernity: Language Ideologies and the Politics of Inequality* (Cambridge: Cambridge University Press, 2003).
31. Holbraad, *Truth in Motion*, 25.

of culture and nature, then musical disciplines face a particularly thorny problem; in the name of diverse forms of contemporary critique, they have tended to affirm both the values of nature (as science) and of culture as a human universal and a given (natural scientific) positivity, a distinction between the given and the made that is assumed as valid for all peoples. But this positivity of cultural diversity is not only a problem of the history of anthropological relativism. It is a problem that coagulated in musical disciplines through a naturalization of musical diversity in ethnomusicological discourse, thus divorcing ethnomusicology from the continued critique of the anthropological object that transformed anthropology itself through creative relations with the fields of history, philosophy, and literary criticism, and more recently through encounters with the problem of climate change. Indeed, for anthropology itself—to name just one field with which ethnomusicologists formerly dialogued—this has implied the need to generate "a new anthropology of the concept that corresponds to a new concept of anthropology, in which the conditions of ontological self-determination of the studied collectives prevail absolutely over the reduction of human (and non-human) thought to a dispositive of recognition" (*MC*, 16). The very notion of Gaia, used in the title of this section, has increasingly been employed as a term that displaces the taken-for-granted notions of nature, earth, culture, human, and so forth in anthropology. This is because of the central place given to rethinking the conceptual order within the political recasting that the crisis of the environment poses for all disciplines.

Returning, then, to music studies: I believe that the reaffirmation of the values of musical analysis, of musico-cultural relativism, of a postcolonial critique based on the constant confusion between Western ontology and epistemology (knowledge as being), and of the rejection of the drastic need to rethink the political stakes provoked by climate change is deeply rooted in certain political positivities that prevail within the notion of music itself in Western disciplinary contexts. This is something that emerges in the understandings of diversity and sustainability, and their relation to music in ecomusicology.

On Music as Political Positivity: Diversity as Cultural Capital

The political purpose of ecomusicology is most frequently framed in terms of "making music serve the interests of sustainability."[32] As such,

---

32. Pedelty, "Ecomusicology, Music Studies, and IASPM," 162.

different books and articles in ecomusicology often begin by denouncing problematic environmental-musical relations and then seeking out the multiple ways that music might productively engage in sustainable development.[33] As a form of activism, the language of sustainable development has tended to permeate ecomusicological discourse as that which accounts for the political response to the crisis of environmentalism.

As Jeff Todd Titon notes, the transference of ideas from ecology to cultural heritage has been a determining factor in the transformation of the language employed by institutions such as UNESCO—for example, a shift from the language of folklore to the "safeguarding" of cultural heritage.[34] This shift has also given rise to a series of critiques of top-down institutional models. Based on such critiques, scholars have proposed a number of more collaborative models that are designed to better address musical diversity and different modes of ecological relation.[35] In this scenario, as Marc Perlman points out, a nature characterized by biodiversity (or threatened by its disappearance) corresponds to a notion of (equally threatened) diverse musics of the world—in short, a comparison and "juxtaposition of species diversity with musical diversity."[36]

This parallelism between musical diversity and biodiversity participates in a broader discussion that goes beyond questions of sustainability and is found in the ecologization of music since the 1970s. As David Ingram observes, "ecophilosophical speculation" on music has been a central problematic in the history of Western music philosophy, particularly

33. The notion of music sustainability has been developed primarily by Jeff Todd Titon. See his "Economy, Ecology, and Music: An Introduction," *The World of Music* 51, no. 1 (2009): 5–15, and, in the same issue, "Music and Sustainability: An Ecological Point of View," 119–37. Other texts that explore the issue within ecomusicology include Mark Pedelty, *Ecomusicology: Rock, Folk, and the Environment* (Philadelphia: Temple University Press, 2012); Nancy Guy, "Flowing Down Taiwan's Tamsui River: Towards an Ecomusicology of the Environmental Imagination," *Ethnomusicology* 53, no. 2 (2009): 218–48; and Aaron S. Allen, "'Fato di Fiemme': Stradivari's Violins and the Musical Trees of the Paneveggio," in *Invaluable Trees: Cultures of Nature, 1660–1830*, ed. Laura Auricchio, Elizabeth Cook, and Giulia Pacini (Oxford: SVEC, 2012), 301–15.

34. Titon, "Music and Sustainability."

35. Titon, for example, has sought to decenter the top-down discourse of resource management of intangible cultural heritage through the search for collaborative modes of preserving endangered music through the use of the notion of ecosystem and principles derived from it. See Titon, "Music and Sustainability"; and Pedelty, *Ecomusicology*.

36. Marc Perlman, "Ecology and Ethno/musicology: The Metaphorical, the Representational, and the Literal," *Ecomusicology Newsletter* 1, no. 2 (2012): 15–21, esp. 15.

with questions surrounding music's capacity to tune the relation between humans and the world.[37] Ingram posits "an ecologization of sound" across "a wide range of popular music styles" in Anglo-America since the 1970s and examines "the different ways in which they have mediated American relationships between nature, technology, and environmental politics" (*JG*, 16). In his excellent book *The Jukebox in the Garden: Ecocriticism and American Popular Music Since 1960*, Ingram explores several recent "eco-philosophical claims." The first is an "environmental ethics," in which it is claimed "that music is a form of utopian expression that prefigures a better society in the future, including a healed relationship between music and the natural world" (*JG*, 15); the second claim posits the "utopian promise of popular entertainment"; while the third ("eco-listening") asserts "that the activity of listening itself has a special role to play in the formation of ecological awareness" (*JG*, 15–16). After mapping out these different claims, Ingram addresses how they take hold across "a wide range of popular music styles" and then examines "the different ways in which they have mediated American relationships between nature, technology, and environmental politics" (*JG*, 15).

The ecologization of sound is thus closely associated with the notion that music, sound, and listening are understood as that which politically resolves the separation between nature and the human or the conflictive relations between humans, understood as part of the ecological crisis. This corresponds to a conceptualization of music as that which produces community and of listening as the much-needed suture for the torn relations both between humans and between humans and the environment. Allen, for example, develops this idea of the specificity of music:

> The environmental crisis . . . is also a failure of holistic problem solving interpersonal relations, ethics, imagination, and creativity. In short, the environmental crisis is a failure of culture. Humanist academics (particularly philosophers, literary scholars, and historians) work to understand the people, cultures, and ethical situations that created, perpetuate, attempt to solve, and face this crisis. In such a context, musicologists have perspectives and insights to offer, especially because of the ubiquity of music, the importance that most

37. David Ingram, *The Jukebox in the Garden: Ecocriticism and American Popular Music Since 1960* (Amsterdam: Rodopi, 2010). Hereafter, this work is cited parenthetically as *JG*.

people accord to it, and the communicative and emotional powers associated with music and the communities who make, enjoy, and consume it.[38]

Music, in such accounts, produces the bonding of a group through the feedback between culture as it resides in particular objects (such as music) and culture as constitutive of the social as such.[39] In this feedback, community is understood as that which is produced by the relation between identity (as the social dimension of music) and representation (as that which the cultural object provides). I have no doubt that music can potentially provide unique possibilities and tactics in the mobilization of the political. But the problem with many ecocritical accounts of the political in music is much deeper in that "the recalcitrance of nature," on the one hand, and "the autonomy of the individual," on the other, become the ground for understanding personhood, sociality, and the collective for all musics of all peoples.[40] Why has this understanding of music as embodying the Good in a notion of the political that reaffirms the transcendental autonomous individual and nature become so central to the utopianism of ecophilosophical speculation in contemporary Euro-America?

An initial answer might begin with the observation that the rise of musical ecologization coincided with an epistemic turn in the understanding of culture in the 1980s and 1990s. George Yúdice characterizes this epistemic turn as a new understanding of culture as a resource. This contemporary notion of culture as resource emerged in the interrelationship between multiculturalism, neoliberalism, and the fracturing of the political in the midst of the economic reorganization of late twentieth-century forms of globalization.[41] As Yúdice stated in 2003, in the era of globalization, "culture is increasingly wielded as a resource for socio-political amelioration, that is, for increasing participation in this era of waning political involvement,"

38. Aaron S. Allen, "Prospects and Problems for Ecomusicology in Confronting a Crisis of Culture," *Journal of the American Musicological Society* 64, no. 2 (2011): 414–19, esp. 414.
39. See Roy Wagner, *The Invention of Culture* (Chicago: University of Chicago Press, 1981). For how this feedback is central to the notion of cultural policy, see Toby Miller, *The Well-Tempered Self: Citizenship, Culture, and the Postmodern Subject* (Baltimore, MD: Johns Hopkins University Press, 1993).
40. Marilyn Strathern, *The Gender of the Gift: Problems with Women and Problems with Society in Melanesia* (Berkeley: University of California Press, 1988), 21.
41. George Yúdice, *The Expediency of Culture: Uses of Culture in the Global Era* (Durham, NC: Duke University Press, 2003).

and he argued that this shift "has given the cultural sphere greater pro-
tagonism than at any other moment in the history of modernity."[42] Through
this shift, the political itself was displaced as a positivity associated with
the idea of culture as diversity. Roberto Eposito has said that one of the
major problems of modern political philosophy is that the very significance
of the terminology of the political is taken for granted and normativized,
paradoxically neutralizing the very idea of the political itself.[43] In this case,
that which is increasingly taken for granted is the notion that the political
increasingly resides in the cultural, thus giving rise to the idea of culture
as capital. If we recall the different "ecophilosophical claims" of music analyzed by Ingram, we see, likewise, that the political properties attributed
to music, sound, and listening in its engagement with ecology are all, by
default, taken for granted as a self-evident positivity.

I would like to propose that during the second half of the twentieth
century, as part of the rise of culture as resource, the link between different
forms of "ecophilosophical speculation" and music, the expansion of cultural diversity understood as the preservation of multiple heritages, and the
increased capitalization of culture as a mode of political action, a prevailing Euro-American ontology of music, sound, and listening has emerged
in which these are understood politically as that which sutures torn relationships either between humans and the environment or among humans.
This is an acoustic ontology that increasingly prevails in the conceptual
order that defines the place of music, sound, and listening in the modern public sphere.[44] Here, the political value of music (understood as that
which enables the social) gets enmeshed with the affective potentialities of
sound (as a taken-for-granted positive political outcome of acoustic potentialities). To culture's increasing enmeshment in "the immaterialization of
capital"[45] correspond other forms of immaterialization and deracination as
well, and sound/music is particularly suited for such immaterialization precisely because of the historical difficulty of grasping its "object," as explored
in the previous section.

Consider, for example, the enmeshment of the above with the difficulty of grasping "the object" of the environmental crisis, or the expansion

42. Yúdice, *The Expediency of Culture*, 9–10.
43. Roberto Esposito, *Términos de la Política* (Barcelona: Herder Editorial, 2008).
44. By this I do not mean to imply that this is the only possible political imbrication of this
relation. But it is a very strongly prevailing one in contemporary modern politics.
45. Yúdice, *The Expediency of Culture*, 9.

of notions of immateriality associated with techniques of sound production—particularly those that increasingly define the practices of media production in the digital era—and the implications for sound/music becoming
a central contemporary sphere of the arts under this emerging aesthetic/
ecological regime. Both the general ecological aesthesis described by
Ingram under the rubric of "ecophilosophical speculation" and the affective, aesthetic, and activist responses it generates are partially related to
what Timothy Morton calls "hyperobjects." A hyperobject can be anything
from climate change to plastic bags, the biosphere to nuclear waste, the
waterways altered by hydroelectrics to oil spills. Despite their many differences, hyperobjects share a number of properties. As Morton elaborates,
hyperobjects are

> *viscous*, which means that they "stick" to beings that are involved
> with them. They are *nonlocal*; in other words, any "local manifes-
> tation" of a hyperobject is not directly the hyperobject. They involve
> profoundly different temporalities than the human-scale ones we are
> used to. . . . Hyperobjects occupy a high-dimensional phase space
> that results in their being invisible to humans for stretches of time.
> And they exhibit their effects *interobjectively*; that is, they can be
> detected in a space that consists of interrelationships between aes-
> thetic properties of objects.[46]

Many of these properties are reminiscent of classical ideas associated with sound, primarily, those according to which sound's potentialities
are confused with its essence. Jonathan Sterne has exposed a number of
these ideas as an "audio-visual litany," observing the tendency to emphasize sound's capacity to (1) affect beings by "immersing" them in its invisible
reverberation, (2) alter a person's sense of time and space, and (3) mediate
between entities and between entities and the world.[47] To him, this is part of
a long history of association between "sound, speech and divinity," in short,
of a cosmology that is confused with an epistemology (a way of knowing)
and with the potentialities of an object.[48] Again, I do not deny these and
other potentialities in the properties of sound. But recognizing potentialities
is not the same as proposing an inherent ontology or political outcome in

46. Timothy Morton, *Hyperobjects: Philosophy and Ecology after the End of the World*
(Minneapolis: University of Minnesota Press, 2013), 1; original emphasis.
47. See Sterne, *The Audible Past*, 16–18.
48. Sterne, *The Audible Past*, 18.

which such potentialities are prefigured as actualizations that only take one form: as a positivity of the political in music, sound, and listening.[49]

It is not by chance that the historical period in question (the end of the twentieth century) is also associated with a media aesthetic that is more and more oriented toward sound, a media aesthetic tied—in Steven Shaviro's terms—to a structure of feeling that is "expressive," in the sense that "it gives sounds and images . . . to a kind of ambient, free-floating sensibility that permeates our society today, although it cannot be attributed to any subject in particular."[50] With the word *expressive*, Shaviro "means both *symptomatic* and *productive*." He elaborates:

> These works are symptomatic in that they provide indices about complex social processes, which they transduce, condense, and rearticulate in the form of what can be called, after Deleuze and Guattari, "blocs of affect." But they are also productive in the sense that they do not *represent* social processes, so much as they participate actively in these processes, and help to constitute them. Films and music videos are *machines for generating affect*, and for capitalizing upon, or extracting value from, this affect.[51]

For Shaviro, finally, these modes of production "generate subjectivity, and they play a crucial role in the valorization of capital."[52] Thus, at the same time that notions of the political become enmeshed with culture, the immaterialization of culture itself, the hyperobjects of environmental thinking, and the affective dimensions of cultural objects are increasingly understood as a problem of relationality.

But as Marilyn Strathern has taught us, the question of "relations" emerges as a much-needed value precisely (and perhaps only) when domains or entities are considered a priori as separate. This explains why the ecological appeal to positively constituted notions of music and listening "takes place in a cultural context where relations are imagined as existing *between* individuals,"[53] and *between* individuals and the environment.

---

49. As a contrast in the relation between speculative philosophy and the politics of the acoustic, see Steve Goodman, *Sonic Warfare: Sound, Affect, and the Ecology of Fear* (Cambridge, MA: MIT Press, 2012).
50. Steven Shaviro, *Post-Cinematic Affect* (Ropley, UK: John Hunt, 2010), 2.
51. Shaviro, *Post-Cinematic Affect*, 2; original emphasis.
52. Shaviro, *Post-Cinematic Affect*, 3.
53. Marilyn Strathern, *Kinship, Law and the Unexpected: Relatives Are Always a Surprise* (Cambridge: Cambridge University Press, 2005), 50; original emphasis.

Relationality emerges as an eminent *value* to be sought, cultivated, and restored primarily when the person is conceived as an autonomous individual and the separation between nature and humans is perceived as a problem to be resolved.

Moreover, conflict—which might otherwise be understood as an everyday feature of existence—is violently repressed as a constant feature of sociality. In the understanding of sound/music and listening as that which eminently enables (communitary) relations, conflict is excised from an imagined (musically) unified community, and by that fiat the political emerges as an outside of music. As noted by Samuel Araujo and the Grupo Musicultura, in both the musicological and ethnomusicological tradition, conflict and violence "signal either a social or personal disturbance of an implicit regular order, or an eventual denial of a given order," instead of being understood as "conditions of knowledge production."[54] Thus, in many historical studies of music, "all difference is read as opposition and all opposition as the absence of a relation: to 'oppose' is taken as synonymous with 'to exclude.'"[55]

Within this framework, non-Western cultures are frequently brought into the discussion of music and ecology as exemplars of those for whom such separation is not problematic. For example, what anthropologists have historically called "animism" is often appropriated by the acoustics of ecology (under multiple disciplinary guises) through the idea that indigenous cultures have an acoustic nondifferentiation between humans and animals that Westerners lack.[56] As Viveiros de Castro states,

> In these post-structuralist, ecologically-minded, animal-rights centered times . . . savages are no longer ethnocentric or anthropomor-

54. Samuel Araujo and Grupo Musicultura, "Conflict and Violence as Theoretical Tools in Present-Day Ethnomusicology: Notes on a Dialogic Ethnography of Sound Practices in Rio de Janeiro," *Ethnomusicology* 50, no. 2 (2006): 287–313, esp. 289.
55. Eduardo Viveiros de Castro, "Culture: The Universal Animal," in *Cosmological Perspectivism in Amazonia and Elsewhere*, ed. Giovanni da Caol and Stéphane Gros, HAU Masterclass Series, no. 1 (2012): 83–103, esp. 93, accessed July 20, 2014, www.haujournal .org/index.php/masterclass/issue/view/Masterclass%20Volume%201.
56. For different versions of this idea with different political and musico-philosophical implications, see Bernie Krause, *The Great Animal Orchestra: Finding the Origins of Music in the World's Wild Places* (New York: Little, Brown, 2012); Tina K. Ramnarine, "Acoustemology, Indigeneity, and Joik in Valkeapää's Symphonic Activism: Views from Europe's Arctic Fringes for Environmental Ethnomusicology," *Ethnomusicology* 53, no. 2 (2009): 187–217.

phic, but rather cosmocentric or cosmomorphic. Instead of having to prove that they are humans because they distinguish themselves from animals, we now have to recognize how *in*-human *we* are for opposing humans to animals in a way they never did: for them nature and culture are part of the same sociocosmic field. . . . [T]heir views anticipate the fundamental lessons of ecology we are only now in a position to anticipate. (*MC*, 95)

In this case, the complicated history of sound and music as phenomena that lie "between nature and culture" becomes entangled with the radically anthropocentric notion that animality is the common condition of the human and the nonhuman.

The history of Western music's analytical categories—melody, rhythm, and, perhaps most crucially of all, the voice—is traversed by a zoo-politics of the acoustic that is obsessed with separating the human from the nonhuman.[57] Music, like language, has been a fundamental "anthropotechnology" used in projects that seek to "direct the human animal in its becoming man" and that are central to Western philosophy and to the establishment of the human as a separate political community.[58] But the relationship between the human and the nonhuman is not necessarily understood in the same way by different ontologies of the acoustic.[59] The challenge, then, is how to understand different modes of constituting what Roy Wagner calls "invention" (the made) and the related counterinvention of the "given" in sound.[60] As expressed by Viveiros de Castro, building on Wagner, "Cultures (the human macrosystems of convention) are distinguished by what they define as belonging to the sphere of responsibility of

57. See Ana María Ochoa Gautier, *Aurality: Listening and Knowledge in Nineteenth-Century Colombia* (Durham, NC: Duke University Press, 2014).
58. Fabián Ludueña Romandini, *La comunidad de los espectros. 1. Antropotecnia* (Buenos Aires: Miño y Dávila, 2010).
59. As a general introduction in English to this idea and to different conceptions of personhood in the non-Western world, see Marshall Sahlins, *The Western Illusion of Human Nature: With Reflections on the Long History of Hierarchy, Equality, and the Sublimation of Anarchy in the West and Comparative Notes on Other Conceptions of the Human Condition* (Chicago: Prickly Paradigm, 2008); and Eduardo Viveiros de Castro, *Cosmological Perspectivism in Amazonia and Elsewhere*. The questioning of an ontology determined by subject-object distinctions is also a central topic of philosophy today. For an introduction to this topic, see *The Speculative Turn: Continental Materialism and Realism*, ed. Levi Bryant, Nick Srineck, and Graham Harman (Victoria: re.press, 2010).
60. Wagner, *Invention of Culture*.

the agents—the world of that which is 'constructed'—and by what belongs (because it is counterconstructed as belonging) to the world of the 'given,' that is, to the non-constructed" (*MC*, 31). This is not an issue of how to "include" the human *in* the environment but rather of asking how the given and the made are conceptualized and thereby related to the reformulation of notions of production, habitation, the acoustic, and form.[61]

Although almost all accounts of ecomusicology reference Steven Feld's work as an important antecedent, none, to my knowledge, has explored its full importance. My purpose is not to analyze Feld's work in detail but rather to elaborate a key insight in his work: that exploring different forms of relationality and alterity is not about dissolving the human into the natural through a transhuman extension of music or sound but rather that such an exploration helps us arrive at questions about music and ecology through the exploration of different ontologies that do not take the idea of nature and culture for granted. Moreover, not only Feld but other authors who worked on questions of indigeneity in the 1980s began an exploration of the acoustic that established important links with structuralism as a key entry point into a heritage of thought that dealt centrally "with the problematic nature of the given."[62] Although in ecomusicology what is identified as the main political task is a form of political activism, it is important to note that for many involved in addressing the crisis of climate change, a crucial task is to take the time to *think* its political implications. Instead of dismissing the legacy of differently positioned ethnomusicologists and anthropologists who have been working with the problematic nature of sound and of nature since the 1980s, perhaps it is time we acknowledge that this is a history of thought that proposes a radically different set of possibilities than that proposed by ecomusicology today. It is beyond the scope of this essay to analyze such literature. I simply wish to point to possible directions.

61. For anthropological work on recasting notions of production and creativity based on different understandings of the given, the made, and perception, see, among others, Strathern, *The Gender of the Gift*; Tim Ingold, *Being Alive: Essays on Movement, Knowledge and Description* (London: Routledge, 2011); and Viveiros de Castro, *Metafísicas caníbales*.
62. Patrice Maniglier, *La vie énigmatique des signes: Saussure et la naissance du structuralisme* (Paris: Scheer, 2006), 12–13. Hereafter, this work is cited parenthetically as *LVE*.

Structuralism and Acoustemology:
Steps toward an Acoustic Multinaturalism

Feld coined the term *acoustemology* to "shift attention" to "sound as a way of knowing . . . worlds."[63] In the introduction to the third edition of *Sound and Sentiment*, he writes about his shift from an "anthropology of sound," which appeared in the first publication of the book in 1982, to the development of acoustemology in the 1990s. I quote him at length:

> I coined this new term to join acoustics and epistemology, to argue for sound as a capacity to know and as a habit of knowing. I needed a way to talk about sound that was neither a matter of critiquing the anthropology of music or language nor of extending their scope to include environmental ambiences and human-animal sound interactions. I wanted to have a new all-species way to talk about the *emplaced copresence and corelations of multiple sounds and sources*. I wanted to have a new way to talk about how, within a few seconds, and often in the absence of coordinated visual cues, Bosavi people know quite precisely so many features of the rain forest world, like the time of day, the season, the weather history. I wanted to link this kind of tacit knowledge, as well as active eco-acoustic knowing, to expressive practices, to the way Bosavi listening habits and histories figure in the shaping of poetic, vocal and instrumental practices.[64]

Feld's work emerged in the early 1980s, at a moment when questions about studying modes of artistic production—weaving, singing, making masks, and so on—and their relation to different understandings of the nonhuman were a central topic in anthropology. These preoccupations in anthropology grew out of structuralism's emphasis on questions surrounding symbolism and myth. Also central to ethnomusicology in this period is Anthony Seeger, for whom questions about nature and culture and their relation to understandings of music were fundamental. In general, though, such questions were soon relegated to a secondary place in ethnomusicology, in large part because of the rise of popular music studies and

63. Steven Feld, *Jazz Cosmopolitanism in Accra: Five Musical Years in Ghana* (Durham, NC: Duke University Press, 2012), 7.
64. Steven Feld, "Introduction to the Third Edition," in *Sound and Sentiment: Birds, Weeping, Poetics, and Song in Kaluli Expression*, 3rd ed. (Durham, NC: Duke University Press, 2013), xxvii; my emphasis. Orig. pub. 1982.

the problems posed by World Music. Simultaneously, in France, the decline of structuralism in philosophy was so dramatic that it was almost "as if it had never existed" (LVE, 8). Finally, the radical critique of anthropological structuralism in the United States resulted in its near expulsion from the American academy.

Interestingly, neither Feld (who initially proposed the notion of anthropology of sound) nor Seeger (who initially proposed the notion of musical anthropology) saw themselves as developing *new* fields; with those terms, they sought only to signal that they were reconsidering how to configure questions regarding sound. The problem that both of them (as well as others in anthropological linguistics) posed was how to conjoin the linguistic structuralism of Ferdinand de Saussure with the anthropological structuralism of Claude Lévi-Strauss with questions of sound/music.

It is important today to reconsider the legacy of this work in light of the renewed interest in the relation between ecology and acoustics. I would therefore like to close by making some suggestions as to why it is important to link the historical moment of structuralism with present-day rearticulations of ontological questions regarding the "given" and the "made" in issues of sound.

I see the legacy of these texts that sought to recast questions of expressive culture in relation to the nonhuman "not as heritages to either reject or preserve, but as tentatives, efforts, works, for questions that are perhaps still open."[65] As is evident, today these questions are not only open but have gained increasing political urgency on the face of climate change. A crucial dimension of the structuralist legacy, and of Feld's and Seeger's work, is the way they have *posed* questions about the sounds they have worked with. Even if we disagree with their postulations, the important issue is the room they gave for a problematic to unfold as such—as a problematic that, rather than requiring a solution, requires time to (re)think how it is addressed as such.

For Patrice Maniglier, "the structuralist movement did not consist in attributing a common function (communicating) to an ensemble of heterogeneous phenomena (languages, rites, etc.), but in recognizing the equally problematic nature of the given in disciplines marked by the heritage of comparativism" (LVE, 16). Although Maniglier's work is centered on a rereading of Saussure, what he says in terms of language can be appro-

---

65. Patrice Maniglier, "Introduction: Les années 1960 aujourd'hui," in *Le moment philosophique des années 1960 en France*, 18–19.

priated easily for music, since, as Maniglier himself states, the problem ultimately "is posed equally in all the disciplines that have cultural facts as their object" (*LVE*, 16).

To summarize and simplify a complex issue that I can only begin to articulate here: It is "impossible to establish a strict criterion of analysis" with regard to sonorous domains because "of the liminal problem of individuation of perceptive phenomena" such as music, sound, or language. Neither the physical manifestation of sound, nor the performativity of sound, nor questions of formal analysis, nor questions posed solely as "social" questions of music resolve the issue of the liminal nature of the acoustic and how to analyze it. Such questions, moreover, are not solved either by a turn to sound or to a "sonic ecosystem," because these commonly offered solutions ultimately leave untouched the central problematic regarding the taken-for-granted assumption about nature (as the given) and culture (as the made).[66] Thus, the appeal to structuralism (and to the questions opened by it) is one that insists on the openness of structure itself: "structure does not designate the form of a given totality, but, on the contrary, the means of making a diagnosis of real discontinuities behind apparent continuities. . . . It does not provide a common method, but rather a common problem that was constructed in different ways" (*LVE*, 17). In this way, "the structural disciplines are confounded with the movement of extension of the linguistic problem [hence, the comparison between anthropology of music and linguistics] not because these would define a unified empirical domain upon which would rest an exportable method, but because different disciplines, for singular reasons, proper to their history (in particular . . . the way they bring into evidence the comparative fact), found themselves confronted by a new type of positivity, a new way of being a fact" (*LVE*, 17). Thus, "the voyages of the structural method" (*LVE*, 17) pose crucial philosophical questions regarding the problem of difference at the center of acoustic entities.

Particularly important for linking acoustemology and structuralism is the latter's rejection of "metaphor as the essence of representation" and a reorientation of thought "towards semiotic processes such as metonymy, indexicality, literality."[67] Acoustemology's own exploration of indexicality and

---

66. The idea of a "sonic ecosystem" is used by Tina Ramnarine. Although I find this particular term problematic, her work on postcolonialism, indigeneity, and music is crucial to any discussion of ecology and music. See Ramnarine, "Acoustemology, Indigeneity, and Joik in Valkeapää's Symphonic Activism."
67. Eduardo Viveiros de Castro, "Intensive Affiliation and Demonic Alliance," in *Deleuzian*

metonymy in sound, of different ontologies and understandings of alterity, and the link to the history of structuralism, in turn, leads us to thinking of acoustic multinaturalism. I will briefly provide one short example from the historical colonial archive as a way to close.

In his *Views of Nature; or, Contemplations on the Sublime Phenomena of Creation: With Scientific Illustrations* (1810), Alexander von Humboldt described his trip down the Orinoco, the Casiquiare, the Rio Negro, and the Apure, in what today is southern Venezuela and part of the larger Amazon region. Humboldt's travels through the Casiquiare and the Orinoco region in general made him acutely sensitive to the changing sounds of nature during day and night. Part of Humboldt's attentive listening became a general law, known as "Humboldt's acoustic effect," which describes the increase of the volume of a sound by night and in lower temperatures. More important for this essay, though, is the passage in which he describes his first experiences listening to human and animal sounds along the river on the banks of the Apure:

> After eleven o'clock, such a noise began in the contiguous forest, that for the remainder of the night, all speech was impossible. The wild cries of animals rung through the woods. Among the many voices that resounded together, the Indians could only recognize those which, after short pauses, were heard singly. There was the monotonous, plaintive cry of the Aluates (howling monkeys), the whining, flute-like notes of the small sapajous, the grunting murmur of the striped, nocturnal ape (Nycthipithecus trivirgatus, which I was the first one to describe), the fitful roar of the great tiger, the cougar or maneless American lion, the peccary, the sloth, and a host of parrots, parraquas (Ortalides), and other pheasant-like birds. . . . If one asks the Indians why such a continuous noise is heard on certain nights, they answer, with a smile, that the "animals are rejoicing in the beautiful moonlight, and celebrating the return of the full moon." To me the scene appeared rather to be owing to an accidental, long-continued and gradually increasing conflict among the animals. . . . Further experience taught us that it was by no means always the festival of moonlight that disturbed the stillness of the forest; for we observed that the voices were loudest during violent storms of rain,

---

Intersections: Science, Technology, Anthropology, ed. Casper Bruun Jensen and Kjetil Rödje (New York: Berghahn, 2009), 219–53, esp. 221.

or when the thunder echoed or the lightning flashed through the neck of the woods.[68]

While Humboldt sees conflict in the noise produced by the animals, an idea that he develops further in the text as reflecting humanity's own undesirable and problematic dispositions, the Yekuana, rather, hear the animals as celebrating the return of the full moon, having, as it were, their very own feast or ritual. In this cannibal order of things, a mouth is an organ that swallows as much as it emits sounds: this is why the function of a mouth is conceived not so much as distilling the essence of sound into abstract ideals expressed by a unique subject with a unique voice but rather as transforming them through acoustic digestion into vocalization. Indeed, as Anthony Seeger has shown, in the Amazonian complex, new songs are learned as part of interspecies communication, that is to say, from "outsiders"—be they foreigners, birds, or other nonhumans.[69] Hence, although both Western philosophies and Amerindian ones affirm that humans and nonhumans have voices, the nonhuman becoming of the human voice implies, in Amerindian ontologies, a radically different understanding of alterity.

Historically, the mode of understanding of Amerindian anthropomorphism has been the idea of animism. But a long lineage of primarily South American (or South Americanist) and Melanesian anthropologists has challenged the idea of animism by proposing the terms *perspectivism* and *multinaturalism* to explain the indigenous understanding of the relationship between the human and the nonhuman. The Brazilian anthropologist Tânia Stolze Lima summarizes the critique of animism and the proposal of perspectivism in this way: "A proposition such as 'the Juruna think that animals are humans,' besides deviating appreciably from their discursive style, is a false one, ethnographically speaking. They say that 'the animals to themselves are humans.' I could, then, rephrase this as 'the Juruna think that the animals think they are humans.' Clearly the verb 'to think' undergoes an enormous semantic slippage as it passes from one segment of the phrase to the other."[70]

68. Alexander von Humboldt, *Views of Nature; or, Contemplations on the Sublime Phenomena of Creation: With Scientific Illustrations*, trans. E. C. Otté and Henry G. Bohn (London: Henry G. Bohn, 1850), 198.
69. Anthony Seeger, *Why Suyá Sing: A Musical Anthropology of an Amazonian People* (Urbana: University of Illinois Press, 2004). Orig. pub. 1987.
70. Tânia Stolze Lima, "The Two and Its Many: Reflections on Perspectivism in a Tupi Cosmology," *Ethnos* 64, no. 1 (1999): 107–31, esp. 113.

It is thus possible to rewrite Humboldt's words. Instead of saying the Yekuana believe that the "animals are rejoicing in the beautiful moonlight, and celebrating the return of the full moon," we could say that the Yekuana think that the animals think they are rejoicing in the beautiful moonlight and celebrating the return of the full moon.[71] Clearly, the acoustic order undergoes an enormous semantic slippage with this displacement.

In this perspectivist ontology, whether a sound is produced by humans or animals depends on the ear that hears it. While the animals of the rain forest hear their own sound as celebrations of the full moon as if they were human, and the Yekuana hear it as animals that think they are celebrating as humans, Humboldt hears it as noise that drowns conversation. Unlike Humboldt, who hears animal noise, the Indians, by contrast, recognize not only that there are animals that sound like peccaries, macaws, and monkeys, but also that they hear their own sound as human, since humanity, not animality, is the common condition that is shared.

In principle, then, what is common to animals and humans is the capacity to produce expressive sound. That is, all species have the capacity to think of themselves as social collectivities, as having homes, undertaking rituals, singing, and so on. It is the perspective according to which each species conceives of this voice that differs. If animals conceive of themselves as singing and having voices, this does not mean that all beings share the same point of view: "numerous peoples of the New World (very likely, all) share a concept according to which the world is composed of a multiplicity of points of view: all existents are centers of intentionality, that apprehend other existents according to their respective characteristics and capacities" (MC, 33). Thus, "a similitude of the souls does not imply that these souls share what they express or perceive. The way that humans see animals, spirits and other cosmic actants is profoundly different from the way that those beings see them and see themselves" (MC, 35). This "perspectivism," or "multinaturalism,"[72] resides in the differences in thinking and sensing bodies—not so much as "physiological functions" but rather as "effects that singularize each species of body, its forces and weaknesses: what it eats, its forms of moving, of communicating, where it lives, if it is

---

71. Lima, "The Two and Its Many," 113.
72. Eduardo Viveiros de Castro, *From the Enemy's Point of View: Humanity and Divinity in an Amazonian Society*, trans. Catherine V. Howard (Chicago: University of Chicago Press, 1992), and also his *Metafísicas caníbales*; Lima, "The Two and Its Many," and her important work, *Um Peixe Olhou Para Mim: O Povo Yudjá e a perspectiva* (Sao Paulo: Editora UNESP; ISA, Rio de Janeiro: NuTI, 2005).

gregarious or solitary, timid or arrogant" (*MC*, 55). Thus, "the body, [under-stood] as a bundle of affects and capacities, lies at the origin of perspec-tives" and permits the generation of "relational multiplicities" (*MC*, 55).

So the fundamental insight, let us say, is not that the bird thinks of its birdsong as a song in a ritual feast, while a person hears that same birdsong as simply the sound of a bird. This would be a cultural relativism in which the idea of culture is simply extended to other species. Rather, the sonorous object (that is, ritual song / bird sound) does not have an essence but is conceived as a multiplicity through which a relation is con-stituted—as such, alterity is *inherent* to things or, in this case, to specific acoustemes. Alterity is thus understood "as a condition of the possibility of being."[73] Thus, multinaturalism is not so much "a variety of natures" (apply-ing the notion of relativism to nature) but rather "variation as nature" (*MC*, 58). In this world, "nothing is created, all is appropriated."[74]

The question of music and environmentalism rests, finally, on acknowledging the political importance of different ontologies across cul-tures and history, not on reaffirming the idea of nature as central to a new disciplinary subdivision, even if the political implications of ecological con-cern are the common cause of our shared interests. As noted by Lévi-Strauss, in mythical narration, "things that emit sound" (the things he refers to in this case are stones and wood) often act as "operators" that "possess other sensory connotations" and "express, as a totality, a set of equiva-lences connecting life and death, vegetable food and cannibalism, putre-faction and imputrescibility, softness and hardness, silence and noise."[75] The presence or absence of sound therefore stands as the very mediator of the presence or absence of life, showing us how myths (or cosmology) help tie events to structures. But the acknowledgment of such a relation, based as it is on admitting the agentive acoustic dimensions of nonhuman enti-ties in the affairs of humans, hinges on an understanding of the relations between humans and nonhumans that unsettle the historically constructed boundaries between nature and culture, the human and the nonhuman in Western modernity.

73. Sahlins, *The Western Illusion of Human Nature*, 47.
74. Marshall Sahlins, *What Kinship Is—And Is Not* (Chicago: University of Chicago Press, 2013), 57.
75. Claude Lévi-Strauss, *The Raw and the Cooked* (Chicago: University of Chicago Press, 1983), 153. Orig. pub. 1964.

By Way of Recapitulation

For the last few decades, the discussion of power-knowledge relations has transformed the way we practice social sciences and the humanities and is an intensifying discussion in the sciences, as well. Such a discussion has not escaped the industrial-technological complex's global
lobbying efforts and their need to ally themselves with neoconservative
scientists who have helped them in their political efforts by seeking to
debunk the drastic political implications of climate change for humans as
a species and for the world as we know it.[76] Such a perverse alliance is
based deeply on sustaining the relation between modernity, science, and
unfettered capital growth fueled by a debt economy, developmentalism,
consumerism, and identity.[77] By contrast, we also find a growing relation
between scientists and different fields in the social sciences and humanities that calls for a deep need to rethink this disciplinary division and ontological assumptions of this epistemological structure that has prevailed in
our scholarship, giving rise to discussions on posthumanism and a post-
social anthropology. These are not simply discussions about how to name
changing academic disciplines. As has been recognized by many scholars
who have denounced the entrenched alliance between developmentalism,
disciplinary history, and Western ontology, one of the fundamental political
needs posed by the existential implications of climate change—the end of
humans as a species and of the world as we know it—is to take the time
needed to think.[78] The way we engage with the politics of the knowledge
economy, in other words, is a central aspect of what is questioned by the
political urgency of climate change.

As such, one needs to question whether the central objective of
sound/music scholars concerned with the environment is to create a sub-
disciplinary field centered on the issues of "nature, culture, and music" or,
to the contrary, to take the time to drastically rethink the political implications of keeping the underlying ontology that such a relation implies. Also,
one cannot but help notice the radical absence, in the discussions in ecomusicology, of a broad transdisciplinary discussion on the great amount of

76. For a summary of the lobbying efforts of the "carbon lobby," see Hamilton, *Requiem
for a Species*.
77. See Hamilton, *Requiem for a Species*.
78. See, among others, Hamilton, *Requiem for a Species*; Leff, "Sustentabilidad y racionalidad ambiental"; and Isabelle Stengers, *Une autre science est possible: manifest pour
un ralentissement des sciences* (Paris: La Découverte, 2013).

literature that has emerged in response to such a crisis. Finally, perhaps it is time not only for a deep engagement with such a transdisciplinary discussion but also for a deep critical engagement with pioneering areas within musico-anthropological studies that have questioned our very concepts of sound/music. It is not by chance that such studies invariably have dealt with indigenous cultures in different parts of the world. This does not mean that suddenly it is time for all of us to "go native." To the contrary, indigenous ontologies from different parts of the world provide models even if, and especially when, they do not resonate with our own categories of knowledge and being.[79]

79. Eduardo Viveiros de Castro, "Outros valores, alem do frenesí do consumo," *Outras palavras: Comunicação compartilhada e Pós-capitalismo*, September 20, 2012, accessed June 18, 2104, outraspalavras.net/posts/outros-valores-alem-do-frenesi-de-consumo/.

Sign, Affect, and Musicking before the Human

Gary Tomlinson

1. Introduction

The thoughts offered here were set in motion by music (or *musicking*), in the course of a project to describe its emergence across evolutionary timescales;[1] but they range across several topics and disciplinary terrains. Musicking points with exemplary clarity, first, toward an intersection of evolutionary thinking in biology with the humanistic enterprise of semiotics. This crossing will lead to another, a conflicted one: the crossing of an *affect theory* that proposes an extended phenomenology with the *realism*

1. Gary Tomlinson, *A Million Years of Music: The Emergence of Human Modernity* (New York: Zone, 2015); also Tomlinson, "Evolutionary Studies in the Humanities: The Case of Music," *Critical Inquiry* 39, no. 4 (2013): 647–75. I am grateful to the editors of this special issue, Jairo Moreno and Gavin Steingo, for their close reading of an earlier version of this essay and perceptive comments on it; the misconceptions and missteps that remain are, of course, my own. The essay originated, meanwhile, as an address to the conference "Sound and Affect: Voice, Music, World," at SUNY Stony Brook, April 18–19, 2014; I am grateful to the organizers, Judith Lochhead, Eduardo Mendieta, and Stephen Smith, for the invitation to participate.

boundary 2 43:1 (2016)   DOI 10.1215/01903659-3340673   © 2016 by Duke University Press

that recently has, in certain precincts of philosophy, advanced an innovative ontology. I will aim to spotlight both certain missteps of the phenomenology and opportunities afforded by the ontology. The foundational role of musicking will frequently recede, but it will not be lost from sight.

If we take the defining project of that strain of the humanities now labeled "posthumanism" to be a thinking-beyond the human and anthropocentrism,[2] we can readily see that, deployed historically, such an effort will encounter not only the nonhuman but also the *pre*human. For reasons that will be surveyed later on, aligning musicking along such a deep-historical axis offers a leverage to this effort that is the more powerful because of the ways musicking stands apart from language and symbolic cognition. These latter two activities are often taken to demarcate and distinguish the human from the non- and prehuman, but musicking, properly understood, can have the reverse effect. This proper understanding concerns itself not especially (as might be assumed) with the putative nonhuman "music" found in the world today—birdsong, whale songs, and much more; thinking of these complex communicative activities as music has, for a long time, confused more than it has clarified. The understanding we seek instead scrutinizes *human* musicking for access to a broad communicative stream in the biosphere that encounters much more than the human alone: a *parahuman* stream that will further the aims of the posthumanist project.

This understanding of musicking does not, however, approach all the conformations in the biosphere that might be thought of as communicative. Instead it runs toward biosemiotic questions that will draw distinctions even while urging parahuman inclusiveness. Human exceptionalism is seen to fade, but broader exceptions in the biosphere take shape. These exceptions oppose, then, certain moves in the recent theorizing of affect, which have tried to knock down distinguishing markers in the world of lived experience and to create a single spectrum of affective intensities extending throughout the biosphere (and even beyond it). Musicking has been a touchstone for some who have thus extended vague notions of affect or experiential intensity, and it figures importantly in one of their founding texts, *A Thousand Plateaus*.[3] They, however, have misunderstood musick-

2. Cary Wolfe, *What Is Posthumanism?* (Minneapolis: University of Minnesota Press, 2010), is a chief account of the topic, working along Derridean lines with a large admixture of the systems theory of Niklas Luhmann; see esp. the introduction and chaps. 1–3.
3. Gilles Deleuze and Félix Guattari, *A Thousand Plateaus: Capitalism and Schizophrenia*, trans. Brian Massumi (Minneapolis: University of Minnesota Press, 1987); Deleuze

ing and read Gilles Deleuze and Félix Guattari inadequately; our adjusted view once again has an effect opposed to far-flung extensions of affect.

Something related to posthumanism's attempt to think beyond human exceptionalism has also characterized the recent turn in philosophy called *speculative materialism* or *speculative realism.* The stakes of this turn are a refuting of the correlation between thought and the world by which the latter was taken to conform to the former—Kant's "Copernican Revolution" in epistemology. For Quentin Meillassoux, a leader in the new direction, this "correlationism" has been, since Kant, the founding premise of the Western tradition, the humanism that has determined and beleaguered the ontologies of Hegel, Heidegger, Wittgenstein, and many others down to our own day. To overturn it requires recalling an earlier mathematization of knowledge (if with a new mathematics, unknown to Galileo or Descartes or even Leibniz and Newton) and using this other dispensation to locate a place for a knowledge of events for which there could be no sentient observer, no possibility of a Kantian correlation (the Big Bang, for example). In pursuing this strategy, Meillassoux moots the possibility of knowledge of past events conceived as *of the past* rather than as a retrojection of present correlational consciousness—the mode of most twentieth-century historicisms, which have in general followed in the Kantian tradition.[4] Both the impetus to break down correlationism and the reconceiving of historicism intersect with the posthumanistic superseding of humanism. As we will see, the second of these moves in particular can profit from an erecting of distinctions that some posthumanistic work, particularly concerning affect, flattens.

The direction taken here, finally, is not toward effacing differences but instead toward shifting the lines drawn and rethinking the terms that enable us to draw them.

2. Biosemiosis and Musicking

To present musicking in a way that facilitates an approach different than usual to the human/nonhuman frontier is to raise the question of its connections to a broad biosemiotics. This, in turn, broaches other fron-

---

and Guattari, *Capitalisme et Schizophrénie 2: Mille Plateaux* (Paris: Éditions de Minuit, 1980).
4. Quentin Meillassoux, *After Finitude: An Essay on the Necessity of Contingency*, trans. Ray Brassier (London: Continuum, 2008), esp. chaps. 1, 4–5. Hereafter, this work is cited parenthetically as *AF*.

tiers: far reaches of the sign, of agency, of affect. At the farthest reach, we witness these phenomena emerging from a universe of information indifferent to the presence of organic life; to this place we will return. More locally, a biosemiotic approach, in developing a general theory of the sign in the biosphere, loosens the grip of language and the symbol on our views of the emergence of the human. From a historical vantage, this is necessary since any view of the emergence of humanity must find ways to conceive presapient hominins equipped with nothing like modern musicking, language, or symbolic cognition, but instead deploying protolinguistic and protomusical behaviors in sophisticated social negotiation. Linguocentric and symbolocentric approaches to deep histories of the human are ubiquitous, but they build barriers, posit revolutionary shifts, and encourage catastrophism where instead continuities are called for. Biosemiotics helps us to envisage a more far-reaching semiosis, a nonsymbolic making of signs that embraces but exceeds the human.

   To analyze this sign-making, biosemioticians have turned to the ideas of Charles Sanders Peirce.[5] The leverage Peirce offers comes, in general, from his focus on the *process* of signification rather than the *structure* of the sign.[6] This process involves nested relations among his three famous types of signs (icon, index, and symbol), such that indices rely on icons and symbols rely on indices and therefore icons as well. Peirce's thinking on these relations was shifting and complex, but it pointed toward a stable foundation for signification, an ontological a priori to it that he termed *thirdness*. He realized that signification of whatever kind involves not only the relation of sign to object (secondness) but also *a relation to this relation* of a third element. This third element is arguably Peirce's signal contribution to semiotics; he called it *interpretant*.[7]

5. See, for example: Thomas A. Sebeok, *Signs: An Introducton to Semiotics*, 2nd ed. (Toronto: University of Toronto Press, 2001); Sebeok, *Global Semiotics* (Bloomington: Indiana University Press, 2001); Terrence Deacon, *The Symbolic Species: The Co-evolution of Language and the Human Brain* (London: Penguin, 1997); Deacon, "The Symbol Concept," in *The Oxford Handbook of Language Evolution*, ed. Maggie Tallerman and Kathleen R. Gibson (Oxford: Oxford University Press, 2012), 393–405; and Deacon, "Beyond the Symbolic Species," *Biosemiotics* no. 6 (2012): 9–38; Paul Kockelman, "Biosemiosis, Technocognition, and Sociogenesis: Selection and Significance in a Multiverse of Sieving and Serendipity," *Current Anthropology* no. 52 (2011): 711–39; also Kockelman, *Agent, Person, Subject, Self: A Theory of Ontology, Interaction, and Infrastructure* (Oxford: Oxford University Press, 2013).
6. See Kockelman, *Agent, Person, Subject, Self*, 13–14.
7. For Peirce's views discussed in this section, see Charles Sanders Peirce, *The Essen-

The biosemiotician's interpretant builds on this Peircean concept. It names an element of organismal activity or experience, an *attending to* stimuli that connects them and makes one of them a sign in relation to the other, the object. The interpretant marks an organism's experience of a relation external to itself, the fold or wrinkle that constructs a relation to a relation and thereby draws bits of information into a semiotic process. The attending aspect here is central.[8] It points up the relation of Peircean semiosis to what philosophers working in the phenomenological tradition call intentionality (briefly, the capacity of mind to be directed toward something); and it extends this capacity and its semiotic concomitants very far beyond human minds—however far, indeed, we extend the phenomenon of attention itself.

In evolutionary terms, this sweeping semiosis is always niche-constructive, though niche construction need not always be semiotic. The biocultural coevolution of hominins and many other lineages (especially, though arguably not only, among mammals and birds) may be thought of as one among several general types of niche construction. It is necessarily semiotic, given the nature of culture, defined minimally as the transmitting of behaviors learned within a generation to successive generations; but most instances of coevolution are nonsemiotic (I'll come back to examples later). This difference between semiotic and nonsemiotic coevolution marks in the biosphere the limit of signs and the distinction of sign from information (to which I'll also return). The interpretant defines, ultimately, ecological entailments circumscribing certain kinds of organisms, sentient organisms, let us imprecisely say. It thus extends semiosis far out through the biosphere, rendering large reaches of it—but not all of it—a *semiosphere*.[9] This is the vast network of semiotic acts mediating between certain organisms and the surrounding world of information, including other organisms.

At first blush, all this might seem to move far from Peirce's own, human-centered semiotics and his conception of the interpretant; but it

---

tial Peirce: Selected Philosophical Writings, ed. The Peirce Edition Project (Bloomington: Indiana University Press, 1998), 2:4–11, 161–64, 401–21; Peirce, "Logic as Semiotic: The Theory of Signs," chap. 7 in *Philosophical Writings of Peirce*, ed. Justus Buchler (New York: Dover, 1955); and Peirce, *Selected Writings*, ed. Philip P. Wiener (New York: Dover, 1966), 381–93.

8. Kockelman describes the interpretant simply as a "change in attention"; see *Agent, Person, Subject, Self*, 14.

9. The term was coined by Juri Lotman in the early 1980s; see Lotman, "On the Semiosphere," *Sign Systems Studies* 33, no. 1 (2005): 205–29.

does not. Through the interpretant, the sign becomes for both Peirce and the biosemioticians a constructive, poietic moment of the perceiver's projection of itself into its environment. The engagement of the perceiver is a reactive *making* of signification, not a passive registering of it or a happening upon it. This making is a two-way street, as is all niche construction: the organism, opening out to aspects of its environment, is shaped and constituted at the same time as it shapes and constitutes. The nature of this poietic mutuality can take several forms, as Peirce made clear in discerning three hierarchically ordered kinds of interpretant. "In all cases," he wrote, the interpretant "includes feelings; for there must, at least, be a sense of comprehending the meaning of the sign. If it includes more than mere feeling, it must evoke some kind of effort. It may include something besides, which, for the present, may be vaguely called 'thought.' I term these three kinds of interpretant the 'emotional,' the 'energetic,' and the 'logical' interpretant."[10] Note two things here: the alliance of feelings and meaning in *all* signs, and therefore even in the most basic, far-flung kind of interpretant; and the distinction of meaning, present in all interpretants, from *thought*, limited to the third, rarest type.

If Peirce's semiotics has been foundational in extending signification and describing a semiosphere, its impact on music studies has hardly been less important. Already in 1944, Susanne Langer's *Philosophy in a New Key* employed Peircean categories in an attempt to reconcile Eduard Hanslick's musical formalism with Ernst Cassirer's philosophy of symbolic forms.[11] Langer exercised a strong influence on Leonard Meyer's watershed study *Emotion and Meaning in Music* and thus initiated a whole genealogy in studies of musical expression and perception.[12] Recent outgrowths

10. Peirce, *The Essential Peirce*, 409.

11. Susanne K. Langer, *Philosophy in a New Key: A Study in the Symbolism of Reason, Rite, and Art* (Cambridge, MA: Harvard University Press, 1944). Hanslick's *On the Musically Beautiful* (*Vom musikalisch-Schönen*), first published in 1854 and reprinted many times into the twentieth century, described a uniquely musical formalism that has remained ever since a strong current in musical thought. It is by the measure of this formalism that other arts, from poetry to architecture, came more and more to be seen as "aspiring" to the "condition" of music, to recall Walter Pater's famous phrase. The formalism opened new conceptions of the distance between music and language; Langer's important book attempts to draw together many strands, including a Wagner-derived theory of myth and an early anthropological theory of ritual; but its chief ingredients are Hanslickian musical formalism and a theory of signs joining Peirce with Cassirer.

12. Leonard B. Meyer, *Emotion and Meaning in Music* (Chicago: University of Chicago Press, 1956).

of this family tree with explicit Peircean orientation include works of music theorists Jean-Jacques Nattiez and Naomi Cumming, of ethnomusicologist Thomas Turino, and of philosopher Charles Nussbaum.[13]

These writers have emphasized the index and indexicality—Peirce's semiotic function of pointing, deixis, contiguity, in-touch causality, and embodiment—as basic to musical expression, far more so than Peirce's other sign types, icons, and symbols. Some of these writers have also considered the interpretant, and Cumming is particularly rewarding in this regard. This is not to say they ignore symbolism. They cannot do so, for musicking, like all other aspects of human culture, is always suspended in symbolic webs and transformed by them, and it is only in deep-historical perspective that we encounter anticipations of musicking and language in a presymbolic space (n.b.: anticipations—not musicking and language in their modern forms). Nevertheless, the effort of these theorists is at heart one of describing how musical signification is rooted in indexicality rather than symbolization and conveys meaning without semantics and many other features that language requires. Peirce's emphasis on semiosis as a process of construing perceptions and constructing signs, rather than on the sign as representation, has suited well this effort.

In its overweening indexicality, modern musicking is allied with our ancestors' presymbolic communicative sociality—their protolanguage, protomusic, and technosociality—all of which relied on the burgeoning of a deictic and proximate signification long before symbolic cognition or human modernity.[14] Modern musicking adds much to this ancient indexicality, especially a systematizing of indices, through combinatorial and hierarchic organization, that presapient hominins three or five hundred thousand years ago could not command.[15] This systematizing is akin to the indexical formalization Michael Silverstein recognizes in the pragmatics of modern language, which creates a metapragmatic level manifested in all discourse

13. Jean-Jacques Nattiez, *Music and Discourse: Toward a Semiology of Music*, trans. Carolyn Abbate (Princeton, NJ: Princeton University Press, 1990); Naomi Cumming, *The Sonic Self: Musical Subjectivity and Signification* (Bloomington: Indiana University Press, 2000); Thomas Turino, "Peircean Thought as Core Theory for a Phenomenological Ethnomusicology," *Ethnomusicology* 58, no. 2 (2014): 185–221; Turino, "Signs of Imagination, Identity, and Experience: A Peircean Semiotic Theory for Music," *Ethnomusicology* 43, no. 2 (1999): 221–55; Turino, *Music as Social Life: The Politics of Participation* (Chicago: University of Chicago Press, 2008), esp. chap. 1; and Charles O. Nussbaum, *The Musical Representation: Meaning, Ontology, and Emotion* (Cambridge, MA: MIT Press, 2007).
14. See Tomlinson, *A Million Years of Music*, esp. chaps. 3 and 5.
15. Tomlinson, *A Million Years of Music*, chap. 4.

and especially pronounced in activities such as ritual,[16] except that meta-pragmatics hovers close above the symbols of language, while the musical systematizing of indices points away from them. Musicking in its modern form thus offers a circumstance close to unique in communication: a complex, combinatorial, and hierarchic formalization of nonsymbolic signs. But let me be clear about the import here of *modernity*: much evidence indicates that this formalization marshals a constellation of panhuman capacities that have existed for between forty and seventy thousand years.

Modern musicking (in this sense) relies on the kind of indexical semiotic labor broadly dispersed through the semiosphere, far beyond humans or the hominin lineage alone. For nonhuman animals, indexicality represents no half measure of semiosis but instead semiotic fullness, the consummation of the sign. The index, for biosemioticians, is the place where experience and learning have reshaped a sign-making that would otherwise remain flatly iconic, a question of difference or its absence; and in nonhuman signification in the world today there is arguably no semiosis other than these—that is, no symbolism. Human musicking, then, merges a systematic cognition characteristic of our species with an indexical response to experience that is far more widespread. In this it restrains the human sign-making machine even from the midst of a hypertrophied symbolism, beckoning toward both the parahuman and the prehuman. Musicking stands *before* the human, both chronologically and in the sense of a coeval challenging of human exceptionalism.

3. Sign and Information

What Peirce called the *emotive* interpretant, his most basic and widespread type, adduces a foundational affective aspect of semiosis—and of musicking, too, as an aspect or kind of semiosis. This affect of biosemiotics, however, cannot be reconciled easily with that described by an affect theorist like Brian Massumi. Massumi, translator of Deleuze and Guattari's *A Thousand Plateaus*, followed them in defining affect as a pre- or proto-emotional experience of intensity, "a prepersonal intensity corresponding to the passage from one experiential state of the body to

16. See Michael Silverstein, "Metapragmatic Discourse and Metapragmatic Function," in *Reflexive Language: Reported Speech and Metapragmatics*, ed. John A. Lucy (Cambridge: Cambridge University Press, 1993), 33–58; Silverstein, "Indexical Order and the Dialectics of Sociolinguistic Life," *Language and Communication* 23, nos. 3–4 (2003): 193–229.

another and implying an augmentation or diminution in that body's capacity to act."[17] This seems to be on the right track, separating affective experience from Cartesian-style catalogs of discrete emotions; and the idea of a shift in experience recalls the interpretant-generating wrinkle and organismal engagement of biosemiotics. But Massumi takes pains to dissociate his affect from consciousness—hence, it would seem, from agency—and especially from signification all told. In an influential essay of 1995, he described intensity, or affect, as "a non-conscious, never-to-conscious autonomic remainder." The "autonomous system" of affect "is not semantically or semiotically ordered"—not ordered, that is, "as a conventional system of distinctive difference."[18]

We can see, first of all, that Massumi has engaged here in some sleight of hand, substituting a local precinct of signification for the whole of it; for his idea of conventionalized difference pertains only to the Peircean symbol, not to semiosis in general. "Signification" and "semiosis," in Massumi's account, seem thus to circle back toward language, and it is on the basis of this linguocentrism that he opens his divide between them and affect. Language, he writes later, creates a level of "qualification" that does not correspond to the plane of intensity but instead typically interferes with it; it can only "amplify intensity" by "making itself functionally redundant."[19] Massumi's nonconscious intensities, meanwhile, pose a strange kind of experience, one that shifts without awareness or attention and then "implies" altered capacities. For higher animals, his affect includes processes such as those of the autonomic nervous system; but can we reasonably maintain that autonomic changes are always experiential, or

17. Massumi, in Deleuze and Guattari, *A Thousand Plateaus*, xvi.
18. Brian Massumi, "The Autonomy of Affect," *Cultural Critique*, no. 31 (1995): 83–109; the essay was republished as chap. 1 of Massumi, *Parables for the Virtual: Movement, Affect, Sensation* (Durham, NC: Duke University Press, 2002). Here also is Eric Shouse, glossing Massumi's position: "An affect is a non-conscious experience of intensity; it is a moment of unformed and unstructured potential. Of the three central terms in this essay—feeling, emotion, and affect—affect is the most abstract because affect cannot be fully realized in language, and because affect is always prior to and/or outside of consciousness (Massumi, *Parables*). Affect is the body's way of preparing itself for action in a given circumstance by adding a quantitative dimension of intensity to the quality of an experience. The body has a grammar of its own that cannot be fully captured in language because it 'doesn't just absorb pulses or discrete stimulations; it infolds contexts . . .' (Massumi, *Parables* 30)." See "Feeling, Emotion, Affect," *MC Journal* 8, no. 6 (2005): ¶5, journal.media-culture.org.au/0512/03-shouse.php.
19. Massumi, "The Autonomy of Affect," 86.

are they so only when they bring about a shift of attention? Is my peristalsis experiential and affective, or does it come to be such only when my indigestion or my postprandial torpor makes itself felt or known?

The biosemiotic interpretant, instead, involves meaning in its shift of experience or attention; "there must," as Peirce said, "be a sense of comprehending the meaning of the sign." The interpretant also incorporates an irreducible element of agency, for it is a function of the organism's relation to its surroundings, a reaction to or imposition on it by which the organism produces sign and object. Such consciousness, or awareness, marks the moment of shifting attention; by another name, it marks a *salience* that rises up in the relation of animal to itself and its environment, through processes we understand only imperfectly.[20] The biosemiotic approach recognizes the shifting intensities of Massumi's affect and certainly allows for organismal shifts without awareness or consciousness; but it encompasses affect within the semiotic process, involving it always in agency and meaning. It extends agency and meaning as far as poietic interpretants can be found in the animal kingdom. How far, then, can we track this animate making of signs?

To answer this question will be to define the emergence of semiosis from *information*. It is clear, to start, that the sign cannot be coextensive with information; the sign is not environmental stimulus alone, but instead results from a particular process enacted *upon* information that makes a relation to a relation. This difference is described, from other angles, by several approaches to a definition of *information*. Claude Shannon, launching the information age in 1948, did not so much define information as quantify it.[21] His famous diagram of communication—the schematic showing information source and destination, transmitter and receiver, and in the middle the all-important channel with its inevitable noise—reserves no place for anything like Peirce's interpretant. It could not do so, because Shannon's account was one of secondness, not thirdness, as is made clear by his rigorous disregard of any content or "meaning" transmitted. That is: *Information entails no relation to a relation* but is instead a more basic corre-

20. See, for example, Duane M. Rumbaugh, James E. King, Michael J. Beran, David A. Washburn, and Kristy L. Gould, "A Salience Theory of Learning and Behavior: With Perspectives on Neurobiology and Cognition," *International Journal of Primatology* 28, no. 5 (2007): 973–96.
21. C. E. Shannon, "A Mathematical Theory of Communication," *Bell System Technical Journal* 27, no. 3 (1948): 379–423, 623–56, viewed at http://cm.bell-labs.com/cm/ms/what/shannonday/shannon1948.pdf; see pp. 379–80.

spondence distanced along a channel. In framing the fundamental problem of communication as "reproducing at one point either exactly or approximately a message selected at another point," Shannon captured the essential reduplicative nature of informational secondness. Information can be quantified prior to any content it might carry, but not prior to its transmission from sender to receiver. The very phrase "information transmission" is a tautology, for information comes about only in a doubled existence.

More recently, Jerry Fodor emphasized this reduplication and gave us something closer to a definition of information; again the key term of contrast is *meaning*. Fodor wrote, "There is a lot less meaning around than there is information. That's because all you need for information is reliable causal covariance. . . . Information is ubiquitous but not robust; meaning is robust but not ubiquitous."[22] Reliable causal covariance captures the tautology of all information. As a postulate of minimal requirements, it sets the bar very low, pervading the cosmos with information in all manner of simple and complex systems. From our Peircean vantage, we might say that in a situation of secondness nothing more than reliable covariance—but a good deal less—is possible. As there is no third term to intervene and connect two terms—that connection producing the sign—there remain only two possibilities: a conformation/correspondence/covariance or its absence.

Information in Fodor's sense is not restricted to the biosphere, then, but ubiquitous far beyond it. Understanding this has recently helped biologists concerned with the origin of life, such as Stuart Kauffman, to breach what had once seemed an impermeable barrier between the living and nonliving. But the Fodorian conception also marks the foundational place of information *within* the biosphere. We can no longer think of the protein-producing interactions of DNA, RNA, and amino acids in living cells without thinking of information and its reliable causal covariance. It is no accident that physicist Erwin Schrödinger characterized life in informational terms exactly during the World War II years that saw the development of Shannon's mathematical theory—a decade *before* the structure of DNA was determined.[23]

In conversation some years ago, I asked Kauffman for a biologist's definition of information, and he paused only briefly before responding: "A

22. Jerry Fodor, *A Theory of Content and Other Essays* (Cambridge, MA: MIT Press, 1990), 93.
23. Erwin Schrödinger, *What Is Life? The Physical Aspect of the Living Cell, with Mind and Matter and Autobiographical Sketches* (Cambridge: Cambridge University Press, 2006); the lectures "What Is Life?" were delivered in Dublin in 1943.

bacterium swimming up a glucose gradient"—not a definition, but an adroit and exemplary instance. To say that the bacterium is *not* processing information would defeat any useful definition of the term. But at the same time, it makes little sense to think of a bacterium forming meanings or indulging in interpretant poiesis, of its *agency* (I'll come back to this point). It makes little sense, in other words, to think of a bacterium in terms of thirdness; its relation to the world is one of sheer secondness. This contrast between the bacterium and animals distinguishes a fundamental pair of overlapping functions in the biosphere. Since Fodorian information characterizes all organized systems, all living things are *information processors*; but only some living things, a slim minority at that, are *sign-makers*.

4. Orchid and Wasp

Placing limits on signs in the far broader field of information opens fascinating questions regarding the emergence and proliferation of semiosis in a portion of the biosphere and a slice of its history. What thresholds needed to be crossed in the complexity of living organisms in order for thirdness to appear? Was the crossing inevitable in a biosphere burgeoning in complexity, say, about 550 million years ago? Was there a certain kind of complexity within organic design that could not but be accompanied by an emergent semiosis?

Entertaining these questions, posed here in deep-historical terms, illuminates a divide between types of coevolution that evolutionary theorist Rick Prum exemplifies in a different way, by contrasting the roots of a plant with its flowers.[24] To describe the natural selection that resulted in plant root systems, he notes, we need little more than knowledge of the nutrient requirements of plants and of the physical conditions in which many of these nutrients may be obtained—solubility of nutrients, osmosis and diffusion mechanisms across cell membranes, and so forth. This is true notwithstanding the coevolutionary feedback dynamics of many sorts that arose in the course of root-system evolution among different species of plants, other organisms, and the nonliving environment, all of which would figure in a fuller account of the niche-constructive history of any species. The flower, on the other hand, requires from the start a different kind of explanation, one that takes account of coevolutionary feedback. This is because the

24. Richard Prum, "The Evolution of Beauty" (talk given at the Whitney Humanities Center, Yale University, January 2013).

selection for flowers depended (largely, if not exclusively) upon the inter-actions of plants with animate organisms, pollinators such as flying insects and birds. As these constructed their niches, so flowers constructed theirs, in a shifting mutuality of selective pressures.

The Peircean perspective allows us to see something further about Prum's phylogeny of flowers. It is not merely coevolutionary from the start; it is also *fundamentally but not wholly* semiotic. The animate organisms creating the feedback loops whereby selective pressures were altered and reshaped were not mere information processors; the cells of the root sys-tem were this, covarying reliably with gradients and other factors in the soil around them. The pollinators, instead, were sign-makers, generating inter-pretants that guided their behaviors; for them the flowers pointed to—were indices of—their own requirements. This semiosis, then, entered as a cru-cial aspect into the coevolutionary feedback by which flowers, information processers but not sign-makers, evolved.[25] I observed before that not all coevolution need be semiotic; now we see that many nonsemiotic organ-isms emerged from niche-constructive interactions with semiotic ones.

The relation of flower and animal pollinator can also be described without reference to semiosis, and Steven Shaviro, working from Deleuze and Guattari's *A Thousand Plateaus* and Alfred North Whitehead's *Process and Reality* to put Kant's aesthetic judgment on a Darwinian footing, has recently pursued this avenue.[26] Shaviro's key term is *beauty*, which, he agrees with his sources, arises as a process enacted between flower and pollinator. Beauty does not inhere in an orchid, and neither is it a pure projection onto the flower by a wasp; instead, it comes about as a rela-tion between the two or through an "aparallel evolution" of them (to use a phrase from *A Thousand Plateaus* that seems to do the same work as the more transparent *coevolution* of the biologists).

Shaviro follows Whitehead deeply into this process. Orchid and wasp are connected to one another through what Whitehead called *prehensions*,

---

25. In saying this of the flower, I am aware of—if not convinced by—recent extensions to plants of semiotic agency (as opposed to complex information processing and trans-mission). For an overview of early work in this field, see Kalevi Kull, "An Introduction to Phytosemiotics: Semiotic Botany and Vegetative Sign Systems," *Sign Systems Studies* 28 (2000): 326–50. For an introduction to current debates concerning plant cognition, learning, and more, see Michael Pollan, "The Intelligent Plant," *New Yorker*, December 23, 2013.
26. Steven Shaviro, *Without Criteria: Kant, Whitehead, Deleuze, and Aesthetics* (Cam-bridge, MA: MIT Press, 2009), 2–4; also chap. 3.

"concrete facts of relatedness" by which the two are brought into a *nexus* that mutually constitutes both as "actual entities" or "actual occasions."[27] Such networks of mutual constitution stand at the heart of Whitehead's processualism: "*how* an actual entity *becomes* constitutes *what* that actual entity *is*" (*PR*, 23). A prehension, then, is "referent to an external world," and in this it has a "vector character"; this directedness involves purpose, valuation, causation, and, most basically, emotion or feeling (*PR*, 19). A flower's beauty results from what Whitehead termed a *proposition*, a prehension in action along which change in the world comes about (paraphrasing Shaviro) or (quoting Whitehead) "an element in the objective lure *proposed for feeling*" by the prehension, which, "when admitted into feeling . . . constitutes *what is felt*" (*PR*, 187). Shaviro concludes simply: "Something *happens to* the wasp" that "encounters the orchid"; from this prehension or proposition of feeling arises felt beauty.[28]

I will return to Whitehead's prehensions and feelings below, but for now I note that in Shaviro's nonsemiotic analysis of wasp and orchid, we once again veer toward affect theory—and also toward its discontents. We end up with something like Massumi's agentless affect, since the wasp's active changing of the world seems to disappear in its experience of the flower's proposition. The wasp is swept up in a process that alters it (as an occasion in the world) and from which emerges its feeling; only then, maybe, does its agency kick in, as it flies to the flower. To be sure, Whitehead's phrase "admitted into feeling" needs here to be taken into account, as it seems to hint at an agency like that in the Peircean interpretant. In the interpretant, however, the agency of the semiotic partner is never obscured.

An additional difficulty concerns the term *beauty* itself. Shaviro's notion of a wasp experiencing beauty cannot be mere poetic license, for its implications are large. They are so because affect theory, when it is not busy divorcing agency and meaning from animal experience and thus *narrowing* semiosis toward the human (a stance of anthropocentrism), pursues an almost opposite course along which capacities and percepts of a distinctly human cast are *widened* implausibly beyond the human (anthropomorphism). Shaviro moves in this direction when he likens wasp to gardener in the full version of a quotation excerpted above: "The orchid is not beautiful in itself: but something *happens to* the wasp, or to the gardener,

---

27. Alfred North Whitehead, *Process and Reality*, ed. David Ray Griffin and Donald W. Sherburne (New York: Free Press, 1978), 22. Hereafter, this work is cited as *PR*.
28. Shaviro, *Without Criteria*, 3; see Whitehead, *PR*, 187.

who encounters the orchid and feels it to be beautiful." Gardener and wasp both perceive or construct beauty, and we can see that it is Whitehead who has sponsored Shaviro's rejection of human exceptionalism in the assimilation of the two. The move is a laudable one, in keeping with the best aims of posthumanism in general; but if not carefully made, it comes at a price. Let us see how this price is paid in a strain of affect theory different from Massumi's.

5. Difficulties of Ubiquitous Agency

With its distinction of signs from information, the approach I have outlined makes apparent the *continuity* between humanity and a broader community of life as well as an equally evident *discontinuity*: the uneven, partial distribution of agency and meaning in that community. It extends agency and meaning as far as the sign itself, far beyond the human, but at the same time not as far as all life, and certainly not beyond the biosphere. This is a position of exceptionalism, to be sure, but of a broad, latitudinarian sort.

Rejecting this position leaves two alternatives, both unacceptable. I have already suggested the first: a retreat to a narrow exceptionalism in which signs and semiosis (often confused, in this position, with symbolism) are the sovereign attainment of humans alone, or perhaps of humans and a few other species. In this move, the rich, complex experiential world of *animal making* far beyond the human is effectively reduced to causal covariance, information alone, nonsemiotic secondness. The implausibility of this reduction is apparent to any observer of that making among higher animals in the world today, which evinces agency and experience of meaning, two hallmarks of thirdness and the interpretant. It is apparent also in a deep-historical perspective, where continuities in the emergence of human particularity are sought. Here the biosemiotic perspective offers a new set of positions on the coevolutionary and biocultural processes that resulted in distinctive human capacities. The perspective thereby supersedes both the simple pronouncements of human uniqueness that have characterized archaeological descriptions of the modernity of *Homo sapiens* and also the many functional models offered to back such pronouncements that feature catastrophism and rely on one-off mutations, language genes, behavioral revolutions, and other unexplained eruptions of discontinuity.

The second alternative to the biosemiotic approach avoids this anthropocentrism but swings far in the other, anthropomorphic direction. It proposes a fantastical extension of meaning and agency through the whole of the biosphere and, in some positions, far beyond it. This option has been taken by some recent affect theorists, who seem to react to the exclusion of consciousness and agency from affective intensities such as Massumi's by filling the cosmos with both. The option has found advocates also in a broader attempt to rethink the object on philosophical grounds—an "object-oriented ontology" that shades often into a revival of an ancient panpsychism. I will consider these one at a time.

A good example of the hyperextension of meaning and agency comes in William Connolly's recent response to Ruth Leys's critique of affect theory.[29] To save his view of affect, Connolly wishes to extend agency and intentionality very far indeed—and far beyond consciousness. To do so, he cites Kauffman's bacterium and glucose gradient, the example of information from my dinner-table conversation, which Kauffman later worked up in a book. Kauffman wrote, "Let us stretch and say it is appropriate to apply [agency] to the bacterium. We may do so without attributing consciousness to [it]. My purpose in attributing actions (or perhaps better, protoactions) to a bacterium is to try to trace the origin of action, value, and meaning as close as I can to the origin of life itself."[30] We note immediately Kauffman's qualifications of the notion even of bacterial action, let alone agency: "Let us stretch and say . . . actions, or perhaps better, protoactions." We note also Kauffman's frank special pleading. He *wants* to make not just agency but value and meaning as closely coterminous with life and its origin as he can manage. There is a metaphysics at work here, one signaled in the title of Kauffman's book, *Reinventing the Sacred: A New View of Science, Reason, and Religion.*[31]

More important, however, is the fact that Kauffman's definition of agency is sweepingly broad—too broad, finally, to be of use in affect theory; Connolly does not cite this part of the discussion. An agent, Kauffman specifies, is any system of self-generating, self-sustaining complexity, able minimally to carry out thermodynamic work, bounded by a membrane, and with receptors to detect food or avoid poison. "Virtually all contemporary cells," he says, "fulfill this expanded definition."[32] It may be that the catch-

29. William E. Connolly, "The Complexity of Intention," *Critical Inquiry* 37, no. 4 (2011): 791–98; also Ruth Leys, "The Turn to Affect: A Critique," in the same issue of *Critical Inquiry*, 434–72.

30. Quoted from Connolly, "The Complexity of Intention," 793.

31. Stuart A. Kauffman, *Reinventing the Sacred: A New View of Science, Reason, and Religion* (New York: Basic Books, 2008).

32. Kauffman, *Reinventing the Sacred*, 78–79. Kauffman has devoted much of his career

ment of "agency" can be usefully applied to all cells—to a cell in my liver, for example, or to a cell in a leaf, as well as to the bacterium; if it is, however, the word loses its power to characterize the more local affective experiences of more complex organisms.

We can underscore this point with a Kauffmanesque thought experiment. Imagine with Connolly that a single bacterium, without central nervous system, nucleus, or any other bounded organelles, evinces an agency (or merely an intentionality) linked to affect. What mechanisms would experience or express this? The answer would need to be the receptors and mechanisms of action they involve: the flagella and their molecular controls that enable the cell to "swim" toward increasing glucose concentration. But then how do we avoid extending agency farther? We would need to think, for example, of the agency of the mechanism of coding and translation that builds the proteins for the flagellum—amino acids locking in order onto translating messenger RNA. But if we extend agency this far, mustn't the regress continue, to the atomic valences in the molecules that bring about the bonding on which protein coding depends? We are getting close to the electrons-with-feelings of some of the wilder affect theorists.

But we have at hand a category other than affect or intentionality for all these phenomena. It is information—reliable causal covariance. The bacterium is an information processor par excellence, indeed a miniature miracle of information processing. We may wish to follow Kauffman and, by lexical convention, apply the term *agency* to all this complexity. But the disadvantage of doing so, as I have said, is that the term ceases to do useful work in our conversations about the far less widespread phenomena of affect, interpretant-making, and meaning; and the advantages of doing so are unclear at best, except in the service of a metaphysics like Kauffman's. So let us say again: information is basic to life, and much else beyond, while semiosis is more narrowly distributed, and only within the biosphere. Distinguishing the two offers a way of modeling fundamental differences that have formed across the history of the cosmos. Agency, meanwhile, may be coterminous with semiosis (in the Peircean view) or there may be some other way of thinking of it, but it cannot both be extended to the

---

to describing autocatalytic systems in aggregates of molecules, or, as they are also termed, autopoietic systems. See, especially, his earlier books, *The Origins of Order: Self-Organization and Selection in Evolution* (Oxford: Oxford University Press, 1993) and *Investigations* (Oxford: Oxford University Press, 2000). For a classic account of autopoiesis, see Humberto R. Maturana and Francisco J. Varela, *Autopoiesis and Cognition: The Realization of the Living* (Dordrecht: Reidel, 1980).

limit of life or, beyond that, of information and also be usefully related to affect.[33]

The extension of agency is allied in Connolly's thinking, as it is in that of other affect theorists, with a narrowing misapprehension of the idea of signification. (We have already witnessed this narrowing at work in Massumi's position.) In these views, the sign often comes to seem synonymous with *representation*, a term, in this usage, opposed to embodiment and embodied experience; or with *conventionalization*, which seems to some of these writers to define the sign but of course is limited in Peircean semiosis to one (rare) type of signs, symbols; or even with *ideology*, an effect of human culture and society and their patterns. If signification is made coterminous with ideology or even conventionalized signs, it certainly cannot be extended far beyond the human. Meanwhile, accepting a representational view of the sign pushes us once again back toward human exceptionalism and Kant's epistemological revolution.

No such limitations are found in the approach I've advocated here, combining a broad extension of the sign, conceived not as representation but as relation to relation, with an ontological distinction of signs from information. The realm of the sign is seen to be vast but not without limit; from both of these features the model gains its heuristic power not only to efface the border between the human and nonhuman but also to describe biocultural, coevolutionary processes that arise in all cultural animals and from which human modernity may plausibly be supposed to have emerged.

33. There is another possibility regarding the agency of bacteria, one that is mooted by Connolly ("The Complexity of Intention," 793): that it can be an emergent product of bacterial collectivities and their internal relations. The complexity of such aggregates is great (and fascinating), but the burden of demonstrating the heuristic advantage that comes from the application to it of the term *agency* is a large one. Moreover, invoking *emergence* as a magic word wherever complexity appears in the world or when old-style, reductionist causal accounts falter is an ever-more frequent expedient in humanistic and social science accounts, an expedient that seems to me to lurk in Connolly's recourse to the emergent agency of bacterial colonies. This is not to doubt in general the importance of emergent complexity in explanatory accounts across many disciplines, only to insist that it amount to more than an incantatory invocation—as it does in Kauffman's earlier work (see the preceding note) or in Terrence Deacon's thought, for example, "The Hierarchic Logic of Emergence: Untangling the Interdependence of Evolution and Self-Organization," in *Evolution and Learning: The Baldwin Effect Reconsidered*, ed. Bruce H. Weber and David J. Depew (Cambridge, MA: MIT Press, 2003), 273–308. For my modeling of emergent processes involved in the biocultural evolution of *Homo sapiens*, see *A Million Years of Music*, chaps. 1 and 6–7.

6. Whitehead's Feeling, Harman's Relations

On the other hand, *suppose rocks have feelings*. Then we might as well attribute to them agency also. Such a revival of panpsychism is the direction in which some have carried the new ontologies of objects, and this brings us to the second anthropomorphic trend named above, the philosophical extension of affect, experience, agency, and even mind.

Both modest "object-oriented" ontologists and more radical panpsychists have relied on Whitehead's post-Kantian, processual ontology, introduced above. The crux of the matter involves Whitehead's vector-like prehensions, activated in the form of propositional feelings, and the emotional experience that results from them. Remember the orchid, wasp, and gardener, and imagine now (as Whitehead did) that the entity-constituting emotional involvement extends not only to the gardener, or even the gardener and wasp, but to the orchid also. Now extend the realm of feeling with another example: a lizard seeking the warmth of a rock that has been sitting in the sun. In this circumstance, Whitehead would say, prehensions, or propositional vectors, extend in several directions: between lizard and rock, rock and sun, lizard and sun. These prehensions alter in greater or lesser degree the actuality as entity-in-process (or as *occasion*) of lizard, rock, and sun, and they do so in ways involving causation, valuation, purpose, and, most basically, feeling. Whitehead thus gave the term *feeling* a new, technical status; he meant it to capture an aspect of the mutual, causal alterations that shape all entities.

Now take a further step, with object-oriented ontologist Graham Harman. For him, these feelings, or prehensions, are indistinguishable, whether it is the lizard or the rock or even the sun that prehends. Their categorical sameness challenges the Kantian tradition, in which "human access" to reality has been privileged; now we describe equivalencies to human access: lizard access, rock access, sun access.[34] In Shaviro's reading of Harman, this position is tantamount to panpsychism; "'human access,'" he writes, "is no different in kind from the sort of mental or epistemological access that all entities have to whatever other entities they encounter. I prehend the sunlight that warms me . . . in much the same way that . . . fire prehends the cotton that it consumes." Here the granting to fire of a "mental access" is arresting (at least), but for hardcore panpsychists it follows, as Shaviro shows, from Whitehead's defining of cognition, thought,

34. See Graham Harman, *The Quadruple Object* (Winchester, UK: Zero Books, 2010), 44–47, 118–19. Hereafter, this work is cited as *QO*.

and mentality as outgrowths of his fundamental *feeling*. Affective relation is a component of all the constitutive relationality in the world and, as such, sponsors all these other relations and their breadth.[35]

It is evident, however, that there is a large gap between Whitehead's feeling and the affect of affect theorists. Likening the two runs the obvious risk of an unintended category switch, in which a colloquialism ("feelings") is mistakenly taken to be synonymous with a carefully defined technical term. Feeling, in Whitehead's sense, cannot aid in attempts to define and distinguish affect from such things as Cartesian emotions; at least, if it is posited to do so, its efficacy will need to be established from the ground up according to the principles of Whitehead's ontology. In this, Whitehead's feeling is like Kauffman's agency: each term has been co-opted to denote so encompassing an aspect of reality that it has been made inapt for the more quotidian uses to which affect theorists put it.

Harman's position, on the other hand, amounts to much more than inadvertent category switching or wide-eyed panpsychism. For him, objects "perceive" insofar as they stand in relation to one another, not as a simple fact of their existence or their endowment with some soul-like quality (*QO*, 122). He uses the example Shaviro cites of fire and cotton related through prehensions—it is a favorite of his—to advance not an all-out panpsychism but a "polypsychism," in which all objects might relate to one another (thereby "perceiving") but do not necessarily do so.

This points to a fundamental tenet of Harman's object-oriented ontology: its division of real and sensual objects. Real objects are autonomous from what encounters them, standing outside relationality and withdrawing from the "experience" of other objects; Harman relies on Heidegger's tool analysis to describe this category. Sensual objects are objects as they enter into relations with other objects, "encrusted with accidental qualities" as a result of those relations; this category Harman adapts from the intentionality or attending-to of Edmund Husserl and Franz Brentano (*QO*, chaps. 2–3 and pp. 47–48). In relation to Whitehead, we could put Harman's position this way: his sensual objects are like Whitehead's objects, connected by prehensions and emerging as occasions through

---

35. Steven Shaviro, "Consequences of Panpsychism," www.shaviro.com/Othertexts /Claremont2010.pdf; 6, 13–14. Whitehead was more careful than some modern-day panpsychists to distinguish the special way he used the word *mental*: "Mental activity is one of the modes of feeling belonging to all actual entities in some degree, but only amounting to conscious intellectuality in some actual entities"—in effect, another Whiteheadian redefinition for special purposes of a commonplace term; see *PR*, 56.

relational processes; but his real objects propose something essential about objects that departs from Whitehead's thinking.

The fundamental "ontological rift" (*QO*, 119) for Harman, then, comes not between human perceptions and the rest, in the Kantian manner, but between real objects and relationality—that is, sensual objects. The power of this formulation is considerable, but so also is its tendency to flatten the other rift I have pointed to: the rift, or, better, the deep-historical rupture that introduced signs into a cosmos of informational causality alone. There is little place in Harman's ontology for the difference between Peircean secondness and thirdness, little place also for the difference in the biosphere between more and less complex organisms. Insofar as his sensual object is a matter of an intentionality made ubiquitous—objects directed toward or attending to other objects, thereby "encountering" or "experiencing" them—it is like Whitehead's prehensional feeling. Both conceptions aim to characterize all relationality at a foundational level—in this they converge on my information, sharing with it both conformational and causal aspects;[36] but neither conception has much to say about semiotic agency and its particular, redoubled relationality.

Assimilated to information, Whitehead's feeling and prehensions and Harman's perceptions and encounters among objects might be seen as *solidifying* the borderline between information and sign, indeed as helping us to pinpoint a categorical difference in relations of entities in the world, rather than dissolving the cosmos into a puddle of undifferentiated affect. This difference, as we can now reaffirm from another vantage, intersects obliquely with the old border between the living and nonliving. Information and its relationality range freely across this border; semiosis, meaning, affect, feeling (in the affect theorists' various senses), experience, and consciousness all are far more narrowly circumscribed.

7. Biosemiosis and Musicking Again: *A Thousand Plateaus*

The close bond of semiosis with affect, feeling, or emotional intensity should come as no surprise to affect theorists, since it is basic to *A Thousand Plateaus*, a touchstone of their approach. Deleuze and Guattari start from a position akin to Whitehead's processualism, defining affect as the

36. On the "conformal" "phase" of feelings, see Whitehead, *PR*, 164. For Harman, causation must of course originate in the sensual (i.e., relational) realm, but it asymmetrically involves real objects also; see *QO*, 74–76.

forces of *becoming-animal*, the animal drives that are the de- and reterrito-
rializations of assemblages.[37] From Spinoza's *Ethics*, they borrow a distinction of active and passive affects, reframing these, then, as the capacities
for action and for undergoing that characterize any animal and connect it to
the network of intersecting assemblages that make up the abstract machine
of nature. Affective assemblages themselves are coalescences of relations
that resemble Whitehead's networks of entities connected by prehensions
or Harman's relations of objects—or at least resemble the small portion of
these that form within the animal/animate realm. Deleuze and Guattari see
no objectification or frozen representation here; indeed, they single out,
as a primary failing of psychoanalysis, its view of the (human) animal as a
fixed representation of the drives in it, rather than as a becoming-animal
shifting with the flux of its assemblages. For them, in sum, "Affects are
becomings."

Representation and objective fixity, then, are foreign to affect as
well as the assemblages it de- and reterritorializes; but must signification
also therefore be divorced from affect, in the manner of Massumi? By no
means, and not only for the reason, already raised, that signification and
representation cannot be taken to be synonymous. Deleuze and Guattari
define affect as what an animal can *do* in its assemblages; the assemblages themselves, in which becoming-animal occurs and to which that
becoming gives shape, appear as arrays of environmental entailments or
affordances in which animals' capacities intersect with each other and with
the nonanimate world. The sum of an animal's affects, all its capacities for
acting and undergoing, provides the measure of its becoming; and for this
reason counting or tallying animal affects is for Deleuze and Guattari *nothing other than ethology itself.* To make and exemplify this point, they rely
on Jakob von Uexküll and his famous analysis of the *Umwelt* of the tick.[38]
With this move, their position on affect migrates from touchstone of affect
theory to touchstone of biosemiotics, since Uexküll is the forefather of that
field, and his tick its semiotic, interpretant-generating exemplar. Uexküll's
Umwelt is not a territory in which a distinct animal eats, mates, and defends
itself. Instead it is an assemblage, affectively and semiotically made and
unmade in the relations of becoming-animal.

37. See Deleuze and Guattari, *A Thousand Plateaus*, chap. 10; for the following two para-
graphs, see esp. 254–60.
38. See Jakob von Uexküll, *A Foray into the Worlds of Animals and Humans, with a
Theory of Meaning* (1934–40), trans. Joseph D. O'Neil (Minneapolis: University of Minnesota Press, 2010).

Deleuze was well aware of this semiotic orientation. In an interview with Catherine Clément on the 1980 publication of *Mille Plateaux*, he explicitly connected animal assemblages, ethology, and semiotics. "We are trying," he said, "to substitute the idea of assemblage for the idea of behavior: whence the importance of ethology, and the analysis of animal assemblages, e.g., territorial assemblages. . . . In assemblages you find states of things, bodies, various combinations of bodies, hodgepodges; but you also find utterances, modes of expression, and whole regimes of signs."[39] Here fixed "animal behavior" is transformed into becoming-animal and assemblage-making, and these in turn are allied to semiosis. Deleuzians and affect theorists alike are quick to connect "affect" in *A Thousand Plateaus* with Spinoza, and fair enough. They are considerably slower to explore its rich, essential connection to Uexküll's semiotic ethology—a cherry-picking that has obscured much.

Peircean semiotics in *A Thousand Plateaus* is not restricted to the becomings of nonhuman animals, of course. One of the central chapters in the book is devoted to distinguishing the several "regimes of signs" Deleuze mentioned in the interview, and it starts from ideas of Peirce, "the true inventor of semiotics."[40] From my parahuman, biosemiotic perspective, this chapter is of limited relevance, as it concerns the need to reassert a specifically linguistic pragmatics submerged in the post-Chomskyan era and hence attends mostly to language and symbol. But one distinction drawn here stands out for our purposes: an arrangement that aligns the index with territorialization ("the territorial states of things constituting the designatable"), the icon with reterritorialization ("operations . . . constituting the signifiable"), and the symbol with deterritorialization ("a constant movement of referral from sign to sign").[41] It would be a mistake to oversolidify or rigidify this scheme, since territorialization, deterritorialization, and reterritorialization are, throughout *A Thousand Plateaus* and beyond, not opposed to one another but linked as processes of formation and change in assemblages. (Deterritorialization, Adrian Parr has written, "inheres in a territory as its transformative vector"; again we drift close to Whitehead's prehensions.)[42]

39. From "Eight Years Later: 1980 Interview," in Gilles Deleuze, *Two Regimes of Madness: Texts and Interviews, 1975–1995* (New York: Semiotext(e), 2007), 175–80, esp. 177. My thanks to Jairo Moreno for drawing this interview to my attention.
40. Deleuze and Guattari, *A Thousand Plateaus*, chap. 5; for Peirce the inventor, see 531n41.
41. Deleuze and Guattari, *A Thousand Plateaus*, 112.
42. *The Deleuze Dictionary*, ed. Adrian Parr (New York: Columbia University Press, 2005), 67.

Nevertheless, we can push the indexicality/territoriality alliance here in directions that will allow us to follow Deleuze and Guattari's discussion of musicking and the refrain along a specifically semiotic path.

It is important to do this because musicking attracts affect theorists like moths to a candle, usually because they think it accommodates their vague ideas of intensities unfettered by sign, meaning, or agency. Here is Jeremy Gilbert, for example: "Music has *physical effects* which can be identified, described and discussed but which are not the same thing as it having [*sic*] *meanings*, and any attempt to understand how music works in culture must . . . be able to say something about those effects without try-ing to collapse them into meanings."[43] Here a hoped-for, embodied affect-without-meaning is mooted; but "meaning" seems restricted to something representational or symbolic, in the Massumian manner of linguistic mean-ing—a bird or a cat could not have it. With Gilbert's mention of culture, also, we are on the verge of rehabilitating the pernicious old nature/nur-ture chasm (which Whitehead and Massumi, along with many others, had wisely thrown out).[44] It is hard to tell how close to the edge Gilbert comes, but Eric Shouse, elaborating Gilbert's views, jumps over:

> Music provides perhaps the clearest example of how the intensity of the impingement of sensations on the body can "mean" more to people than meaning itself. . . . In a lot of cases, the pleasure that individuals derive from music has less to do with the communication of meaning, and far more to do with the way that a particular piece of music "moves" them. While it would be wrong to say that meanings do not matter, it would be just as foolish to ignore the role of biology as we try to grasp the cultural effects of music.[45]

What is missing from both Shouse and Gilbert, obscured by their eagerness to discover embodied intensities without meaning, is any appre-

43. Jeremy Gilbert, "Signifying Nothing: 'Culture,' 'Discourse,' and the Sociality of Affect," *Culture Machine* 6 (2004), accessed August 19, 2014, at www.culturemachine.net/index .php/cm/article/viewArticle/8/7.
44. Here, for example, is Massumi: "It is meaningless to interrogate the relation of the human to the nonhuman if the nonhuman is only a construct of human culture. . . . The concepts of nature and culture need serious reworking, in a way that expresses the irre-ducible *alterity* of the nonhuman in and through its active *connection* to the human, and vice versa. It is time that cultural theorists let matter be matter, brains be brains, jellyfish be jellyfish, and culture be nature, in irreducible alterity and connection" ("The Autonomy of Affect," 100).
45. Shouse, "Feeling, Emotion, Affect," ¶11.

ciation of the complex, hierarchized, formalized, and combinatorial cognition, perception, and action that must be in play for musicking to emerge from the more general stream of acoustic stimuli. The effects they value in musicking could just as well pertain to the impact of a foghorn blaring unexpectedly in the darkness, or the explosion of a volcano, or the bark of a dog or buzz of a mosquito. We may welcome such terminological expansiveness, like a band of Italian Futurists, and want to extend thus the catchment of "music." As in the cases of Whitehead's feeling and Kauffman's agency, however, we do so only by disqualifying the term for other, more discerning uses.

Deleuze and Guattari, for their part, instead tried to take account of such musical formalizations. They concluded their chapter linking Spinozist affect, becoming-animal, and Uexküll's tick with a section on *becoming-music*, and they followed this with a long chapter on music and the refrain (*ritournelle*).[46] The gist is that the refrain is a frozen territoriality—here we are back to Uexküll, since it is birdsong and its territorial imperatives that Deleuze and Guattari play upon—which poses a block of content captured in an assemblage that stands at the heart of music, but *is not itself* music. Music comes about with the deterritorializing of the refrain in a process in which machinic transversals cut across its assemblage: the Beethoven machine, the Berio machine, the African shrike machine.[47] An assemblage is thus opened to other assemblages; interassemblages result that are at once new structurings of refrains, remaking their selective pressures or territories. The voice poses the refrain, but the "machining" of the voice (*machination de la voix*) creates music. Musicking is a surmounting of the fixed imperatives of vocal repetition, the frozen "mate with me" or "get off my land" messages of the birdsong. Or, to allude to one of the recurring issues in Deleuze and Guattari's thought, the refrain is *actual*, but musicking *virtual*: a set of immanent vectors of sound formalizations that undermine all tendencies to sameness of what returns (the *ritournelle*).

46. Deleuze and Guattari, *A Thousand Plateaus*, 299–350.
47. "A machine," they write, "is like a set of points that insert themselves into the assemblage undergoing deterritorialization, and draw variations and mutations of it" (Deleuze and Guattari, *A Thousand Plateaus*, 333, trans. modified; see *Mille Plateaux*, 411). Manuel De Landa ranks among the most important commentators on the Deleuzian/Guattarian abstract machine; of his several accounts, my favorite is the least systematic: *A Thousand Years of Nonlinear History* (New York: Zone, 1997). For De Landa's recent thoughts on the assemblage, see *Deleuze: History and Science* (New York: Atropos, 2010), esp. chaps. 1, 3, and 4.

Musicking, then, affirms the becoming and change immanent in all repetition and signification; this is its exemplary force for Deleuze and Guattari. The indexicality of the refrain, its alliance with territoriality, is seen to be subject, like all other becomings-animal tallied in ethology, to the transformations of the assemblage. Indexicality and musicking alike are caught up in the parahuman, semiotic play of transversals that *re*territorialize as they *de*territorialize. These transversals constitute new territorial outcomes, in the interassemblage, of machinic operations. There is something *systematic* about this animate building of interassemblages; *semiosis broaches new possibilities for order in the biosphere's machinic transversals.* For musicking's part, the transversals are well described as the formalizations of its indexical signs. These are never static, always becomings; they arise in all the things we might call musicking, human and nonhuman, but they assume outlines of advanced formalization in human musicking, marking large differences between a Beethoven machine and a shrike machine. (To underscore these differences, minimized in Deleuze and Guattari's account, and not to devalue the immense complexities of nonhuman communication, I have here pursued parahuman semiosis through human musicking alone.) As these formalizations assume fleeting, territorial arrangement, they affiliate human musicking with rites and religion, with social difference and transcendence, perhaps with fascist force, as Deleuze and Guattari assert. This is the effect of the refrain-as-actual, but it is unmade by musicking-as-virtual. This power of musicking opens onto affective and signifying realms that are characteristically human but that extend continuously far beyond the human. Deleuze and Guattari never lost sight of these continuities of affect, sign, and meaning, and musicking is one of their signal exemplifications of all three. These are lessons affect theorists who tarry in musical locales need to remember.

8. History vs. Historicism: Meillassoux

The revival of Whitehead and his prehensions and the new object-oriented ontology of Harman are aspects of the recent development of speculative materialism I described briefly in my introduction. This line of thought counters Kantian humanism and its aftermaths, especially the fundamental correlation in which knowledge of the world is seen to arise from the nature of human access to it, *given* only through our *being*. It is evident why this move away from the Kantian base would appeal to all the positions encountered above opposing human exceptionalism: not only panpsych-ism but affect theory, Shaviro's aesthetics, and my biosemiosis.[48]

But there is, I think, a special connection between the biosemiotic approach and Quentin Meillassoux's brand of speculative materialism, introduced in his manifesto *After Finitude*. This connection concerns life and the life sciences, and in it the import of biosemiosis can be seen in a bright light while an opportunity not seized by Meillassoux can be defined. I conclude with a gesture toward this double opening: toward parahuman biosemiosis philosophized, and toward an adjusted view of the question, central to Meillassoux's project, of the relation of science to a nonhuman past or future.

This question, though it cannot be simply answered, can be simply put: If all knowledge is shaped by human access to the world, what is the nature of the knowledge created by modern science concerning the world at a time when there were (or will be) no humans to gain this access? Less plainly: If knowledge is subject to the limits and conditions laid out in Kant's transcendental idealism, in this way given to human comprehension and made in it, how is it that "science thinks . . . *a time which, by definition, cannot be reduced to any givenness which preceded it*" and allowed it to emerge (*AF*, 21)? Meillassoux pursues this puzzle by reconsidering sev-eral starting points for post-Cartesian thought: not only Kantian correla-tionism, but, before it, Hume's questioning of the grounding of causality and Leibniz's principle of sufficient reason. The resolution Meillassoux sketches is mathematical, since mathematics (he argues) offers access to the world that is absolute without being transcendental or relying on metaphysics. He exemplifies this through Georg Cantor's set theory (also developed by his teacher Alain Badiou), which demonstrates the "transfinite," that is, the impossibility of totalization even in a set of infinite members (*AF*, 103–5). The point is neither easy nor fully explicated by Meillassoux, but we can attempt to sum it up this way: the world is contingent because in it cau-sality and laws can find no stable ground. Mathematics can model this con-tingency without recourse to metaphysical presumptions because it can model absolute realities that are nontranscendental (i.e., nontotalizable). Without this mathematical means, we are cast back onto the attempt to

48. These affinities, however, might in some cases prove illusory. I have suggested, for example, how the extension of affect far beyond the human can amount to anthropocen-trism or anthropomorphism—neither one an effective countering of Kant's humanistic idealism.

sidestep or evade contingency, a project inevitably reliant on illusions of transcendentalism and of special human access. "Whatever is mathematizable," in sum, can be posited as an ontological fact without involving thought or the transcendentalism of its correlations; so mathematization defines a thought "able to think a world that can dispense with thought" (*AF*, 116–17).

This role for mathematics, according to Meillassoux, renovates the mathematization of nature that defined the Galilean and Cartesian inauguration of modern science. It reasserts the noncorrelational thought of science in its pre-Kantian form and moves to close the "schism" between philosophy and science opened by Kant. His shaping of knowledge according to the conditions of human access to it was not, after all, the "Copernican Revolution" he thought it to be, since it was not a decentering of humanity in the cosmos like the real Copernican Revolution, from which the Galilean/Cartesian mathematization followed. It was instead the opposite: a reinstalling of humanity in its central place, nothing less than a "Ptolemaic counter-revolution" (*AF*, 118–19).

In the wake of this Kantian "reversal of the reversal" (*AF*, 119), this recentering of decentered humanity, historicism assumed its modern shape. Historicism, for Meillassoux, is a "topsy-turvy" affair, in which the temporality of thought of the past is always reversed by correlational access to it: "You thought that what came before came before?," the Kantians ask; "Not at all: for there is a deeper level of temporality, within which what came before the relation-to-the-world is itself but a modality of that relation-to-the-world." For the correlationist, "the deep meaning of the prehuman past consists in its being retrojected on the basis of a human present." Historicism and the philosophy that sponsors it both fail to face squarely the "*paradox of manifestation*" presented by science, the sheer fact of "empirical knowledge of a world anterior to all experience" (*AF*, 123).

Meillassoux's critique of correlationist historicism suggests an opportunity hidden in his argument to define further this kind of knowledge before experience. He does not seize the opportunity, for it depends on recognizing *two* revolutionary turns in modern science, not just one, and he attends only to the first. In addition to his Galilean mathematization of nature, arising from the Copernican decentering of the human, there is, no less powerful, the *Darwinian historicization of life*.[49] If Galilean/Cartesian

49. I am not the first to point to a Darwinian inadequacy in Meillassoux's conception of science; for a response along different lines than mine, see Martin Hägglund, "Radi-

mathematics proffered a contingent but absolute *means* for understanding nature without humanity, Darwin's variation with selection discovered a *process* leading to a parallel but independent understanding. It is an abstract machine in the Deleuzian sense, a virtual operation immanent in the realm of life by which life *must* manifest itself to thought as a linearity that reaches back to a time without thought. Natural selection and variation built a time machine that opposed the formation of history as retrojection even as this historicism was getting started. Thinking the machine manifested previously inconceivable dimensions and categories of pastness (though, in the midst of the Kantian regime, these needed to be disguised under labels such as a historicist "prehistory").

In the wake of Darwin, his machine, modified and enriched across the last century, spawned others that widened his historicization from life to nature as a whole, from the speciation of living things to the Big Bang. These other Darwinian machines, defined as often as not by Meillassoux's mathematics, generate chaotic recursivity, spontaneous order, and emergent complexity of all sorts. They also are time machines, involve processes of feedback and/or selection, and are indifferent to humanity and its being-in-the-world. (Meillassoux may conceive his mathematics as just such a virtual time machine, though this is not clear in *After Finitude*; however this may be, when he asks, "*What is it that happened 4.56 billion years ago? Did the accretion of the earth happen, yes or no?*" [*AF*, 16], the opening for his question is a Darwinian more than a Cartesian or Galilean one.) In the operation of all these machines, the upside-down temporality of Kantian historicism is turned right-side up again. The reversal of the reversal is reversed. The past recovers its pastness, and mind is understood not as that which grants access to the world but as one among numberless end points arising from what came irrevocably *before*.

The Darwinian and post-Darwinian machines are at root anti-Kantian. Indeed, they point up a real irony of correlationism: transcendental thought thinking its history—that is, thinking *how transcendental thought could arise in a biosphere without it*—requires models of process and continuity which it itself threatens to make inconceivable. The catastrophism I mentioned before, appealed to in most models of the emergence of human modernity, is a gauge of the effectiveness of the threat, and also a measure

cal Atheist Materialism: A Critique of Meillassoux," in *The Speculative Turn: Continental Materialism and Realism*, ed. Levi Bryant, Nick Srnicek, and Graham Harman (Melbourne: re.press, 2011), 114–29.

of *in*effective understandings of Darwin's achievement. Rightly conceived, that achievement amounts to a qualitative challenge as radical as the Galilean/Cartesian quantitative one to the defining of knowledge by means of human access.

The drawing of wide, parahuman borders that I have done in this essay is therefore not a reinstituting, on another scale, of metaphysics or Kantian epistemology—not merely an extension to dolphins or geckos of the correlational access assigned by others only to humans. Instead it stakes an ontological claim afforded by these two scientific revolutions— but especially by the second, since this was the turn in our thought that guaranteed a historicism beyond the human. What is to be gained in not allowing such borders to be effaced is a precision in describing an empirical past that poses us as its future—which is to say that the borders delineate a deep-historical projection that is something other than a retrojection. What would it be like, finally, to *think* the burgeoning of semiosis from within a cosmos organized by information alone? Or the emergence of affect and mind from a biosphere without them? Or the advent of the human from a nonhuman world? This is the history of the future that Darwin's machine holds out to us.

Black Music Labor and the Animated Properties of Slave Sound

Ronald Radano

Introduction

In his 1924 essay on black labor, W. E. B. Du Bois reflected on the significance of African American work life in the development of US industrial and economic strength.[1] Recalling his depiction of a southern culture built upon "[the] blood and dust of toil" in *The Souls of Black Folk*, Du Bois described how the engines of US capitalism and the material wealth of the nation were an outcome of the slaves' hardship and involuntary forms of labor.[2] "It was black labor," Du Bois wrote, "that established the modern

I'm grateful to Jairo Moreno and Gavin Steingo for their polite nudges to read slave music through political economy and for then helping me to draw out the theoretical breadth of my argument through meticulous, close readings. I also want to thank Florence Bernault, Colleen Dunlavy, and Viren Murthy for their valuable comments and suggestions.

1. See W. E. B. Du Bois, "Black Labor," chap. 2 in *The Gift of Black Folk: The Negroes in the Making of America*, with an introduction by Glenda Carpio (New York: Oxford University Press, 2007), 13–28.
2. W. E. B. Du Bois, *The Souls of Black Folk*, ed. David W. Blight and Robert Gooding-Williams (1903; repr., Boston: Bedford Books, 1997).

boundary 2 43:1 (2016)   DOI 10.1215/01903659-3340685   © 2016 by Duke University Press

world commerce, which began first as a commerce in the bodies of the slaves themselves." Particularly important about black labor for Du Bois was that it provided something beyond mere economic and material gain. While seated at the very foundation of modern capitalism, the laboring of blacks was not simply an abstract force or labor-power; it identified a reconfiguring of labor.[3] While far from unexploited (in most instances, slaves did not even own their labor), black laboring nonetheless linked to the "Negro spirit," whose unique qualities amplified and extended the power of a newly conceived, modern black subjectivity that informed a greater American way of being: "a tropical product with a sensuous receptivity to the beauty of the world." The reluctance on the part of black workers, judged by many white owners and slave drivers to be a symptom of torpor and "laziness," offered, in actuality, an additional inspiration for the nation.[4] Configured negatively, "laziness" marked a refusal by the slave "when he did not find the spiritual returns adequate," offering an orientation to labor that would enable the United States to grow "economically and spiritually at a rate previously unparalleled anywhere in history."[5]

Du Bois's portrayal of slave labor can seem, at times, disturbingly resonant with a kind of romance consistent with any overarching generalization about the complexities and nuances of lived, social experience. But the notion that blacks had introduced another kind of labor, an aesthetically informed, performative, *living* labor "not as easily reduced to be the mechanical draft-horse which the northern European labor became," is nevertheless instructive. It proposes a readjustment of the universalist equalization of labor as labor-power, as a commodity-form that is quantifiable, exchangeable, and knowable, as it gestures toward a newly imagined quality and condition, of being-in-labor. For Du Bois, one of the grand ironies of US slavery was how black laboring brought about the possibility of a healthier, embodied form of living, a way of being produced by those who had been previously denied the status of human. And critical to the

3. Du Bois, The Gift of Black Folk, 9. The distinction between laboring and labor-power is fundamental to profit and exchange-value. See G. A. Cohen, Karl Marx's Theory of History: A Defence, expanded ed. (1978; repr., Princeton, NJ: Princeton University Press, 2000), 43.
4. Du Bois, The Gift of Black Folk: for "tropical," 9; for "laziness," 10, 19. Syed Hussein Alatas explores the same figuration of laziness in Southeast Asia in his The Myth of the Lazy Native (London: F. Cass, 1977).
5. Du Bois, The Gift of Black Folk, 9–10.

new formation of this new kind of labor were the musical practices inextricably attached to the slaves' laboring acts.[6]

In a subsequent chapter in *The Gift of Black Folk*, "The American Folksong," Du Bois expands upon the burdens of slave labor as a determining force in the invention of African American music. If the slave songs had been "nurtured by that mother of woe, human slavery," they had ultimately arisen, "till out of suffering and toil there sprang a music which speaks to the heart of mankind."[7] In the modern day, Du Bois could still hear "the plaintive quality that is ever present in the Negro voice," extending forth from "a background of tragedy." Yet these songs of the slaves had also reversed the course of influence, transforming the character of labor itself into "the peculiar contribution which the Negro made." Slave singing had reorganized labor, tempering the rapacious drive for profit and bringing forth "spiritual returns adequate." So powerful were these songs in their intervention into the orders of work behavior that they represented one of African America's most lasting contributions, a mode of performative action of such value that it deserved acknowledgment as a "gift, . . . one of the greatest that the Negro has made to American nationality." The alignment of an alternative labor marked "lazy" by whites with the most celebrated of African American gifts, what was called at the time of slavery and well into the twentieth century (and thus throughout this essay) "Negro music," now offered to the modern nation as a whole a way of imagining another kind of living, a "renewed valuation of life," suggestive of a different conception of what being a US citizen might mean.[8]

It's useful to reflect on these words for a moment, given how important labor was to the formation of US black music and the larger structures of American racial identification. While it is not uncommon for historians to acknowledge African American music's emergence and significance under slavery, they have, by and large, left unconsidered its constitution

6. Marx famously employs the expression "living labor" in *Grundrisse* (London: Penguin Books, 1973), e.g., 299. For a fascinating genealogy of the concept, see Mario Sáenz, "Living Labor in Marx," *Radical Philosophy Review* 10, no. 1 (2007): 1–31. For "draft-horse," see Du Bois, *The Gift of Black Folk*, 9.

7. Du Bois, *The Gift of Black Folk*: for "nurtured," 101. Du Bois here is quoting Natalie Curtis Burlin.

8. Du Bois, *The Gift of Black Folk*: for "plaintive quality," 102; for "gift," 18–19. Du Bois writes, "While the gift of the white laborer made America rich, or at least made many Americans rich, it will take the psychology of the black man to make it happy" (19). For "renewed valuation," 9; for the "laziness" of blacks, 10.

as a peculiar and disruptive labor form whose very peculiarity was indicative of wider conflicts in the epistemological orders of the US South. Such
evening-out of social and phenomenological orders—narrating slave music
as a purely musical form whose semiotic and affective potential could only
reflect, and thus be contained within, a common, overarching southern
experience—has tended to co-opt black musical particularity, representing it as a minoritarian resistance practice existing largely outside of economic processes while also comfortably situated within an otherwise stable
and coherent social reality.[9] Literary and cultural critics, moreover, have
provided many powerful insights into the disruptive performativity of slave
music, opening up new ways of comprehending the significance and consequence of slave sounding practices and their relationship to the precari-
ousness of black subject formation. And yet there has still been a tendency
across black cultural studies to interpret the slaves' performances as a
kind of static, musical indigeneity or radical alterity, whose aesthetic value
and form, while arising from the economic processes of southern slave
society, also purportedly remained qualitatively distinguished from the
complex social history that brought "Negro music" into public knowledge
and conception.[10] While both bodies of scholarship have contributed greatly

9. A chief reference in the study of slave song as a resistance form is Lawrence Levine's
magisterial *Black Culture and Black Consciousness*, a book written at a moment when
cultural and social historians were vigorously advocating "bottom-up" approaches.
More recently, slave music receives frequent, if passing, reference in a variety of historical studies. See, for example, Philip Morgan, *Slave Counterpoint: Black Culture in
the Eighteenth-Century Chesapeake and Low Country* (Chapel Hill: University of North
Carolina Press, 1998).
10. In his influential book *In the Break: The Aesthetics of the Black Radical Tradition* (Minneapolis: University of Minnesota Press, 2003), for example, Fred Moten (looking back to
James A. Snead's seminal theoretical gesture, "in the cut"), proposes a comprehension
of slave music as a tear or break in the conception of the commodity-form resulting from
the slave's expressive terror—as a "thing" that actually speaks. In this sounding, one
locates an aggressively antifoundationalist and acutely Derridian expressive "origin" that
resists objectification as it complicates the very conception of black subjectivity. Moten's
reading is inventive, even if it relies too heavily on a single, canonical text (Frederick
Douglass's 1845 autobiographical *Narrative*) in order to make broad claims about slave
music, slave history, and black music history and culture more generally. What concerns
me more, however, is his rather loose reading of the commodity-form, which he proposes
solely in terms of exchange-value, giving little attention to its basis in labor. The commodity, in the form of the slave commodity, he suggests, possesses an "inspirited materiality" (11), relating to the prediscursive scream that arises from torture and exists prior
to economic relation. This, he implies, endures as a core radicalism, becoming, through

to historical and aesthetic knowledge of black music's significance, they have tended to forestall understanding of Negro music's importance as a foundational black cultural practice whose very constitution as "music" was part and parcel of the formation of race *and* capitalism in the US antebellum South. Whether by situating Negro music as an isolatable, autonomous form existing within the commonsense realities of southern white knowledge, or by claiming for it an ontological separability inextricably linked to a precarious black personhood of broad historical endurance, contemporary scholarship on slave musicality has ironically downplayed its anomalous social and economic character, thereby obscuring a radicalism arising from within the very structures of slave capitalism. This inner radicalism related directly to the economic logic of slave labor, being part and parcel of a value in which exchange identified only one aspect of its complex constitution. In the slaves' sounding practices, we can locate a fundamentally social and economic, disruptive power key to the formation of Negro music's cultural value.

At times, antebellum Negro music seemed to be little more than a conventional commodity-form, being an exchangeable kind of labor performed by those who otherwise had no opportunity for investment in the economic project of slavery and southern industry. As a mode of performance that, by the 1840s, was becoming increasingly conspicuous in everyday antebellum society, the slave sounding practices that accumulated under the category "Negro music" arose from and were born under the economic logic of slave capitalism and its mechanisms of exchange. At the same time, however, Negro music ultimately operated in ways inconsistent with that same logic, exposing differences that became apparent at precisely the moment when its conception as a discursive category in the social order took shape. Its perceived qualities of physical excess and embodiment— identified in the incessant references to the music's extremes of emotion, naturalness, and "soul"—were symptomatic of its anomalous position in the epistemological orders of white mastery. While seemingly at the seat of slave labor and white property ownership, Negro music also appeared to exceed those legal and social markers and claims. Its fundamental excess related directly to the slaves' status as property that had seemingly come

---

Douglass, the basis of "a theory of value" (11). I'm seeking here a more specific grounding of slave musicality in the economic and the social, one that finds a critical linkage to subject formation among and between blacks and whites. For Snead's essay, see "Repetition as a Figure of Black Literature," in *Black Literature and Literary Theory*, ed. Henry Louis Gates Jr. (New York: Routledge, 1984), 59–79.

to claim a property of its own, and this property of a property would always remain with the slave, even as that slave, as chattel, might be bought or sold. We can accordingly explore the theory that Negro music identified a new kind of cultural form emerging out of foundational acts of reification, whose racialized performativity made its labor seem strangely inaccessible and secret, yet always on display. This economically based cultural formation was fundamentally different from the inanimate, fetishized commodity, whose labor is obscured. Here, in Negro music, labor could be readily seen and heard, but, for whites, it always remained ultimately out of reach. At once conspicuous and hidden, slave performative labor revealed the qualities of embodiment and fleshliness materialized in Negro music's many acts of audition.

In this essay, I want to plot out a thesis for the modern origins of US black music, arguing that its uncanny properties of embodiment were the result of its early public formation under slavery—when "Negro music" assumed a social category whose performance-based inventions ultimately confronted and collided with its own classification as a property of labor. In the new social category of Negro music, slavery had brought into being a most peculiar entity consistent with the Peculiar Institution as a whole: a form of unwieldy Negro ownership of a possession whose power and significance arose out of the contested interplay of relations distinguishing social and ontological categories of slave and free. The concept of Negro music signaled a new coalescence emerging out of a structural dislocation of slave subjection and white mastery, whereby a quality of black labor as "Negro sound" marked the invention of a property-form and economic value existing within and against antebellum market exchange. Although slave performances remained fundamentally linked to everyday field labor, their sounding practices soon emerged to test the category and legitimacy of "Music" precisely because they always appeared to exceed possession within the white southern economy in which they were constituted.[11] In the context of US antebellum slavery, African America had brought into being its foundational, inalienable possession, a racialized surplus whose aesthetic and cultural value accrued as a condition of the slaves' reification. And as it circulated as part of the southern economy and across the northern continent in the 1840s and 1850s, Negro music's value would grow in

---

11. I capitalize "Music" throughout this essay to identify white conceptions of an autonomous art form. The "music" in "Negro music" remains uncapitalized in order to underscore how its status remained in question. It might most properly be indicated as "Negro M/music," but I've chosen this simpler form for the sake of clarity.

step with rising public awareness that the slaves were in possession of a cultural practice seemingly energized and enlivened by its inextricable attachment to themselves. It is this fundamental energy—a fleshly power that might even propose a certain agency and enchantment—that I'll be identifying here as animation.[12]

Propertied Labor

An analysis of black musical labor and the production of Negro music begins with the peculiar quality of the producer itself, with the slave as a "species of property." Unlike the Enlightenment's "Man," whose subjectivity and sovereignty related to an inalienable condition of liberty as property—in the words of John Locke, "Every Man has a *Property* in his own *Person*. This no Body has any Right to but himself"—the slave's humanity had been forcibly reconstituted as something akin to the products and productive means of southern agrarian economy—to the work horses, hogs, and fowl with which they were routinely compared. Negro slaves endured a precarious existence in late antebellum contexts, being commonly perceived as literal versions of work. Slaves epitomized reified living forms; less than human, they were laboring machines "attached to the soil" that had undergone "recoordination of eyes, nerves, muscles, and hands."[13] Purchase of

12. I can only gesture here to a rich and complex body of literature on inalienable possessions and their relationship to practices of exchange. Among the critical texts, see Annette B. Weiner, *Inalienable Possessions: The Paradox of Keeping-While-Giving* (Berkeley: University of California Press, 1992), and Bill Brown's rich and provocative essay, "Reification, Reanimation, and the American Uncanny," *Critical Inquiry* 32, no. 2 (Winter 2006): 175–207. David Graeber provides a useful, if idiosyncratic, synopsis of the anthropological texts in his book *Toward an Anthropological Theory of Value: The False Coin of Our Own Dreams* (New York: Palgrave, 2001). For work in related disciplines, see Avery F. Gordon, *Ghostly Matters: Haunting and the Sociological Imagination* (Minneapolis: University of Minnesota Press, 1997); Jane Bennett, *Vibrant Matter: A Political Ecology of Things* (Durham, NC: Duke University Press, 2010). For "energy" and its implications, see Fred R. Myers and Barbara Kirshenblatt Gimblett, "Art and Material: A Conversation with Annette Weiner," in *The Empire of Things*, ed. Fred R. Myers (Santa Fe, NM: School of American Research Press, 2001), 277. (I refer again to the same body of literature at the end of the present essay.)

13. "Species of property" was commonly employed in primary historical sources. For a modern, secondary reference, see Steven Hahn, *A Nation under Our Feet: Black Political Struggles in the Rural South from Slavery to the Great Migration* (Cambridge, MA: Belknap Press of Harvard University Press, 2005), 71. Locke continues, "The Labor of his Body, and the Work of his Hands, we may say, are properly his." John Locke, "Property," chap. 16 in *Second Treatise on Civil Government* (1689), press-pubs.uchicago.edu

slaves in southern slave markets accordingly involved an assessment of the quality and condition of these means. The slave body was rendered an assembly of components requiring close examination before purchase. A prospective buyer might size up the condition of the slave by checking skin quality and color, strength of limbs, coordination, demeanor, and disposition. Buyers could approach purchase this way because they understood slaves as beings beneath the category of Man. In fact, their inferiority had become an apparent necessity; it was fundamental to the white southerner's self-conception of him- or herself as willful and free.[14]

By the 1840s, the category "slave" had been established in the context of the antebellum South as a determining measure of social and economic value, representing a critical component of the white majority's supremacist understanding of itself: masters in possession of individualism and reason. As propertied labor, slaves gave material form to the presubjective, disharmonious condition that conceptualized white humanity and society as a "harmoniously organized whole."[15] Representing the most valuable form of property in the land, slaves identified the principal means by which whites measured their rank. The greater the number of slaves owned, the higher one's social position and power, and in the act of ownership, the slave master realized his freedom. "To own, to possess, to understand the *meum et tuum* [mine and yours]," wrote the proslavery political theorist Louisa McCord, "is one of the first distinguishing characteristics of reason, and in proportion as man becomes enlightened on this point, he rises above the beast."[16] Unlike the slave owners of antiquity, however,

---

/founders/documents/v1ch16s3.html. For "attached to the soil," see Loren Schweninger, *Black Property Owners in the South, 1790–1915* (Urbana: University of Illinois Press, 1990), 146; for "recoordination," see Walter Johnson, *River of Dark Dreams: Slavery and Empire in the Cotton Kingdom* (Cambridge, MA: Harvard University Press, 2013), 162.

14. Walter Johnson, *Soul by Soul: Life Inside the Antebellum Slave Market* (Cambridge, MA: Harvard University Press, 2001).

15. "Organized whole" appears in Frédéric Bastiat, "Economic Harmonies" (1850), a section on "Natural and Artificial Social Order," *Library of Economics and Liberty*, online website, www.econlib.org/library/Bastiat/basHar.html. See also Sean Wilentz, *The Rise of American Democracy: Jefferson to Lincoln* (New York: Norton, 2005), 791; Eric Foner, "The Meaning of Freedom in the Age of Emancipation," *Journal of American History* 81, no. 2 (September 1994): 435–60; Susan Buck-Morss, *Hegel, Haiti, and Universal History* (Pittsburgh, PA: University of Pittsburgh Press, 2009); James L. Huston, *Calculating the Value of the Union: Slavery, Property Rights, and the Economic Origins of the Civil War* (Chapel Hill: University of North Carolina Press, 2003); Robin L. Einhorn, introduction to *American Taxation, American Slavery* (Chicago: University of Chicago Press, 2006).

16. Louisa McCord, "Slavery and Political Economy," in *Political and Social Essays*, ed.

whose human possessions attended to life's necessities so that they could enter the *polis* and exercise their rights and freedom, antebellum slave owners of the US South aimed above all to put their freedom to action in order to accumulate money and capital. The fact that slaves were a measure of material wealth meant that they could serve in the same way as other forms of capital in the market economy. Not only could slaves be bought and sold; they could also stand up as collateral for borrowing, bringing into play a variety of practices of mortgaging and trading between animated and inanimate property-forms.[17] All of this suggests why virtually all white southerners were so deeply committed to slavery even though only a minority of whites actually owned slaves. Notions of capital accumulation and ownership were inextricably linked to racial category and to its claim as the economic basis of production. As Edward Baptist has summarized, "the entire structure [of the southern economy] was bottomed on, founded on, funded by the bodies of enslaved people."[18]

The embeddedness of slavery in the functions of the US economy has inspired many contemporary historians to argue that despite its reliance on unfree labor, the southern economy might best be recognized as a dimension of a greater transatlantic capitalist enterprise. Recalling a posi-

---

Richard C. Lounsbury (Charlottesville: University Press of Virginia, 1995), 435. For more on McCord, see Elizabeth Fox Genovese, *Within the Plantation Household* (Chapel Hill: University of North Carolina Press, 1988), esp. chap. 5.

17. Hannah Arendt, *The Human Condition*, 2nd ed. (1958; repr., Chicago: University of Chicago Press, 1998); Bonnie Martin, "Mortgaging Human Property," *Journal of Southern History* 76, no. 4 (November 2010): 817–66.

18. Edward E. Baptist, "Toxic Debt, Liar Loans, and Securitized Human Beings," *Common-Place* (online journal) 10, no. 3 (April 2010). See also Baptist, *The Half Has Never Been Told: Slavery and the Making of American Capitalism* (New York: Basic Books, 2014). The fundamentally racial basis of the southern economy even made whiteness itself a critical form of property. The legal category named "property-in-slaves" identified the generative mechanism for the creation of the very notion of whiteness, as it established as "free" those individuals in possession of land and chattel. It was only they—property-owning white males—who enjoyed the privilege of voting rights and who could participate in what was called representative democracy. Cheryl I. Harris identifies a critical shift occurring with the Naturalization Act of 1790, when voting rights were extended to unpropertied, white men, which "shift[ed] the property required for voting from land to whiteness." See Harris, "Whiteness as Property," *Harvard Law Review* 106, no. 8 (June 1993): 1710–91, esp. 1744. See also Amy Dru Stanley, *From Bondage to Contract: Wage, Labor, Marriage, and the Market in the Age of Slave Emancipation* (Cambridge: Cambridge University Press, 1998); Alexander Keyssar, *The Right to Vote: The Contested History of Property in the United States* (New York: Basic Books, 2000).

tion taken by Du Bois a century earlier, these scholars have demonstrated how a political structure once thought to have been a kind of in-between, "neither feudal . . . nor capitalist" (what Eugene Genovese famously called seigneurialism), largely operated as part of a forward-looking capitalist formation.[19] Rather than identifying an entirely different mode of production, the southern slave empire was, in nearly every measure, a modern capitalist economy parallel to that of the North, differing only in its inclusion of person-slaves as commodity-forms who existed precariously both as part of the relations of production (i.e., contributing to the constitution of the economic structure) and as productive forces (objects of labor-power; as literal means of production). New recognition of the undeniably capitalist character of the southern economy has accordingly made its inconsistencies with Marxist political economy seem less relevant. As Walter Johnson, one of the leading voices in this conversation, has observed, what emerges as the critical question is not whether slave labor fits within the conception of capitalism and its dependency on free, wage labor but rather "what would a theory of political economy that treated the labor, products, and experiences of people of African descent as central to (rather than prior to) the history of Western capital look like?" If US slavery was not fully capitalist because it was labor itself—a body that labors—rather than abstract labor that was being bought and sold, this "comes to seem less a comment on the character of American slavery than a comment on the orthodox definition of the term 'capitalism.'"[20]

19. For a deep background on the matters of slavery and capitalism, including a discussion of Genovese's work, see Stuart Hall's now classic essay, "Race, Articulation, and Societies Structured in Dominance" (1980), reprinted in *Black British Cultural Studies: A Reader*, ed. Houston A. Baker Jr. et al. (Chicago: University of Chicago Press, 1996). Hall quotes Genovese on p. 32. Marx's famous depiction of plantation owners as capitalists appears in *Grundrisse* (London: Penguin Books, 1973), 513. For succinct assessments of Genovese's position, see Walter Johnson, "The Pedestal and the Veil: Rethinking the Capitalism/Slavery Question," *Journal of the Early Republic* 24, no. 2 (Summer 2004): 299–308 (and other essays in the same issue); Johnson, "A Nettlesome Classic Turns Twenty-Five," review of *Roll, Jordan, Roll*, by Eugene D. Genovese, *Common-Place* (online journal) 1, no. 4 (July 2001), www.common-place.org; Gabriel Winant, "Slave Capitalism," *n+1* (online journal) 17 (Fall 2013), nplusonemag.com/issue-17/reviews/slave -capitalism/. Similar reflections appear in the seminal work of Caribbean scholars Eric Williams and C. L. R. James, who sought to cast the strange interplay of differing modes of production largely on the side of capitalism. See also Susan Buck-Morss, *Hegel, Haiti, and Universal History*.
20. Walter Johnson, ed., *The Chattel Principle: Internal Slave Trades in the Americas* (New Haven, CT: Yale University Press, 2005), 8–9.

The new history of southern capitalism represents a critical turn in the way that scholars comprehend the political economy of slavery in the United States. It marks a shift from prior notions of a strange seigneurialism or paternalism to an equally strange mode of modern capitalism whose ideological commitment to "freedom" happened to depend upon the juridical enforcement of institutionalized slavery. Acknowledging the political force of capitalism in its subsumption of enslavement represents a key change in the understanding of antebellum southern culture. Yet as important as the new history has been in exposing the underlying Eurocentrism of free-labor-based Marxist political economy, it also tends to downplay the critical significance of Marx's observation that capitalism and slavery represented two distinctive perspectives of labor, regardless of whether the category "slave" is comprehended as labor-power or not. What matters here is not the conflict of differing modes of production as part of a greater interpretation of historical materialism but rather the way in which slavery and race brought about differing conceptions of labor-based musical performance in its relation to differing subject categories of "Negro slave" and "white mastery." No matter how well inculcated many slaves were within the southern slave economy, their status as "slave," officially, a property without property, established a fundamentally different order of being, an ontological realm whose sound creations coalesced within and against the greater order of capitalist exchange. The slaves' dual status as both sound-making laborer and audible labor was fundamental to the coalescence of what would be named "Negro music." It was, in particular, the social category of audible, embodied labor—a noisy means of production named "slave"—that structured this coalescence as something anomalous to capitalism's formation as an economic system.

The point, then, is not to dally over traditional Marxian orthodoxies but rather to consider how "Negro music," as a property of, and in, labor, emerged as a direct result of its constitution under slave capitalism at the same time that its creation as the property of a property-form underlay its anomalous character and eventual cultural value. It was in the incommensurability of a sound-filled social order of slaves, existing within the bounds of southern capitalism's property relations and prohibitions, where "Negro music" was made. We might do well, then, to expand upon Johnson's question about the insertion of slavery into capitalism in order to ask: What happens to the look of US political economy when the full potential of slave sounding practices is placed front and center? The answer suggests the necessity of a critical move beyond the familiar narrative orders of US history and its commitment to a modern, Enlightenment slave subject struggling to rise above the shackles, in order to consider different orders of audible being, "ways of being human . . . that do not lend themselves to the reproduction of the logic of capital."[21]

Audible Properties

The African and African American slaves who invented the first North American "Negro music" had already been participants in the southern, racial economy from the outset, being identified as forms of labor or productive means—commodities in and of themselves.[22] They lived and worked in an environment in which sound was among the modalities by which their behavior could be disciplined and conditioned for the fundamental purpose of production and profit. From the perspective of many white citizens in the US South, the sounding practices that so frequently accompanied slave behavior extended predictably from the slaves' status as things. Some owners sought to contain the audible aspect of slave bodies by prohibiting singing with the threat of physical punishment. More often, however, the perception of the innate noisiness of the Negro body led many owners to interact with their property audibly by calling them to order as one might herds of cattle or even by attaching bells to a collar in order to discourage them from running away. When they tried to escape ("at every turn advertisements are stuck up for runaway slaves"), masters sometimes attempted to retrieve their property by describing its distinctive sonic features. Among the first representations of Negro music in the eighteenth century were characterizations of the audible black body, bringing into relation the physical qualities of voice with things and creatures in the natural world with which they were commonly associated, as in Cajah, whose "voice sounds as if coming out of a hollow tree."[23]

21. Dipesh Chakrabarty, *Provincializing Europe* (2000; repr., Princeton, NJ: Princeton University Press, 2007), 67. I'm grateful to Viren Murthy for his many insightful elaborations on Chakrabarty's scholarship in the context of contemporary Marxism. See Murthy's informative essay "Looking for Resistance in All the Wrong Places? Chibber, Chakrabarty, and a Tale of Two Histories," *Critical Historical Studies* 2, no. 1 (Spring 2015): 113–53.
22. Daina Ramey Berry notes how monetary value of slaves affected social status among them. "We'm Fus' Rate Bargain: Value, Labor, and Price in a Georgia Slave Community," in *The Chattel Principle*, 55–71.
23. For prohibitions on singing, see Mark M. Smith, *Listening to Nineteenth-Century America* (Chapel Hill: University of North Carolina Press, 2001), 79. For bells attached to a collar, see Smith, *Listening*, 73–74. For runaway slaves, see Lieut. Francis Hall, *Travels*

Into the antebellum period, characterizations of the slave body as an auditory form appeared increasingly in correspondence with interactions between whites and blacks. Everywhere they labored, slaves were perceived also to be making sound. A team of "half starved" Negroes working along Savannah's wharves performed "a kind of monotonous song, at times breaking out into a yell, and then sinking into the same nasal drawl." Rowers in Georgia "accompanied their labour by a wild sort of song," while others—from a group of porters loading luggage in Philadelphia, to a Negro man pushing a wheelbarrow, to a town girl selling pears—continually brought sound and labor into close relation.[24] The very activity of slave labor seemed to possess a fundamental audibility; Negro work itself was inherently audible, suggesting an indexical relation between sound, labor, and the laboring black body that had evolved into a mode of iconicity, a naturalized, commonsense understanding of the audibility of black flesh. A report from Savannah in 1817 verges on a kind of immateriality in which slaves assume a disembodied, audible form: "Nothing is heard near the water but the negroes' song while stowing away the cotton." Yet another report from New York from around the same time, eighteen years prior to the state-wide abolition of slavery, similarly figures black workers metonymically as sound forms: "The Cries of New-York."[25]

To this extent, sound not only marked slaves but also identified them as audible things whose externalized, sonic properties conjoined with other fleshly expressions of Negro behavior. And because audibility identified something fundamental to the Negro's nature, whites sought to exercise that nature in order to control their bodies and improve the character of work. As Mark M. Smith explains in his important accounting of the nineteenth-century US sound world, "Slaveholders . . . stress[ed]

in Canada and the United States in 1816 and 1817 (London: Longman, Hurst, Rees, Orme, and Brown, 1818), 354. For Cajah, see Lathan W. Windley, comp., Runaway Slave Advertisements: A Documentary History from the 1730s to 1790, 4 vols. (Westport, CT: Greenwood Press, 1983), esp. vol. 1, Virginia and North Carolina, entry for Carter Braxton, July 28, 1768, 61.

24. For "half starved," see "The Levee at New Orleans," Illustrated London Times 32 (June 5, 1858), 13–14; for rowers in Georgia, see Hall, Travels in Canada, 216; for porters, see Edward Thomas Coke, A Subaltern's Furlough (London: Saunders and Otley, 1833), 236–37; for wheelbarrow and girl selling pears, see The Cries of New-York (New York: Samuel Wood, 1809), 21.

25. For stowing cotton in Savannah, see William Tell Harris, Remarks Made during a Tour through the United States of America (London: Sherwood, Neely, and Jones, 1821), 69; The Cries of New-York.

the rhythm of industriousness . . . and the sober tones of organic social and economic relations." When effectively harnessed, the slaves' sounding practices could be incorporated into efforts to increase the efficiency of what planters called "Nigger work."[26] Singing, in particular, staved off the condition of sloth. By exciting the Africans' natural qualities of sound making, white mastery sought to contain another natural quality, the propensity toward laziness, and thus help to organize labor in productive ways. In fact, it might even be fair to say that controls of singing functioned materially in the isolation of a productive force, particularly in the large stretch of southern territory where planters commonly relied on gang labor.[27] Clearly some owners thought so. "While at work," a southern planter wrote in his report on the "management of Negroes," "they should be brisk. . . . I have no objection to their whistling or singing some lively tune, but no *drawling* tunes are allowed in the field, for their motions are almost certain to keep time with the music."[28] And because these fleshly, working machines were thought to be natural sound producers for reasons attributable to race and physiognomy ("Niggers is allers good singers nat'rally. . . . I reckon they got better lungs than white [folk]"), they could easily be induced to sing, even if their intellectual limitations rendered such singing basically as noise; "his songs are mere sounds."[29]

---

26. Smith, *Listening*, 20; and Ira Berlin, *Slaves without Masters: The Free Negro in the Antebellum South* (New York: Pantheon, 1974), 236. Peter Van Der Merwe situates black musical performance within this labor context in *Origins of the Popular Style: The Antecedents of Twentieth-Century Popular Music* (Oxford: Oxford University Press, 1989), 63–65.

27. That is, a productive force in ways akin to G. A. Cohen's characterization of food (Cohen, *Karl Marx's Theory of History*, 52). Interestingly, elsewhere Cohen argues against slave religion as a productive force, in spite of its productive consequence, falling back in this instance on Marxian orthodoxy: "this result plainly contradicts the intent of Marx's theory" (33). Gang labor was in place across the southern territories west of the coastal Low Country.

28. Tatler, "The Management of Negroes," *Southern Cultivator* 8, no. 11 (November 1850): 63. Tatler explains that if the slaves are not "brisk," then they should be beaten. Miles Mark Fisher makes a related observation with reference to the productive effects of singing: "In slavery days, songsters were paid to increase the work upon southern plantations by inducing the laborers to sing. These 'singing bosses,' who had a variety of designations, were usually women; they were also heard in Haiti." Fisher, *Negro Slave Songs in the United States* (Ithaca, NY: Cornell University Press, 1953), 21. The source of this rich quotation, however, is unknown; Fisher's citation of Henry Osgood is incorrect.

29. For "allers good singers," see [Frederick Olmsted], "Mississippi Home," *National Anti-Slavery Standard*, 21, no. 1052 (August 4, 1860): 1; for "mere sounds," see Smith, *Listen-*

Singing not only served to discipline slave labor but also reinforced the slaves' status as a different kind of human, to give form to their social reality as chattel property. By forcing slaves to make sound, owners sought for them to reinforce their own subjugation as exchangeable commodity-forms. "The horror they feel in moving further to the South," observed Edward Strutt of Jesus College, Cambridge, in the early 1830s, "may be seen even in the ballads they are said to sing before the whites."[30] Slaves put up for sale would also sometimes be made to sing while marching in a coffle in order to maintain order, extending the organizing powers of collective singing to keep up the pace. In other instances, slaves were forced to perform as part of their display on the auction block, demonstrating to those who might buy them qualities of vitality and vigor.[31] Such displays were unconscionably cruel, in a most obvious way. But they were also symbolically so. Enforced play intensified the perception of slaves as performative things whose seemingly lighthearted actions affirmed their distance from the realities of southern social and economic life. At least a few masters, finally, appeared to ignore the slaves' qualities of audibility altogether. J. Hector St. John de Crèvecouer seemed astonished by how some owners seemed to "become deaf" to slave misery. "They neither see, hear, nor feel the woes of their poor slaves." The sounding slave, constituted as a kind of noisy, audible flesh, could be classified as a commodity that speaks, as in Fred Moten's rendering, except that there was nothing economically fetishistic about it. As previously noted, the slaves' exchange-value did not mask labor but, on the contrary, intensified awareness that these commodities

ing, 69. Neither were the disciplining capacities of singing lost on the slaves themselves. "A silent slave is not liked by masters or overseers," Frederick Douglass famously wrote. "This may account for the almost constant singing heard in the southern states." Douglass, *My Bondage and My Freedom* (New York, 1855), 97.

30. E. S. Abdy, *Journal of a Residence and Tour in the United States of America*, 3 vols. (London: John Murray, 1835), 3:103. The ballad's lyric appears on p. 104.

31. On slave coffles, see Henry Bibb, "The Plantation Song," *National Anti-Slavery Standard* 5, no. 10 (August 8, 1844): 40; John Rankin, *Letters on American Slavery, Addressed to Mr. Thomas Rankin, Merchant at Middlebrook, August County Virginia*, 5th ed. (Boston, 1838), 45–46; Ebenezer Davies, *American Scenes, and Christian Slavery: A Recent Tour of Four Thousand Miles in the United States* (London: J. Snow, 1849), 94; G. W. Featherstonhaugh, *Excursion through the Slave States* (New York, 1844), 36–37. On performance on the auction block, see Eileen Southern, *The Music of Black Americans*, 3rd ed. (New York: Norton, 1997), 159. Saidiya V. Hartman provides a fascinating discussion of both the coffles and the auction block in chap. 1 in *Scenes of Subjection: Terror, Slavery, and Self-Making in Nineteenth-Century America* (New York: Oxford University Press, 1997).

were about production as such.[32] Their audible nature was merely a quality of their thingly, labor-specific form.

In their efforts to render slaves as propertied labor, many masters directed what they perceived to be Negroes' innately noisy nature in yet other ways that might be construed as productive. Across the slave era, observers recorded how the slaves' proclivities for making sound became a resource available for entertaining whites. Colonial and post-Revolutionary reports, for example, show already that owners sometimes extracted additional value from slave labor for their own pleasure, as in the story of the Virginia slave Old Dick, whose young master, Tom Sutherland, "made me play the Banjer" while Tom and others danced a "Congo Minuet."[33] Antebellum accounts describe white owners frolicking among their human herds and ordering them to act out their affiliations with livestock and pets. The former slave James Watkins recalled in his narrative how

> Our masters sometimes brought ladies and gentlemen to look at us, but when we saw them coming towards us we ran to our cribs, fearing lest they should be coming to buy some of us; but we were called back, and had then to amuse them by performing various antics. We had to run on our hands and knees like dogs, and jump over each other like horses, to stand on our heads, to butt one another with our heads like sheep, and to dance and sing, some knocking old tin cans together, others jingling bones, and others beating juba [patting], the forestep, the backstep, the middle step, the juba singing.[34]

In still other instances, slave performance skills even encouraged purchase for purposes of entertainment. Such was the case of Lavinia Bell, a free black girl, who was stolen from her parents in Washington, DC, and shuttled away to Texas, where she was sold to a white, farm family. On their Texas farm, Bell was, according to a newspaper account from 1861,

32. For St. John de Crèvecouer, see Smith, *Listening*, 15. Fred Moten employs this anomaly to suggest the basis of a "freedom drive" and the quality of the "scream" that precedes and is embedded in an otherwise thingly ontology. See Moten, "Aunt Hester's Scream," chap. 1 in *In the Break*.

33. Mechal Sobel, *The World They Made Together: Black and White Values in Eighteenth-Century Virginia* (Princeton, NJ: Princeton University Press, 1987), 34, 37.

34. James Watkins, *Struggles for Freedom; or, the Life of James Watkins, Formerly a Slave in Maryland, U.S.*, 19th ed. (Manchester: James Watkins, 1860), 12. Watkins continues by quoting this lyric of Juba singing: "I went down the sandy point, / And I bought half a yard of waste / And I wrapped it round the lady's waist, / And I asked her how the juba taste. / And juba this, and juba that, / And juba killed the white-haired cat."

"brought up a 'show girl,'" whose owners "taught [her] to dance, sing, and cackle like a hen, or crow like a rooster" for the entertainment of crowds.[35] Bell's novel imitations not only reinforced her subhuman stature but also put on display once more how slave sound production was perceived not as Music but as another kind of amusing or pleasing sound, an audible extension of the Negro's flesh and physicality, its thingly condition.

The inherent audibility of the slave body typically stood well outside the normative measures of Music, even if the slaves' performances, at times, seemed to resemble it. Samuel A. Cartwright's 1851 depiction captures this distinction. According to Cartwright, for the slave, "music is a mere sensual pleasure . . . there is nothing in his music addressing the understanding [of form] . . . his songs are mere sounds, without sense or meaning." As evidence, Cartwright stressed slave music's inferior qualities: "It has melody, but no harmony"; the former being associated with the body, voice ("gratified by sound, as his stomach by food"), whereas the latter connecting to "the mind" and to the rules of European tonality. Vocality and melody, together with the percussive, bodily enactments of patting, stomping, and the like, were merely audible extensions of a living property. As a kind of bodily prosthesis, not sufficiently externalized to be fully expropriated by whites, these sounds simply marked the slaves' natural proclivities toward barbarism, heightened sexuality, laziness, and play, suggesting a peculiar evolutionary manifestation somewhere between animal and human.[36]

Around the same time, however, the perception that slave vocalizations and instrumental playing were merely outward-extending sounds of living property seemed increasingly to be giving way to the opinion that these soundings were a kind of Music. In large part, this shift in perception arose materially, as a consequence of changes in slave performance practices in the routines of entertaining whites. The copious references to slave instrumental practices indicated that more and more slaves were learning to sing and play in ways informed by European-centered musical rules and that these practices—diatonic and pentatonic scales, popular song forms, duple and triple meter, tonal grammar, equally tempered intonation norms—qualitatively reshaped the style of public musical performances that whites most commonly encountered. Even the racially interactive ritu-

---

35. On Lavinia Bell, see John W. Blassingame, ed., *Slave Testimony: Two Centuries of Letters, Speeches, Interviews, and Autobiographies* (Baton Rouge: Louisiana State University Press, 1977), 341–45.
36. Smith, *Listening*, 69.

als relating to the harvest and Christian religious worship, together with the everyday occurrences of singing while laboring, increasingly became sites of potential relation whereby the inherent noisiness of the Negro would be reoriented in ways drawing similarities to European tonality and musical grammar.[37]

The widespread activity of entertainment eventually produced a new category of labor, the Negro musician. Versions of Negro musicians were already in place in the colonial era, being both "well trained as dining room servants and as scientific musicians . . . playing together on various instruments, at balls and parties."[38] As more and more slaves learned to play Euro-Western music, however, their masters turned these newly acquired labor skills into new ways of turning a profit. The archive of slave musical records accounts for numerous references to slave instrumentalists being hired out to perform for whites at plantation parties, at resorts, at carnivals, on steamboats, and in southern towns. The performances were part of a general practice of slave hiring that deeply informed the southern economy and complicated easy distinctions between paid and unpaid labor.[39] By hiring out their slaves, owners could extract even more value from their property. Musical skill offered to these owners an additional means of income, and when slaves would otherwise not be at work, their musical party performances realized a kind of surplus accumulating beyond conventional labor and increasing their economic value all the more. As Dena Epstein discovered in her seminal studies of slave musical practices, "In the larger towns [in the South] it was not uncommon to find an advertisement" of the services offered for hire, inspiring some owners to train their slaves musically with the intention of hiring them out.[40] Others sought to

37. Roger D. Abrahams, *Singing the Master: The Emergence of African American Culture in the Plantation South* (New York: Pantheon, 1992).

38. Dena Epstein, "Slave Music in the United States before 1860: A Survey of Sources (Part 2)," *Music Library Association Notes*, 2nd ser., 20, no. 3 (Summer 1963): 382.

39. For West Virginia resorts, see Wilma Dunaway, *Slavery in the American Mountain South* (Cambridge: Cambridge University Press, 2003). For carnivals and steamboats, see Epstein, "Slave Music," 382. See also Thomas C. Buchanan, *Black Life on the Mississippi* (Chapel Hill: University of North Carolina Press, 2004); John E. Kleber, ed., *The Encyclopedia of Louisville* (Louisville: University Press of Kentucky, 2000). On the general practice of slave hiring, see Jonathan D. Martin, *Divided Mastery: Slave Hiring in the American South* (Cambridge, MA: Harvard University Press, 2004). Martin questions the view that slave hiring was enabling for slaves.

40. Epstein, for example, reports of a free Negro who trained three slaves in "Slave

purchase slaves who possessed such talents already, and those with special talent might work exclusively as musicians. George Walker, a fiddler and bandleader from Virginia, was available "for hire, either for the remainder of the year, or by the month, week, or job." The well-known autobiography of Solomon Northup [Platt Epps] similarly documents the story of a free black stolen away by white traders who recognized in his accomplished fiddling skills high value in the slave trade. Northup claimed that being hired out as a musician made the course of his twelve years of enslavement more bearable. But it was also what apparently led to his enslavement in the first place.[41]

The widening presence of Negro musicians in a variety of public forums marked a critical transformation in the valuation of slave performances as they began to enter into exchange processes. By grouping together a loosely related, heterogeneous range of performance practices and sounding behaviors under a dominant, discursive category—"Negro music"—the southern social world of white citizenry and free and enslaved blacks had elevated the significance of the slaves' sonic interventions, which had assumed something akin to a material, accessible commodity-form, purchasable and exchangeable as slave labor-in-performance. While the audible sounding practices of slaves would always remain inalienable to the extent that the slaves could control the performance and action of their own bodies, the sounds' materializations in public encouraged their abstraction and translation into the category of "Music." This congealment of a newly conceived "Negro music," in turn, prompted narrators from both the South and North to give closer scrutiny to slave musical practices. When a witness marveled over the display of a group of black firemen, "one of them chanting the burden of the song, and the rest at the end of every two lines, striking in, by way of chorus," when Frederick Law Olmstead detailed the extemporaneous performances of a "gang of Negroes . . . rais[ing] such sound as I never heard before, a long, loud musical shout, rising and fall-

---

Music," 382. I employ the term *surplus* in a way akin to the Marxian notion of surplus value, although it is not, strictly speaking, value produced in the context of work labor. Yet it does effectively create capital, profit that could then be invested culturally.

41. For Walker, see Epstein, "Slave Music," 383. Solomon Northup, *Twelve Years a Slave: Narrative of Solomon Northup, A Citizen of New-York* (New York: Miller, Orton, and Mulligan, 1855), chaps. 6, 13, and 15. On the training of a slave in order to hire him out for parties, see Bruce A. MacLeod, "The Musical Instruments of North American Slaves," *Mississippi Folklore Register* 11, no. 1 (Spring 1977): 45.

ing, and breaking into falsetto, . . . the melody was caught by another, and then, another, and then by several in chorus," they were contributing to an emerging discourse of Negro musical distinctiveness, in which the details of responsorial interplay, "improvisatored" practices, and unusual vocal techniques (e.g., "making tubes of their open palms, to give their voices, which, in all conscience, were loun [*sic*] enough, more volume") were now being comprehended in their relation to European musical practices. After the Civil War, this kind of rhetoric would become codified in the landmark study *The Slave Songs of the United States.*[42]

The rising claims of a Negro musicality identified a discernible threat to the proslavery South: in their musicality, the slaves might possess human qualities after all. If, indeed, slaves were capable of producing Music, then so perhaps were they also possessing of other qualities of humanity, qualities of feeling, emotion, thoughtfulness, and intelligence. Accordingly, as abolitionists appealed to the belief that Negro music reflected the struggles and suffering of slaves, proslavery commentators opted for a rhetoric abiding to the claims of playfulness and laziness that accompanied the new blackface minstrelsy. As a result, in the course of everyday commentary, observers seemed at times unsure how to represent this most peculiar new form, Negro music. Sometimes they shifted their opinion in the middle of an essay. Such was the case, for example, of a journalist reporting in a Charleston newspaper, who at first marveled over the talent of "little negro boys . . . aged six to ten years" whose performance as the Ebony Sax-Horn Band would "try the skills and strength of grown men." Still, the band's performance ultimately did not make sense until it was reduced to a modest, audible form for the pleasure of white people. That the boys "should play difficult music, with all the precision of a practiced band, is, if no new thing, at least a very pleasant species of entertainment."[43] A Georgia physician plainly outlined the paradox: "Despite their kinship with hogs in nature and habit, the Negro has music in his soul." This quality of musicality, which he named a "sixth sense," seemed to be something more than "mere sound." While slave musicality served to limit their proclivities of laziness, it also

---

42. "Negro Music," *Daily Herald and Gazette* (Cleveland), August 14, 1838, issue 293, col. A; Olmsted, "Negro Jodling: The Carolina Yell," in *A Journey into the Seaboard Slave States* (New York, 1856), 114–15; for "improvisatored," see "Negro Music," col. A; William Francis Allen et al., comp., *Slave Songs of the United States* (New York: A. Simpson and Co., 1867).

43. John Joseph Hindemann, "Concert Life in Antebellum Charleston" (PhD diss., University of North Carolina, 1971), 199–200.

increasingly complicated the status of the slave itself, both in his or her dis-position as a kind of labor and as a social agent in possession of a powerful aesthetic form.[44]

Animated Properties

There is a curious moment in one of the foundational texts on the history of antebellum slavery, a moment that brings into relief the trans-formative force of the slave sound world. It is the moment when the dis-tinguished historian Kenneth M. Stampp states in passing, "Rarely did a contemporary write about slaves without mentioning their music."[45] Stampp makes this assertion with considerable authority. *The Peculiar Institution: Slavery in the Antebellum South* represented a seismic change in the writ-ing of Southern history, being the first overarching study of US slavery to give voice and representation to the slaves themselves. Stampp achieved this feat through consultation of a massive body of sources, devoted largely to the thirty-year period before the Civil War. The appendix of his 1956 monograph lists over 150 collections and archives that he consulted in the preparation of his book. Stampp's research involved the perusal of many hundreds, if not thousands, of documents housed in national collections and archives, and it is remarkable to think that he had discovered within them so much mention of slaves engaging in musical performance, par-ticularly so after a century or more of virtual silence about black musical invention.[46] Slave society was, of course, a world in which everyday speech was already brimming with references to its most valuable property. As one writer put it in 1828, "the white conversation is apt to be darkened in its complexion; indeed, three quarters of sociable discourse [in southern states] is often engrossed by the topic of slaves."[47] And yet the conspicuous increase in references to slave sounding practices identified a new atten-tiveness among mastery to something once given little regard. We might wonder, accordingly, what was all this chatter about? Why the sudden fas-

44. For the planter's remark, see Hartman, *Scenes of Subjection*, 44.
45. Kenneth M. Stampp, *The Peculiar Institution: Slavery in the Antebellum South* (New York: Knopf, 1956), 368.
46. See my chapter "Resonances of Racial Absence: Black Sounding Practices Prior to 'Negro Music,'" in *Lying up a Nation: Race and Black Music* (Chicago: University of Chi-cago Press, 2003).
47. Arthur Singleton [Henry Cogswell Knight], *Letters from the South and West* (Boston: Richardson and Lord, 1824), 101.

cination with what would seem to be merely an aural accommodation to the mechanisms of labor and to the recent whims of white entertainment?

On one level, white southerners' new interest was consistent with the aforementioned rise in European-informed slave musical practices that had increasingly entered into the forums of white, social leisure. In these instances, Negro music's appeal drew an equivalence to that of the curiosity or trifle; listeners were fascinated with the ability of those deemed subhuman to perform Music, a human, creative form. While such talents may have posed a challenge to the claims that slaves were inferior, most whites, in fact, seemed perfectly comfortable living in a world in which human-things also possessed the curious ability of creating a kind of Music. Indeed, as Saidiya Hartman argues, any sense of humanity that might have been associated with Negro cultural practices likely served to reinforce racial hierarchy. The themes of sorrow and "natural Christian" sensibility suffusing representations of the public genre, the "spiritual," for example, seemed only to affirm the slaves' subjugation by disassociating them from that which was normative and free.[48]

More fundamental was a second outcome of incorporating European practices, namely, how these new performances, despite their abstract form and public availability as Negro music, could never be successfully introduced into the logic of market exchange. The slaves' musical performances had coalesced into a new form of Negro ownership that, while recognized as coherent and tangible, and, indeed, part and parcel of southern, slave capitalism, also exceeded complete possession even by those whites who owned slaves, precisely because slave sounding practices were thought to be inextricably connected to Negro flesh. While the principal object of exchange in these circumstances was the slave musician him- or herself who performed at social events, the audible sound was what distinguished musicians from the more silent others. We can therefore surmise that this condition of audibility would have been fundamental to their subjective makeup. Indeed, this is precisely what Solomon Northup had insisted upon. The inalienable character of Negro music would matter increasingly as slave performances grew more and more conspicuous and exchangeable, establishing forms consistent with Euro-Western musical standards that could be sold and traded. The peculiar, seemingly animated qualities of slave soundings, of an embodiment within the sound itself, which signified to whites the slaves' subhuman status justifying their

48. Hartman, *Scenes of Subjection*. I discuss the public discourse of "spirituals" in "Magical Writing: The Iconic Wonders of the Slave Spiritual," in *Lying up a Nation*.

enslavement, also supplied African Americans with a new kind of material culture. The animated properties of slave sound identified a congealment structured in dominance that conceptualized analytically and retrospectively qualities thought to have existed outside and prior to dominance, and that had become conceived within antebellum social contexts by the 1840s as a property-form inextricably linked to the slave body. This "Negro music" possessed an essential character and value traceable to its qualities of sentience, exteriorized aurally as embodiments of black flesh and sometimes seen as directly linking to an African past. If the slave was a propertyless, propertied thing, it had nonetheless, through some peculiar racial-economic magic, come to possess a lively, animated property of its own.

Seeking to extract and recover from slave sounding practices those sonic qualities of animation existing prior to Negro music, as if they were an absolute set of cultural truths—a "metaphysics of Africanity"—belies what we already know to be a falsehood.[49] The undoubtedly diverse range of meanings and practices that developed as part of black colonial performance remains hidden within the figurations of eighteenth-century representation, occasionally revealed in the interruptions of normative order and depicted as expressions of "noise." Tendencies that seek to isolate a condition of purely African/black orality according to a "Great Divide" separating ocularity and aurality simply perpetuate unprovable distinctions that deny a condition of magic and supernaturalism across the history of Europe.[50] At the same time, we also possess a kind of knowledge about black auditory practices even if it comes to us as second-level mediations. As Susan Scott Parrish writes more generally about colonial black culture in the British Atlantic, "The colonials' perception of black epistemology was not a mere projection . . . it was loosely based upon . . . a belief in the manipulability of a spiritualized nature [that was] common to the plantation and even urban cultures of African slaves in the colonies." The hidden signs of nature, which were linked to plant cures, conjure, and supernaturalism, together with ontological ambiguities of people and gods, the animate and the inanimate, the living and the dead, were "readily apparent and audible to Africans" across the Americas.[51] It would be the efforts to distinguish

49. Hartman, *Scenes of Subjection*, 74.
50. Veit Erlmann, *Reason and Resonance: A History of Modern Aurality* (London: Zone Books, 2010), 14–15.
51. Susan Scott Parrish, *American Curiosity: Cultures of Natural History in the Colonial British Atlantic World* (Chapel Hill: University of North Carolina Press, 2006), 259–60, esp. 260.

black from white that would begin to separate the magical from the secular among eighteenth-century white observers.

Rather than representing this acoustical phenomenology according to the abstract category of "Africanisms," then, we might better comprehend it as an aggregation of practices that variously coalesced within the new regimes of domination radically transforming black subjectivity, including many regions of North America. Distinctive, semiotically rich, and suggestive of an order of thought relationally constituted within and against European-based imperial epistemologies, these cultural practices and coalescences could never be separated from the enduring, material conditions of terror and social fracture so commonplace and ordinary in slaves' experience. In fact, the ecological realms of thought among slaves were likely to have been constituted in connection to British colonial relations between masters and slaves, their secret, surreptitious qualities owing not only to the African-based beliefs in the supernatural but also to the aims and needs of slaves to guard sacrality as a lone possession. Monique Allewaert has suggested, for example, that the relationship between diasporic African supernaturalism and the conditions of social death on a mass scale became central to the emergence among slaves (particularly those maroons living in tropical circumstances) of a distinctive ontology distinguished from European Enlightenment perceptions of the autonomous, complete citizen-subject. This "disaggregated and opened . . . parahuman" personhood, she writes, was "not predicated on the understanding of the body as an enclosed and organic form."[52] Allewaert is proposing that the slave ontology was an order possessing qualities of a relational autonomy to the natural world not entirely subject to, or easily claimable within, a modern, Euro-Western-based epistemology.

When brought into relation with historical and ethnographic studies

---

52. Monique Allewaert, *Ariel's Ecology: Plantations, Personhood, and Colonialism in the American Tropics* (Minneapolis: University of Minnesota Press, 2013). Neil Roberts's fascinating analysis of the space of slave escape appeared too late in the production process to involve in this essay. See *Freedom as Marronage* (Chicago: University of Chicago Press, 2015). For an introduction to a massive literature on African and African-diasporic supernaturalism, see Wyatt MacGaffey, *Kongo Political Culture: The Conceptual Challenge of the Particular* (Bloomington: Indiana University Press, 2000); Vincent Brown, *The Reaper's Garden: Death and Power in the World of Atlantic Slavery* (Cambridge, MA: Harvard University Press, 2008); James Sweet, *Domingos Alvares, African Healing, and the Intellectual History of the Atlantic World* (Chapel Hill: University of North Carolina Press, 2013), 47; and *Sorcery in the Black Atlantic*, ed. Luis Nicolau Parks and Roger Sansi (Chicago: University of Chicago Press, 2011).

of indigenous African musical traditions, the important insights of the new, materialist-oriented ecocriticism of Parrish, Allewaert, and others propose a suggestive body of accumulated evidence, circumstantial as it may be, of a distinctive order of personhood. Whether or not uniformly "parahuman," these identity formations involved processes of relation and exchange in which sound environments and performance practices—together with their outward linkages to animated properties of the natural and supernatu-ral—served to constitute among colonial-era slaves forms of subjectivity that exceeded and supplanted the "metaphysics of Africanity" still claimed by some scholars. If, moreover, we accept the premise outlined in a long trajectory of scholarship devoted to the African diaspora that documents the mediating role of sound formations in enabling exchange and contact between people and their gods, between ancestors and things, between humans and the livingness of the natural world, then we can begin to dis-cern a generative force in sound among North American slaves whose modes of relation and engagement at times conveyed a discernible, ani-mated resonance. This is not to buy into stereotypes of natural musicality or even to suggest more subtly that Africans in North America were somehow unusually equipped to produce musical value; that value would take form later, with the rise of a Negro music within the political economy of the late antebellum South. What is important to recognize, rather, is the extent to which the animated qualities of slave sound had already been part of slave worlds and also been conceived in white frames of knowledge as part of the peculiar qualities of an African subject category of person-thing. Indeed, the attachments of sound to the slave body served as part of the very con-stitution of the Negro as a putatively inferior life-form.

Efforts to comprehend the musical practices of North American Afri-can slaves typically refer to the ritualized settings of ring shouts and Afri-canized Christian worship, as documented by Michael Gomez, Sterling Stuckey, Samuel Floyd, and others. As important as these demonstrative forms were, they were probably no more significant than the more rou-tine, auditory constitutions of place orienting the slaves' lives. The variety of representations of slave soundings noted throughout this essay may be enough already to convince readers that the natural musicality so fre-quently assigned to slaves pointed to the conspicuous presence of sound-ing practices in the constitution of slave sociality and in the slaves' making of the world. There is reason to suspect, in fact, that both colonial and antebellum slaves lived in a profoundly auditory realm, engaging in rela-tions between the worldly and otherworldly through sound, to the point

where clear distinctions between sound and message collapsed, effect-
ing a semiotic mode whereby acoustical properties did not simply signify
the animate but rather embodied it, akin, for example, to the ontological
structuring through sound described by Steven Friedson among the Ewe of
Ghana and the iconicities of style analyzed by Steven Feld in his pioneering
studies of the Kaluli of Papua New Guinea.[53] The significance of the sonic
as a medium of slave ontological constitution seems likely to have been so
central to slave experience that Parrish and others have ultimately come
to challenge the literary centeredness of twenty-five years of black cultural
studies in the United States, proposing that African America's foundational
trope of the "talking book," originally theorized by Henry Louis Gates Jr., be
replaced with what she calls "the talking woods." In this perception, sounds
inhabit, and are fundamental to, ways of knowing and being-in-the-world,
revealing in themselves properties of animation far exceeding in value the
seemingly lifeless and "dead" forms performed by whites. There is a sense,
indeed, that the early attractions to Negro music were consistent with the
processes of capitalism, whereby the dead labor of capital performs vam-
pire acts of resuscitation, as Marx outlines in *Capital*.[54]

   If the animated sounding practices of southern slaves played a generative role in the constitution across the Americas of new black cultural
epistemics, they would undergo a fundamental transformation as slave per-

53. Steven M. Friedson, *Remains of Ritual: Northern Gods in a Southern Land* (Chicago:
University of Chicago Press, 2009); Steven Feld, *Sound and Sentiment* (1982; repr., Durham, NC: Duke University Press, 2012). In his discussion of the Ewe, Friedson describes
sound-induced contact as neither a self merging into a collective body nor an abstraction that aggregates the body, nor the possession of an ontologically coherent body. It is,
rather, something more akin to a becoming, of a loss of individuality yet without the loss
of self. Such a reading, albeit historically out of context, is nonetheless suggestive of the
kinds of relations that many slaves may have also realized.
54. Parrish, *American Curiosity*, 260. Monique Allewaert elaborates on the significance
of Parrish's argument in *Ariel's Ecology*, 21. Henry Louis Gates Jr., *The Signifying Mon-
key: A Theory of African-American Literary Criticism* (New York: Oxford University Press,
1988). As Parrish and Allewaert show, slaves in the US South often saw the borderlands
of the woods as a place of refuge, a potential pathway to escape, and, frequently, a danger zone leading to recapture. As a source of pharmacological needs, for hunting, fish-
ing, and worship, however, the woods played a constitutive role in shaping forms of slave
knowledge. It is no surprise, therefore, that the slaves' musical activities beyond white
supervision frequently took place in these areas. Parrish also proposes that whites were,
in fact, drawn to African-based conceptions of nature at the same time they distinguished
them as racially specified. For Marx's comments, see "The Working Day," chap. 10 in
Capital, vol. 1, trans. Ben Fowkes (London: Penguin, 1990), 342.

formances began to inhabit new orders of knowledge and value in the capitalist economies of the late antebellum US South. This new valuation was constituted only when slave performances coalesced as "Negro music," as anomalous forms of possession whose qualities of racialized fleshliness further troubled the disconnect between white and black worlds under market capitalism. At this historical moment, a new concept of slave musical ownership arises from the very contradiction of slave capitalism, emerging from a wrinkle in a mode of production in which acculturated Africans learned to create a "Music" that would enter exchange in the southern marketplace. Because the performances of Negro music were expressive of the qualities and experiences that distinguished slaves from white mastery, they would always be construed as possessing something more, containing a quality of excess identifying them as "Negro." Increasingly, the racial materiality of Negro music's fleshly qualities would be recognized as a kind of property resembling the colonial European idea of the African fetish, which, as William Pietz famously outlines in a now classic set of essays, similarly arose from "a breakdown of the adequacy of the [existing] discourse[s] . . . to translate and transvalue objects . . . triangulated among Christian feudal, African lineage, and merchant capitalist social systems."[55] What Pietz calls the "irreducible materiality" of the fetish finds a parallel in the animated qualities of Negro music, through which the audible world of eighteenth-century slaves gave way to the belief in the inherent audibility of the slave body. Negro music brought into recognizable sonic form a version of this animated audibility as it also introduced a perception of the form's unobtainability: a secret possession that was knowably unknown in its fundamental connection to a racial fleshliness that was nonetheless resonating outward into southern public culture, bringing to mind what a

55. William Pietz, "The Problem of the Fetish, I," *RES: Anthropology and Aesthetics* 9 (Spring 1985): 6. Pietz continues: "It was within this situation that there emerged a new problematic concerning the capacity of the material object to embody—simultaneously and sequentially—religious, commercial, aesthetic, and sexual values. My argument, then, is that the fetish could originate only in conjunction with the emergent articulation of the ideology of the commodity-form that defined itself within and against the social values and religious ideologies of two radically different types of noncapitalist society, as they encountered each other in an ongoing cross-cultural situation" (6–7). On the concept of the fetish, see also Peter Pels, "The Spirit of Matter: On Fetish, Rarity, Fact, and Fancy," in *Border Fetishisms: Material Objects in Unstable Spaces*, ed. Patricia Spyer (New York: Routledge, 1998); Rosalind Morris, "Fetishism: Overview," in *New Dictionary of the History of Ideas*, ed. Maryanne Cline Horowitz, 6 vols. (Detroit: Charles Scribner's Sons, 2005), 2:822–26.

later music theorist and composer, Arnold Schoenberg, would call in a different cultural setting, "the instinctual lives of tones."

Property's Properties

Historians have been acutely aware that US slaves, despite being a species of property, also owned forms of property in the face of official, legal sanctions against it.[56] These property-forms were mainly material goods, variously acquired, that could improve the quality of their lives. In the work of Dylan Penningroth, however, the long-recognized existence of slave property receives new attention, and its significance is shown to be more far-reaching and complex than previously understood. Penningroth's account outlines the manifold ways in which the accumulation of money and the acquisition of property coursed through the slaves' lives. Some slaves took on additional labors (planting, sewing, carpentry, etc.) for barter or cash; others hired fellow slaves and even their own children from their masters; still others succeeded as entrepreneurial middlemen who created complex labor networks in which hired slaves hired other slaves, who, in turn, additionally hired slaves.[57] The economic impetus at the heart of this development was the task system, the principal relation of production organizing slave labor across most of the South, particularly in the context of agricultural work. Under the task system, slaves were assigned a set of duties that they were expected to accomplish over the course of the day. Once completed, slaves were often allowed to work for profit on their own. And because labor under the task system was frequently performed in groups, slaves could help one another, whether it be a man assisting his wife in harvesting crops or a woman stepping in for a friend so that she could take on paying work. As a result of these practices, slaves accumulated money and goods, which they could barter and trade with other slaves, free blacks, and, sometimes, poor whites.

The task system produced a series of labor relations that were

---

56. See, for example, Stampp, *The Peculiar Institution*, 67–72; 414–15. Steven Hahn writes, "We may well have underestimated the extent to which slaves in a great many locales—with or without their owners' approval—bought, sold, and bargained with merchants, shop keepers, peddlers, and neighboring whites" (Hahn, *A Nation under Our Feet*, 27).

57. Dylan Penningroth, *The Claims of Kinfolk: African American Property and Community in the Nineteenth-Century South* (Chapel Hill: University of North Carolina Press, 2003), 81, 83.

acutely interdependent and relational, developing from an expanded sense of kinship. Rather than creating a grand, familial network of clearly identifiable relations, this kinship lineage, Penningroth explains, suggested a far more tentative set of connections, variously competitive and supportive. He shows that these microlabor practices followed the disrupted patterns of social relations under slavery, being consistent with the fractured, precarious quality of the slaves' lives within a regime that questioned their status as subjects in the first place. For this reason, ownership was critical to slaves not only because of the depth of their lack in the face of subsistence but also because the claims of ownership "were tangled in the same threads that tied slaves to each other." The relational nature of slave property—both in the interdependency of labor and in the frequency of several slaves collectively owning valuable possessions—meant that ownership, if precarious and contingent, was also deeply social. These tangles of relation, moreover, crossed over into other realms of exchange, even affecting sacred practices such as conjure, which could be bought and sold as a commodified form of service. As slave property was brought into existence, it would also carry with it differing conceptions of materiality consistent with their experience as slaves and even extending back to African orderings of social property among kin.[58]

The rise of Negro music identifies a peculiar kind of possession whose value, in the first instance, derived from its material tenuousness as a property-form. Being something "owned" and retained within the slaves' flesh, Negro music always remained in the slaves' possession, even when its principal mode of expression—as part of working in the plantation fields—served economically as a natural lubricant within the greater forces of production, warding off what masters perceived to be their inborn tendencies toward laziness. If singing during the practice of labor was itself an unstable, tentative expression, seemingly incoherent, immaterial, and unreliable as a cultural possession, it was nonetheless always retained by and within the slave. As a mode of communication—even when performed in what were likely, at times, halting, stop-start responsorial acts—Negro music continually revealed a potential for reaffirming social relationships, much in the same way that material property-forms reinforced the "threads" of relation making up slave communities. But because the "property" made was not only socially constituted but was also a sonic embodiment of the slaves in their performative relation, it was likely to enable a

58. Penningroth, The Claims of Kinfolk, 6. On conjure as labor, see 101–2.

level of emotion and affective involvement far in excess of material forms. Negro music brought into being a new mode of the sensible in which the auditory was foregrounded. This, in part, might explain why whites were able to comprehend the slaves' singing at work as a kind of pleasure and to witness in their musical relations expressions of happiness, particularly so as the discourse network of southern, plantation fantasy grew increasingly familiar by the 1840s and 1850s. And as the slaves' singing continued, lingering conspicuously in acts of labor, inhabiting and frequently overwhelming the auditory place of southern plantation culture, it also identified an abstracted, semiautonomous quality of Negro being that was only partially under the control of ownership. This newly conceived possession of slaves accordingly brought into public knowledge the fabrication of white loss, a loss materialized in the animated fleshliness of slave sounding practices. As a materially tenuous property in the first instance, the slave possession reveals formally a more complex value, relationally grounded in a reversal of profit and loss. That is, if slave musical performance enabled masters to harness and dominate their human property, it offered to slaves something in return—a payback directed to the property itself. The performances of slaves served routinely to reaffirm social relations in ways that no other cultural practice could, marking the creation of a possession or profit, whose value as animated sound was a product of the slaves' very subjugation.

Slaves were well aware of this new kind of ownership. When they could, they exchanged it as a form of labor within the southern market economy. Exchanging for personal profit was, in fact, fairly common among the most musically talented slaves living in or near towns, whose skills and performances were reported in southern publications: "The negro musician, Hicks" of Columbus, Georgia; "the jolly old negro musician," Ike Fennell, of Memphis, "whose violin has 'many a time and oft' discoursed its bewitching strains for the amusement of almost all our young people." Such reports reach back to the beginning of the century and even earlier, as in the runaway ad for Abram from 1801, a carpenter, who worked as a fiddler without his owner's consent.[59] When Solomon Northup performed for whites, he not only sold his talents for his master but also "returned with

59. For Hicks, see "Local News Items," *Columbus Ledger Enquirer* (Columbus, Georgia), September 2, 1861, vol. 3, issue 288, p. 3; for Fennell (who died on his way to a party to perform "with his band"), see "Local News," *Memphis Daily Avalanche*, March 6, 1867, vol. 9, issue 54, p. 3; for Abram, and for elaboration on the hiring of slave musicians, see Nancy R. Ping, "Black Musical Activities in Antebellum Wilmington, North Carolina," *Black Perspective in Music* 8, no. 2 (Autumn 1980): 149.

many picayunes jingling in my pockets—the extra contributions of those to whose delight I had administered." And when George Walker's owner hired him out to play his fiddle at parties, he requested that they not pay Walker directly, apparently because he had a habit of taking a cut for himself.[60] Musicians with less training or talent also bartered and bargained their performances for all kinds of benefit and profit, whether it be in the form of a few coins, a sip of whiskey, or the granting of some leniency in their tasks.[61] We can imagine, finally, how Lavinia Bell, James Watkins, and Old Dick all sought to gain from their newly conceived and racially specified ownership of Negro music.

It follows, then, that in a most fundamental way, Negro music's ownership by slaves, if not inherently a form of resistance, could be nothing but illicit, identifying a claim upon a property legally owned by whites. What slaves had claimed illegally was a part of themselves, a quality of their own flesh, externalized as animated sound.[62] This is why, after all, musical performances by slaves in more developed, ritualized forms, away from the fields, were so frequently done in private: in nighttime rituals, in the "talking woods" of black sociality where slaves would congregate and claim for themselves their own time and social connections, according to a secret practice they famously called "stealing away."[63] In these instances, slaves frequently engaged in a different kind of relation and exchange, bringing to bear the qualities of animation reaffirming African diasporic practices and the inevitably heterodox reorderings taking place in acts of performance,

60. Northup, *Twelve Years a Slave*, 216. For Walker, see Epstein, "Slave Music," 383.

61. Whiskey was a recurring theme. See Robert Criswell, *"Uncle Tom's Cabin" Contrasted with Buckingham Hall, The Planter's Home; or, A Fair View of Both Sides of the Slavery Question* (New York: D. Panshaw, 1852; New York: AMS Press, 1973); Henry Bibb, *Narrative of the Life and Adventures of Henry Bibb, an American Slave* (New York: Published by the Author; 5 Spruce Street, 1849); Charles Lanman, *Adventures in the Wilds of the United States and British American Provinces*, 2 vols. (Philadelphia: John W. Moore, 1856). For coins, see Edmund Kirke [James Robert Gilmore], *Among the Pines; or, South in Secession* (New York: J. R. Gilmore, 1862).

62. The sense of sound as a legal possession of an autonomous subject becomes a critical issue in legal jurisprudence at the turn of the twentieth century. See Stephen M. Best, *The Fugitive's Properties: Law and the Poetics of Possession* (Chicago: University of Chicago Press, 2004).

63. Hartman elaborates on the significance of stealing away in *Scenes of Subjection*, 65–70. For nighttime rituals, see Stephanie M. H. Camp, "The Intoxication of Pleasurable Amusement: Secret Parties and the Politics of the Body," chap. 3 in *Closer to Freedom: Enslaved Women and Everyday Resistance in the Plantation South* (Chapel Hill: University of North Carolina Press, 2004).

often in the most precarious circumstances. The ring shouts, sermons, tes-
timonies, patting practices, and acts of responsorial singing that show up
sporadically across the historical record identify an archive of another order
of exchange that largely deflected the production-oriented market structures of southern, slave capitalism as it sustained the slaves' dynamic
social relations—relations that may have mimicked the disaggregated relations of subjects theorized in the new ecocriticism. In the antebellum musical performances of the illicit, slaves could recall and reenact realms prior,
creating retrospectively historical linkages to form new kinds of exchange,
building and shaping histories of distinction through acts of singing. The
practice of overturning pots, for example, commonly described as a means
of muffling the slaves' singing, was far more likely an African diasporic practice of calling to the dead for new knowledge, a knowledge "spoken" from the
earth and fashioning a new kind of cultural possession. Increasingly, slaves
would understand these acts as their own according to a Euro-Western
knowledge of ownership in which such ritual practices would be translated.
The illicit forms of ritual property became illicit not simply on their own but
according to their conception within the legitimate orders of the southern,
slave economy and under the juridical laws of ownership.[64] White recognition of slave musical ownership drove their conversations, their chatter,
in its incessant reference to slave behavior and control. Stampp's passing comment pointed to a growing anxiety among whites who seemed to
recognize that there was now something owned by slaves that they themselves had somehow lost, and this *something* seemed to be key to the formation of modern black subjectivity.

But it may be in the more emergent forms of Negro musical property—the "*drawling* tunes," together with all the other pedestrian expressions of sounding and singing during acts of labor—where we can best
locate the slaves' recognition of a foundational value attached to their
audible performances. In these circumstances of work—of slaves performing not only as laborers, but also as *labor as such*—the dominant forms of
capitalism's oppression most conspicuously exposed their weakness. As
suggested previously, there is a tendency in most studies of slave music—
owing, perhaps, to the nature of the evidentiary base on which these studies
rely—to look for the strongest indications of value and authenticity within
the private rituals of slaves, where one might expect to locate expressions

64. James H. Sweet, *Domingos Álvares, African Healing, and the Intellectual History of
the Atlantic World* (Chapel Hill: University of North Carolina Press, 2011), 130–31.

of clear-cut Africanity, black particularity, and authenticity. But the performative orientation and practices energizing those important rituals also drew from another place, from the repeated, daily interactions of workers singing and creating culture out in the open, "under the very nose of the overseers."[65] The slaves' improvised, responsorial performance practices established a material order of relation through sound, a performative dynamic and mode of sociality whose routine involvement and possession was not limited to the musically gifted and whose inevitably haphazard, spontaneous engagements would nevertheless be a defining condition of the slaves' everyday relations among themselves. It was in these performance acts where slave soundings were continually regenerated, reconceived, and discursively constituted, informing the public and private performances of Negro music heard beyond the plantation fields, as aspects of those performances circled back into labor, where whites witnessed a property's properties conspicuously on display—properties constituted in acts of labor and inextricably connected to the slaves' status as labor. Significantly, the activity of slave sounding in the plantation fields was not only an audible manifestation of the laboring body but also a social relation whose racial qualities of laziness, suffering, and play reoriented the very look of black labor. As the sounds of work congealed into the expressions of Negro musical play that entertained mastery at their parties and frolics, they also perpetuated the qualities of fleshliness consistent with the slaves' status as labor. The value of Negro music accrued as an indelible marking of flesh and blood, producing in sound a viscosity inextricably linked to the slave as a commodified form of labor, while also exposing indications of a different ontological order altogether: in Negro music, all could hear, if not effectively interpret, the open secret of animated sound. The material *thickness* of slave sound would carry a significance, a value, an agency not unlike that of the piano player's in Dipesh Chakrabarty's reading of Marx's analysis of productive labor, supplying a "fleeting glimpse" of a different order of relation existing within capitalism and yet not subsumed by it; "one does not gain epistemological primacy over the other."[66]

The presence of slave sounding practices as an animated property

65. Paul Gilroy, *The Black Atlantic: Modernity and Double Consciousness* (Cambridge, MA: Harvard University Press, 1993), 37.

66. Chakrabarty, *Provincializing Europe*, 68. This different order is what Chakrabarty named History 2, an affective, phenomenological realm constituted within and against capitalism, yet existing recognizably prior to and outside of capitalism (History 1). The recognition of History 2 as a realm prior, however, emerges only after and within capitalism.

within a human property explains why its value never seemed to dissipate once African American performance style entered into public circulation, beginning with the forms of blackface musical representations that drew widespread, international appeal beginning in the mid-1840s. The mark of theft that would come to define the character of blackface minstrelsy might better be comprehended in this early period not only as an act of expropriation but also of reclamation, whereby whites sought to reclaim what they saw as an illicit property lost in the sounding bodies of African Americans. Reclamation of racialized property becomes central to the constitution of white subjectivity, its theft marking blacks as "enemy." In order to reclaim, they "must first become the enemy . . . to apprehend the enemy 'from the inside,'" assuming what Eduardo Viveiros de Castro calls "the enemy's point of view." And so it follows that the act of conquering by inhabiting also contributed to the instability of whiteness itself. "Negro melodies" in the United States, observed a bemused English writer in 1851, at the height of blackface minstrelsy's popularity, "are hummed on the streets. Young men when they meet you and wish to appear comical, imitate the peculiar chuckle of the sable race. This painful state of things has been going on for several years." The loss of property and the perpetual effort to reclaim what was, in fact, unreclaimable through incessant, ritual acts of performance would be perpetuated according to the consistency of white mastery's commitment to racial difference. What was inalienable and always in the possession of African Americans lived on as animated form as a result of the enduring structures of racism. Racialized, animated, fleshly sound had assumed the position of a critical value. If abstract labor was for Marx "the secret of the expression of value," it was the animated labor of slaves inhabiting Negro musical property that would contradict the significance of abstract labor and sustain Negro music's racially and economically informed aesthetic value well after the point when slavery had ended.[67]

Into the era of Reconstruction, the age of Jim Crow, and the rise of modern consumer society, US whites would continue in their desperate acts of reclamation. These acts seem somehow desperate because they have always been futile from the outset; the white citizenry of the republic could never successfully regain what had been lost, even as Negro music, then black music, became established as a public category and a commodity-

67. Eduardo Viveiros de Castro, "Exchanging Perspectives: The Transformation of Objects into Subjects in Amerindian Ontologies," *Common Knowledge* 10, no. 3 (Fall 2004): 479; John Delaware Lewis, *Across the Atlantic* (London: George Earle, 1851); Marx, *Capital*, 1:152.

form. In fact, over time, the perceived distance between black authentic forms and white musical imitations appeared increasingly to widen, and the legitimacy of white claims accordingly to falter, even while the fundamental musical similarities between black and white styles grew ever stronger. If the performances of blackface repeatedly decoupled Negro music from the fleshly qualities of the slave body, these mediations never diminished its properties of animation. On the contrary, Negro music's animation seemed to increase and its inalienable qualities to intensify in direct proportion to its circulation; its essential value escalated in both economic and symbolic terms as distinctions between what was real and authentic, and what was counterfeit and fake became murkier. An oft-cited essay from 1855 meant to celebrate Negro music did so by conflating slave creations with their minstrel parodies; William Francis Allen's Reconstruction-era publication that sought to present the slave spirituals in the most positive terms relapses into a rhetorical style consistent with darky tunes.[68] In its circulation, "blackness" arose in ways consistent with a second level of fetishism famously outlined by Marx in volume 1 of *Capital*, in his opening discussion of the relation of commodities. As Negro music circulated as a form of commodified labor performed by black itinerants and professionals, and then as a sound emitted from phonograph records, listeners attached value to its racialized qualities, claiming to hear a distinctive, embodied blackness indelibly marked in the sound itself. No matter how far Negro music traveled in an emerging global economy, it would always refer back to a first order of fetishism based in the European fantasy of Africa: to an untranscended materiality originating in the black body. The animated properties hovering about Negro music in its circulated forms, in turn, suggested a kind of spectral quality of the second order of fetishism and were consistent with Marx's dancing table and commodities that speak. In the twentieth century, this secret value would fuel the creation of countless, celebrated performances and works. Black music's inalienable properties would advance as an open secret whose essence identified a seemingly original blackness despite its profoundly intersocial, heterogeneous formation.

Given Negro music's fundamental qualities of the illicit, it is telling that Du Bois would describe Negro music as a gift, as "one of the greatest that the Negro has made to American nationality." Recent anthropological theorizing of the gift as part of a greater economy of exchange invites

68. Jacob J. Trux, "Negro Minstrelsy—Ancient and Modern," *Putnam's Monthly* (January 1855): 72–79; Allen, introduction, *Slave Songs of the United States*.

a comparative consideration of Du Bois's turn of phrase, appearing as it does at a moment when scholars had already begun to inquire into foreign mechanisms of social relation. We might even read Du Bois's notion of the gift according to the conception famously put forward by Marcel Mauss around the same time: as a key force in a relational economy in Melanesia, as something given with the expectation of receiving.[69] In this sense, Negro music's lazy brand of fleshliness and animated, performative labor-as-play was a gift continually taken and yet never fully received. For to receive it, whites would need first to be willing to give back, to embrace "blackness" as a category of whiteness and Americanness, to recognize both blackness and whiteness as falsities, and to imagine a condition in which "race" becomes a concept beyond conception. Because that seems unlikely to happen—because, indeed, what has historically driven white taking is the very belief that black musical ownership is somehow illicit—an animation lives on today as the negative condition of value in black music and all the musics that receive it within the ideological networks subscribing to race as a concept, suggesting a kind of interruption by black music as an enduring practice that refuses sublation under whiteness and capitalism. This interruption has no doubt had an ameliorative and even ethical effect, producing a kind of enchantment arising from its negative aspect. And yet it is also why we abide by a surreal aesthetic condition in contemporary popular culture in which value is understood according to conflicting racial conceptions, one of the present and another grounded in an anachronistic, antebellum belief in racial essence, in what might be called popular music's long slave era. In the spectral qualities of modern black music's animation, one can locate a double-sided beginning to the nation's audible past, bringing into resonant form Marx's reflection, "we suffer not only from the living, but from the dead."[70]

69. Du Bois, *The Gift of Black Folk*, 18. The illicit in Negro music also suggests that there is a racial aspect informing Western music more generally, if we subscribe to Peter Szendy's interesting rendering of listening as so many acts of theft. See Szendy, *Listen: A History of Our Ears* (New York: Fordham University Press, 2008).
70. Marx, "Preface to the First Edition" (1867), in *Capital*, vol. 1; *Karl Marx: Selected Writings*, ed. David McLellan (Oxford: Oxford University Press, 2000), 454. Bryan Wagner's conclusions about police power and blackness as a condition of statelessness seem resonant with my own discussions of the illicit, if, perhaps, with fewer negatively affirmative possibilities. See his *Disturbing the Peace: Black Culture and the Police Power after Slavery* (Cambridge, MA: Harvard University Press, 2009).

All the Marxes at the Big Store; or, General Fetishism

Peter Szendy

Translated by Charlotte Mandell

What happens when you play the piano in a department store?

Behind this seemingly naive question, behind the somewhat childlike surprise that can be roused when a keyboard is shifted from the concert hall or conservatory to a department store, there is a key issue that could be formulated in this way: at the crossroads of commercial exchanges, in this temple of commodity fetishism that is a department store, the piano and the person who plays it both become the site for an economy of transactions. Or rather, and more precisely, the piano and its pianist appear henceforth as the theater of a whole bodily commerce: what becomes manifest, what is noticed through their *traffic of organs*, is the organological market that they are.

What happens, then, what occurs, when one transposes a piano to make it play in the department store? That will be our insistent question, at once innocent and complex, at once naive and tricky or convoluted. And to try to answer it, the best thing is to witness the transposition of the instrument as it is portrayed by the Marx Brothers in their 1941 film, *The Big*

boundary 2 43:1 (2016)   DOI 10.1215/01903659-3340697   © 2016 by Duke University Press

Store. By following them in this move, we will also meet, on one floor or another of the big store, another Marx, their homonym, who was already there, on the watch, observing the secret life of merchandise.

• • • •

The credits to *The Big Store* are remarkable if you know how to watch them, for the vertical scrolling of the images—namely, the very movement of the cinematographic projections that makes frames follow each other on the unspooling film—are superimposed here and confused precisely with the upward movement of the elevator in a large department store: the viewer's point of view of these credits climbs from image to image as if he or she were climbing from floor to floor in the stock of merchandise exhibited for sale. The cinematography of the gaze marries the ascending mechanism, which is that of the buyer climbing the steps of the sanctuary of consumption.

The stylized images beneath these credits, in the shape of cartoon drawings that succeed each other vertically, give way to the first scene: the camera approaches—horizontally this time—a building identified as the Gotham Conservatory of Music and brings us inside. Close-up of Chico's hands. In front of a few admiring children who are listening to him in silence, he demonstrates his pianistic technique: a rising glissando with the middle finger of his right hand—like an elevator quickly climbing the C major scale key by key—as his straight forefinger is already preparing, like a pointed revolver, to hit the note it is aiming at, that note toward which the whole ascension of this manual elevator is headed. "You see, that's the way to play it," says Chico to those we suppose are his young pupils, in this singular conservatory, teaching a technique that is, to say the least, unorthodox, compared to the codification of piano fingering that developed over the course of the eighteenth and nineteenth centuries. (However, I will note here in parentheses: Chico's technique, that technique we could describe as *indexical*, does bring to mind certain fingerings recommended by François Couperin in his *L'Art de toucher le clavecin* [*The Art of Playing the Harpsichord*] in 1716.)

"You've got to practice," says Chico to his flock, thus encouraging them to replicate, reproduce, his gestures, to copy his bodily movements and organic dispositions as if it were a question of mass-producing images and then mass-distributing them. The film seems to promise what we could call the super-merchandising of Chico's singular digital technique, summoned to join a network of large-scale distribution made up of his students and the students of his students, clones and clones of clones of his glorious body. A network whose support or infrastructure is the keyboard, the real assembly line and production line where the corporeal organology of Marx & Sons, of Chico and his reproductions ad infinitum, is made.

"You've got to practice," he says to his little Gotham Conservatory students, these budding pianists who are called on to spread the image of his corporeal schema. "Not on this piano," replies one of the two movers who, suddenly storming into the room and interrupting Maestro Chico's lesson, threaten to seize the instrument and carry it away. Chico protests; he announces the imminent arrival of his friend, the singer Tommy Rogers (Tony Martin), who has recently become the wealthy heir to half the shares of the Phelps Department Store. Tommy, he says, will be able to help the conservatory survive; Tommy can arrange things so that the piano can stay where it is and the production or reproduction of Chico-at-the-keyboard images will continue.

Thus, even before the plot has moved to the big store, everything happens as if some market had already slipped into Chico's fingers and the keys they travel over, as if some supermarket were already traversing his digital technique and his tactile tactics, ensuring their reproducibility and their coining in multiple copies: the final image we see before the camera leaves the conservatory for the Phelps store is that of the four boys, lined up two by two at two pianos and executing four parallel glissandos with four middle fingers that transport four pointing forefingers, in an elevator-like movement leading to the punctuation of four staccato notes.

• • • •

Thus, what has been foreshadowed from afar, since the beginning of the film, and even before the actual plot gets under way, is the unforgettable scene where Harpo, much later, will play the harp in one of the display rooms of the big store. For there too, when the musician begins making music in the heart of the department store, what he is exposing, what he is causing to appear and become visible, is the infrastructure of exchanges that condition and allow his musical gestures as such.

In this room, luxuriously furnished with antique furniture, Harpo first discovers a music box that has on its turning lid two figurines, led by the small ritornello in a circular round dance. Then Harpo comes upon a mannequin whose posture he immediately mimics, standing next to it like its copy or image. And that is when the cinematographic gaze becomes the instrument of what Marx—the other Marx, the one of *Das Kapital*—described as commodity fetishism, namely, that animism by which things, as soon as they are exhibited for sale on the market, as soon as they refer to each other as exchange-values, are attributed with a soul, an autonomous movement, and even a voice.[1] With the help of a subtle dissolve, Harpo, in fact, takes the place of the mannequin; he becomes the living copy of this copy of the reified human figure so well that he plays, he literally interprets, the animation of the value-bearing commodity. In short, he embodies to the letter what his homonym, the author of *Capital*, called "the fantastic form of a relation between things" (*CL*, 165). The coat described by Karl Marx as representing a "supra-natural property" (*CL*, 149)—namely value—is well and truly endowed with life by Harpo Marx; everything occurs as if the clothes themselves began to move and greet each other, like what occurs in the famous prosopopoeia that concludes the first chapter of *Capital*: "If commodities could speak, they would say this: our use-value may interest men, but it does not belong to us as objects. What does belong to us as objects, however, is our value. Our own intercourse as commodities proves it. We relate to each other merely as exchange-values" (*CL*, 176–77).

Then, as if he were merely embodying that movement of mutual recognition between things, Harpo begins greeting himself in the mirrors. He exchanges a greeting with himself; he exchanges himself, so to speak, for himself in the mirrors of this room where his reflection is mirrored. We hesitate; we no longer know if it's Harpo who is becoming a thing by his reproduction in images or if it's the thing—the coat, the mannequin—that is becoming Harpo by animating itself. And this undecidability, as we will see, is already signaling toward what we will have to call a *general fetishism*.

When Harpo begins playing the harp, filmed in the point of a triangle between two reflections of himself, we witness another scene stemming from what we could call, along with Freud, "animatism."[2] In fact, just

1. Karl Marx, *Capital: Critique of Political Economy*, vol. 1, trans. Ben Fowkes (London: Penguin, 1976), esp. chap. 4 ("The General Formula for Capital"). The matter of the soul of commodities (*Warenseele*) is also discussed throughout the first chapter: "the soul of value" (*Wertseele*) of the coat is "recognized" by the cloth (143); the economist speaks from "the depths of the soul of commodities" (177). Hereafter, this work is cited parenthetically as *CL*.

2. Sigmund Freud, *Totem and Taboo*, trans. James Strachey (London: Routledge and Keegan Paul, 1950), 91: "The technique of animism, magic, reveals in the clearest . . . way an intention to impose the laws governing mental life upon real things; in this, spirits need not as yet play any part. . . . The assumptions of magic are more fundamental and older than the doctrine of spirits, which forms the kernel of animism. Our psycho-analytic point of view coincides here with a theory . . . [which] postulates a pre-animistic stage before

as Harpo had previously become an animated copy of the mannequin, so now it's Harpo's double in the mirror who begins playing notes that Harpo "himself" is not playing. Harpo is the first to be surprised by this autonomy acquired by his copy, but he quickly adapts to it and seemingly derives a lot of pleasure from it, which becomes even more intense when the scene ends with the abyssal multiplication of Harpo in a cascade of images: repeated ad infinitum in countless mirrored copies of himself, he continuously repeats ascending and descending glissandos on his instrument, all the while seeming to sink as well into the horizontal density of the visible, in a striated glissando of himself.[3]

What is happening, then, in this big store that makes Harpo and Chico enter the fantastic world of commodity? Nothing new, of course; nothing other than the observation of what was already there without being visible: namely, the structure of exchangeability inherent in the musician's body, that is, that iterability and equivalence that inhabit each of his or her gestures, allowing their very musicality to be identified in them. For what else does this musicality result from but the possibility that it can detach itself from its singular occurrence? What makes an ordinary body into a musician's body other than the fact that its body language (*gestualité*) begins in a way to float above itself, at once incorporated and disembodied: "material immaterial" (*sinnlich übersinnlich*), as Marx writes about "commodity form" (*Warenform*) (*CL*, 143).

. . . .

To understand how the musicality of a body stems necessarily from what we will soon have to describe as *general fetishism*, we would have to dive back into the long and complex history of keyboard techniques — which I have done elsewhere and will not repeat here.[4] I will simply recall this remarkable statement by Carl Philipp Emanuel Bach in his *Essay on the True Art of Playing Keyboard Instruments* (1753): at bottom, it is a matter, he writes, only of "comfortably getting so to speak as many fingers as we need" (*bequem so viel Finger gleichsam kriegen als wir brauchen*). It is

---

animism, the character of which is best indicated by the term 'animatism,' the doctrine of the universality of life." Freud is borrowing this concept of animatism from the British anthropologist Robert Marett.

3. This scene in *The Big Store* should be compared with the famous mirror scene in *Duck Soup*, where the distinction between the original and the image of Groucho becomes radically undecidable, since they exchange places.

4. See Peter Szendy, *Membres fantômes: Des corps musiciens* (Paris: Minuit, 2002).

a phrase that, if he weren't mute, could have been placed in the mouth of Harpo, who ends up comfortably obtaining, in the mirror of himself, as many Harpos as he needs to form an orchestra with himself.

Even better: it's Chico we could imagine making this old phrase into a new reply to utter with his priceless Italian accent ("as a-many a-fingers as a-we need!"). For it is he who, without ever seeming to make the slightest effort, exemplarily tries to obtain as many fingers as he needs. Even more, always more, not hesitating, in this digital or organic market of exchanges, to profit from the surplus-value of any supernumerary object that can come (dare I say) to hand.

Let's look, leaving the big store for a little while in order to better return to it, at the brief piano recital Chico gives in *Go West* (1940). We witness a kind of infinite digital variation on a tune entitled "The Woodpecker Song." Now we see the forefinger of his right hand detach from the rest of the fingers, as if it had been sent on assignment to an isolated key. Now we see it enter a game of exchanges that, around the pivot of the pinky finger, makes it symmetrically equivalent with the thumb, whose note it repeats two octaves higher. Now it is carried along a rising glissando by the other folded-in fingers, to be propelled by them as their representative to the very top of the keyboard. Now it folds in on itself, curls under, to knock against the raised lid of the piano (thus imitating the woodpecker in the song), as its homologue on the left hand is held in the air, stretched out in its admonishing function, drawing attention to what is being played on the other side. At times, the right forefinger even sways, floating above the keyboard, content to indicate silently the virtual journeys over the keys.

Still, this fetish forefinger, the privileged substitute for the other fingers, is itself substitutable, notably by the middle finger that, during a few measures, can in fact take its place as the pointing or indicating finger. Unless we should think that the forefinger is being doubled, like Harpo in the mirror of the big store, that it is being divided into two forefingers, recto and verso so to speak, two forefingers in one that take turns in one direction and the other on the same repeated key. But in the end, we should enlarge the space of this keyboard economy; we should include in this minimarket of exchanges on the keyboard all the possible substitutes that could be introduced. For example, the apple that Harpo is getting ready to bite: Chico seizes it to make it the prosthetic instrument of exhilarating trills on the keys, which virtuosically conclude this piece of bravura during which exchanging organs (forefinger, middle finger, etc.) and inanimate things (the keyboard, the lid, the apple) will have been confronted with each other.

What can we learn from this brief analysis of Chico's playing? The forefinger is one finger among others that can be exchanged, substituted indiscriminately for some other (the middle finger, the pinky, etc.). But this same forefinger also stands out exemplarily as the absolute finger, since it also has the indexical function of indicating what it is doing (it then becomes, from the left hand to the right hand, the announcer of itself). So it serves a dual purpose, being both an index finger[5] and an index of index. So much so that the index finger detaches from itself, as if to indicate what it will do. Or better, as if to place everything it does within quotation marks. The index finger, in that it is always an index of index, in that it doubles all its gestures with a gesture indicating these very gestures, in that it becomes *its own double*—the index finger constantly grasps, cites already each of its movements as it executes them. And that is why it is, in Chico's fascinating playing, the musical finger par excellence.[6]

• • • •

Before returning with the Marxes to their big store, before we continue to pace up and down with them this bazaar where so many fetishes circulate, we have to pause to try to pin down what appears as a *general fetishism*, according to the expression offered by Jacques Derrida in *Glas*.[7]

5. In the United States, this finger is aptly referred to as the "pointer finger."—Eds.

6. A dozen years before *Go West* and *The Big Store*, in 1929 (the year of *The Cocoanuts*, the Marx Brothers' first film), Walt Disney Studios produced a wonderful little cartoon called "The Opry House" (youtu.be/KjxVJwH_89o). Here we see Mickey giving a piano recital during which his singular fingering technique resembles Chico's in more than one way. Especially by his use of the index finger, which becomes here more than ever indexical or indicative, insofar as he seems to have the ability to control the keys from a distance by pointing at them like a revolver. Thus, little by little, the pianist and his piano detach from each other. Mickey becomes superfluous; he can be completely forgotten, replaced by the piano and the stool, those inanimate things that become animated and play on their own.

7. Jacques Derrida, *Glas*, trans. John P. Leavey (Lincoln: University of Nebraska Press, 1990). Indeed, the expression "general fetishism" already appears in Charles de Brosses's *Du culte des dieux fétiches* from 1760. After discussing "the Yucatan peninsula in America" (46), de Brosses declares that "fetishism is no less general in all the regions of America" (48). Already in the beginning of his book, de Brosses points out the generalization he is about to make based on the "cult . . . of certain earthly and material objects called Fetishes among African Negroes . . . & that for this reason I will call Fetishism": "I ask to be permitted to make common use of this expression: & although in its proper definition, it refers particularly to the belief of the Negroes of Africa, I will point out in advance that I count on using it as well in speaking of any other nation, among whom cult objects are animals, or inanimate beings that are deified; even sometimes in speaking of certain peoples for whom objects of this kind are not so many Gods properly speaking,

For we must understand with the greatest rigor the generalization that is at play: fetishism becomes generalized not when one applies a concept of fetish that remains intact in its formulation to all possible objects or situations but rather when we can no longer distinguish or contrast the fetish-substitute from its thing-origin, so much so that there is no longer anything but fetish, with the temporary and always unstable effects of fetishism in a strict or limited sense.

What are these effects, and how can they be described based on this general fetishism, for which the Marx Brothers' department store is at once theater and allegory? If we turn now to another discourse on fetishism, namely, the brief article that Freud published in 1927 and that served Derrida as a starting point for the generalization he proposed, we find an analysis of the fetish over which we should linger. Not so much for the famous definition Freud gives of the sexual fetish—which is, he says while remarking that he thus risks "arousing disappointment," a "substitute for the woman's (mother's) phallus which the little boy once believed in and does not wish to forego"[8]—but rather for the quasi-cinematographic nature of his description:

> It seems rather that when the fetish comes to life, . . . some pro-
> cess has been suddenly interrupted—it reminds one of the abrupt
> halt made by memory [*das Haltmachen der Erinnerung*] in trau-

---

but things endowed with a divine virtue, oracles, amulets, & protecting talismans: for it is constant enough that all these manners of thinking have at bottom only a single source, & that this is only the accessory of a general Religion widely spread throughout the whole Earth, which should be examined separately, as forming a particular class among the various Pagan Religions" (10–11). After de Brosses, we find a number of authors using the expression "general fetishism," but always, as in de Brosses, to indicate the generalized application of a concept that remains unchanged. Derrida is the first person, to my knowledge, to carry this generalization into the concept itself, when he writes, "Despite all the variations it can be subjected to, the concept of fetish bears an unvarying predicate: it is a substitute—for the thing itself as center and . . . origin of presence. . . . If what has always been called 'fetish,' in all critical discourse, implies reference to a non-substitutive thing, there should be somewhere—and this is the truth of the fetish, the connection of fetish to truth—a decidable value of fetish, a decidable opposition of fetish to non-fetish. . . . And yet, . . . there might be, especially with Freud, enough not to shatter but reconstruct from its generalization a 'concept' of fetish that no longer lets itself be contained in . . . the Ersatz/non-Ersatz opposition" (*Glas*, 209, trans. modified). The de Brosses quotes are from the original 1760 French edition of *Du culte des dieux fétiches*, gallica.bnf.fr /ark:/12148/bpt6k106440f.

8. Sigmund Freud, "Fetishism," trans. Joan Riviere, in *Collected Papers*, vol. 5, ed. James Strachey (London: Hogarth Press, 1953), 199.

matic amnesias. In the case of the fetish, too, interest is held up at a certain point [*bleibt das Interesse wie unterwegs stehen*]—what is possibly the last impression received before the uncanny traumatic one is preserved as a fetish [*wird etwa der letzte Eindruck vor dem unheimlichen, traumatischen, als Fetisch festgehalten*]. Thus the foot or shoe, or part of it, owes its attraction as a fetish to the circumstance that the inquisitive boy used to peer up the woman's legs towards her genitals [*von unten, von den Beinen her*].[9]

The fetish, in short, is the pause of the elevator of the gaze that travels from floor to floor in the movement of general interchangeability. The fetish rises up, it is formed and stabilized, when the cinematography of generalized fetishism freezes in its low-angle shot, when it is stuck at some floor or other of the big store of exchanges: as Paul-Laurent Assoun says so well in his reading of Freudian theory, "everything stems from the 'kinetic' aspect of the scene and its stopping-point," for the "fetish-object" is at bottom nothing but a "*freeze-frame [arrêt sur image]*."[10]

It's from this point that we should now return to *The Big Store*. We had entered, remember, by taking the elevator up through the credits, by merging with this ascending cinematic gaze that made us travel up the stacked heap of merchandise, while still pausing, regularly halting, in this very movement. If it is true that fetishism, as Freud would have us think of it, is both the movement of the circulation of desire passing from substitute to substitute *and* the freeze-frame interrupting this general kinematics, then we should pay extra attention to all elevators that, well beyond the credits at the beginning, constantly pierce through the big store, glide up and down *The Big Store* while making images slip past.[11]

· · · ·

It is impossible to describe here all the occurrences of this glissando of the elevator, which we see everywhere. The famous choral number of sales personnel, led by Groucho to the wild rhythm of a tune called "Sing

9. Freud, "Fetishism," 201, trans. modified.

10. Paul-Laurent Assoun, *Le fétichisme* (Paris: Presses universitaires de France, 1994), 85–86.

11. Corresponding to the credits at the beginning, there is, at the other end of the film, the inscription "The End," which detaches from the background in a swift descending movement in which the floors of the big store stream past one last time, this time from top to bottom.

While You Sell," begins in the elevator, whose symbol also seems to haunt the words sung ("Sales will mount up to the skies!" exclaims Groucho in front of the ecstatic employees). Later on, in the hilarious scene that begins with the arrival of a large Italian family, the father, following Groucho's suggestion, presses a button and thus makes a four-level bed rise up, like an elevator, containing Harpo and Chico, who scroll past as if they were in the frames of a film. In this same scene, Harpo manipulates a generalized keyboard of bed-elevators, making them rise and descend like vast glissandos on the floor-keys of the big store. Finally, just before the happy ending, in the long chase sequence between the store manager and the three Marx brothers, the elevator explicitly becomes the place where the holding or the freezing of the frame is at play: what must be seized, recaptured from the other, is the photograph that constitutes the proof of the conspiracy against Tommy, a photo that travels from hand to hand or floor to floor.

Just as there is everywhere in *The Big Store* what we could call "elevatoriality," so it must be admitted that the principle of the keyboard is at work here well beyond the pianos we see appearing here and there. There is not only the unforgettable typewriter endowed with a flying roller ("typeflying machine"), on the keyboard of which Harpo, in the office of the private detective Groucho, is playing, types with deafening noise and drowns out the tale of the widow Phelps (Margaret Dumont). But it is, in the final analysis, all the striated, or, in one way or another, discretized series that in this sense form potential keyboards, from the strings of a harp to the bells of a giant carillon made up of lamps hanging from the store's ceiling, which Harpo travels across by leaping from one to the other as if he were stringing together the arpeggio of a perfect chord.

In short, the keyboardization of the world is the pleasure taken in this becoming-substitutable of things, the premise for their musicalization, for the celebration of their general interchangeability.

The elevator and the keyboard, as we see, are the two apparatuses, the two mechanisms, that animate the department store of general fetishism: on the one hand, they ensure the streaming of images or the procession of notes; they allow the circulation of exchanges and substitutions without which there would be neither film nor music. On the other hand, they are also striated—key by key and frame by frame; they bear the mark of all the freeze-frames and all the stuck keys where our gaze and our listening are frozen, captured.

Dialect and Dialectic in "The Working Day" of Marx's *Capital*

Rosalind C. Morris

I have always been moved by "The Working Day" chapter of Marx's *Capital* (volume 1).[1] Above all others, it holds me captive with its seamless movement between analytic and descriptive prose, its deft negotiation of argument and polemic. The caustic wit and searing indictments of the text are counterbalanced with unrelenting empiricism to convince readers of the labor theory of value. Much has been done to displace that theory over the last three decades, and consequently, the power of the text as a model of dialectical method has been increasingly overlooked. This is a grave loss, for the chapter is as aesthetically masterful as it is analytically astute. Moreover, and despite being overshadowed by the spectral and specular melodrama of the chapter on the fetish-character of commodities, "The Working Day" is particularly exemplary in its account of how abstrac-

1. Karl Marx, "The Working Day," in *Capital: A Critique of Political Economy*, vol. 1, trans. Ben Fowkes (London: Penguin, [1867] 1976), 340–416. Hereafter, this work is cited parenthetically as *C*, followed by references to the German *Gesamtausgabe* edition, *Das Kapital: Kritik der Politischen Ökonomie. Erster Band. Hamburd 1972. Gesamtausgabe, Band 6* (Berlin: Dietz Verlag, 1987), cited as *MEGA*.

boundary 2 43:1 (2016)   DOI 10.1215/01903659-3340709   © 2016 by Duke University Press

tion works concretely, and how the concrete realizes abstraction. One must therefore attune oneself to the sensuous to grasp its theoretical project. It is for this reason that I speak of being moved.

"The Working Day" moves me in a very particular manner, one whose phenomenal dimension bears theoretical significance. Quite simply, it speaks to me. It does so in the most literal and the most metaphorical senses—assuming the fictitious possibility of distinguishing between these two. No doubt, this sense of being affected and intimately addressed is related to a certain disciplinary affinity. As much as in any other text of Marx's oeuvre, including the ethnological notebooks, "The Working Day" reaches toward ethnography in its reading and deployment of reported speech. The text is built upon an evidentiary scaffold that gives to such speech a singular role—and even the role of signifying the singular. Alongside Edmund Burke and Diodorus Siculus, Hegel, Horace, and, of course, Shakespeare, the discourse of the children employed in factories sounds forth from the reports of the inspectors of factories and the commissions on child labor. Plaintive, unself-conscious, without guile or sentimentality, they give to "The Working Day" a texture, if not a grain, in Roland Barthes's sense.[2] These voices appear only in the form of a trace, it is true. Nonetheless, in their marked exteriority to Standard English, they give to be read the somatic history of a body shaped by the conditions of labor in the factories of industrializing Britain. Transcribed and redacted, but retaining syntactic and grammatical blemishes, the reported speech of the children is sufficiently coarse as to chafe at the seemingly smooth discourse of the phantasmatic worker, whose voice is heard "arising" on the factory floor in the opening pages. And it is in the dialectical movement between these two voicings—of "The Worker," impossibly unitary and in command of the master's discourse, on one hand; and the workers of the factory floor, speaking in a mother tongue they do not fully possess, on the other—that "The Working Day" chapter assumes its force and achieves its performative mastery. This movement calls us to think about the structural relationship between workers and The Worker, between the positing of a class position and the subjection to a system that enables such positing. It opens onto the future history of revolutionary politics and it calls forward the long history of the discourse on class to which Marx was heir and which bore within itself the metaphysical seduction of a historically concluding synthesis.

In evoking these scraps of overheard speech, I do not mean to imply

---

2. Roland Barthes, "The Grain of the Voice," in *The Responsibility of Forms*, trans. Richard Howard (New York: Hill and Wang, 1985).

that "The Working Day" gives voice to the subalterns of the English factory floor. The reported speech of the children is not the presencing of those otherwise dispossessed urchins any more than the citations of ethnography constitute a moment of authentic self-representation, in which cultural others address their future audiences with the truth of their desire to be heard. It is not their subjective consciousnesses that speak from the text; the quotations are merely the evidence of an interpellative exchange in which they perform their own exteriority to dominant discourse, while providing the longed-for information of sociological accounting. Nor does the dramaturgy of the chapter enlivened by this reportage consist in the solicitation of sympathy via the narration of tragedy. To be sure, there is pathos to be found in "The Working Day"'s final capitulation to liberal contract—"the 'modest Magna Carta' of the legally limited working day" (*C*, 416; *MEGA*, 302). But if the chapter speaks, and not only to me, it is for other reasons; it is because it addresses the ear. "The Working Day" chapter addresses the ear through the fiction of a singularity that would be capable of writing itself in dialect, as dialect. In doing so, it makes audible the nature of the Marxian dialectic itself.

This essay is an exploration of the relationship between dialect and dialectic in "The Working Day" chapter of *Capital*. I write the title of Marx's work in English, for it is the English edition that speaks to me, in my mother tongue—though not in the maternal voice. The reasons for this particular resonance are not merely autobiographical, however. For the intimacy between dialect and dialectic becomes most audible in the English version of the text, as it has come to us in the aftermath of Eleanor Marx's editorial restitution of the original English reports cited by Marx in the first German edition and revised in later ones. This, despite the fact that English shares with German the etymological and phonetic linkage between the words, *dialekt*/dialect and *dialektic*/dialectic—an artifact of their shared roots.

In 1847, Marx could write, somewhat sardonically, that it was Proudhon who had made him speak English, but what he meant by English then was the discourse of David Ricardo's economics. Marx's own critique of a language inseparable from liberalism's discourse was made in French and would not be translated into English until 1900. By 1882, however, he could complain about the mistranslations of excerpts from *Capital* in the otherwise enthusiastic reports on his work that had appeared in *Modern Thought*.[3]

3. Karl Marx, "Letter to Friedrich Alfred Sorge, in Hoboken," December 15, 1881, in *Karl Marx, Frederick Engels: Collected Works*, vol. 46, trans. Rodney Livingstone et al. (New York: International Publishers, 1992), 24–25.

It was, however, not only in deference to her father's newly acquired concern with English precision that Eleanor Marx undertook the task of "re-Englishing" the text of *Capital*. She devoted herself to the labor, with more than filial piety, so that it would be immune to the kind of criticism that had been directed at Marx when, in 1872, the Berlin *Concordia* had published an article accusing him of misquoting and even of fabricating citations from the April 1863 speech of British chancellor of the exchequer William Gladstone. Although this was not the case, Engels himself acknowledged that Marx's early reliance on French translations of English-speaking economic theorists had, on occasion, as in his readings of James Steuart, "yielded a different shade of meaning . . . and other similar instances of trifling inaccuracy."[4] He did not deem the translational artifacts significant for the overall argument, however, and insisted that the "laborious process of emendation has not produced the smallest change in the book worth speaking of."[5]

In the case of the restored English reports, then, what is at stake is not a matter of fidelity to the original argument or accuracy of interpretation. It is, rather, the affirmation of a sensuous, phenomenally perceptible dimension to class that can be conveyed and felt across the flat abstractions of the page. This material dimension of an always already dialectical formation will constitute something like a remainder before the fact, that which threatens the fantasy of an identity between the singular and the universal and which therefore demands the dialectical *method*—not merely as an analytical procedure but as the ground of a political practice without guarantees and open to the future. We shall consider both of these dimensions of dialectical practice in the pages below. I will nonetheless begin with a few further remarks about Marx's English, as well his English literature.

Perhaps nowhere else in the world is the intimacy between class and speech so profound than in England, so it is not surprising that it is in the speech of the English workers that the violence of class makes itself detectable in the English edition of *Capital*. For this reason, perhaps, there are no accompanying descriptions of the waifs and hardy young lads who speak in the marked idioms of the workers. Almost nowhere does a mise-en-scène provide this speech with an accompanying image. The language, we might say, is the form of appearance (*Erscheinungsform*) of class. At the same time, and without relinquishing a recognition of the graphological dimension

4. Frederick Engels, "Preface to the Fourth Edition," in *Capital*, 1:114–20, esp. 114–15.
5. Engels, "Preface," 115.

of the entextualized speech, we might refer to this as the form of audibility of class. In the broken syntax, the pronomial confusion, and the grammatical errors of the English reports, so distant from the Standard English in which both Marx and the capitalist speak, one encounters the material—properly audiovisual—trace of a class-divided system. This lack of standardization is precisely what reveals legal and economic equality to be a mere "fiction." Nonetheless, and despite Marx's tendency to reduce the category of fiction to the status of the illusory, on a par with the fetishistic and the occult, it is by reading Marx's "Working Day" chapter *in the mode of literary fiction* that we grasp the particular work that voice does in the theory of political subjectivity elaborated there. The mode of this fiction is characterological, but it is not psychological. And it possesses nothing of the *Bildungsroman*, with its narration of character formation across the lifetime. Nonetheless, the chapter's theme is time: not only the time of labor and labor-time, but the temporal and yet untimely process of positing the future subject of revolution. Let us, then, consider how these two dimensions, the characterological and the temporal, are brought together via the intertextual practice of "The Working Day" chapter, and then proceed to an account of the specific problematic of voice in the development of a dialectical method.

In the Time of Literature

Marx himself gave credit to the "current splendid brotherhood [which included Miss Brontë and Mrs. Gaskell] of fiction-writers in England, whose graphic and eloquent pages have issued to the world more political and social truths than have been uttered by all the professional politicians, publicists and moralists put together."[6] Nonetheless, the uncited intertextual references of "The Working Day" chapter do not embrace the current splendid fiction. Rather, they point backward, to earlier texts, from Shakespeare to the Old Testament/Tanakh. The first such reference occurs when The Worker's voice rises above the "sound and fury" of the production process. The phrase summons Shakespeare's soliloquy on the burden of fate and the futility of life from the latter moments of *Macbeth*, and calls forth the question of time as its corollary. Shakespeare gives to the doomed general a melancholy sense of belatedness that expresses itself in the desire to have his wife's death displaced into the future. Her death has come

6. Karl Marx, abstract of "The English Working Class," in *New York Tribune* (1854), www .marxists.org/archive/marx/works/1854/08/01.htm.

too soon, and Macbeth will not resign himself to the notion that there is a "time for everything," as the narrator of Ecclesiastes would have it, except by assigning "the word" itself to temporal finitude. "She should have died hereafter; / there would have been a time for such a word. / Tomorrow and tomorrow and tomorrow."[7] It is this repetitive drumbeat of time that Marx calls up in the opening section of "The Working Day," but he evokes the final lines of the soliloquy with mordant irony; tomorrow names the horizon of deferral by which value accumulates and to which debt is owed, and time itself is grasped as the object and the medium of capitalism's intervention, the source of its surplus. If, therefore, the fateful word could be temporalized and natural law thereby evaded in the wish fulfillment of Shakespeare's *Macbeth*, it is the naturalization of law that concerns Marx in his account of how capital extracts surplus value from laborers through the theft of their time in "The Working Day." Beyond this revelatory reversal, however, is the embedded biblical referent to which both texts make recourse.

It is, from a certain perspective, possible to read "The Working Day" chapter as an ironic response to the call of the biblical discourse upon labor, one born of the shared question: "What profit hath he that worketh in that wherein he laboureth?" (King James Bible), or as the New International Version bluntly puts it, "What do workers gain from their toil?" (Eccles. 3:9). The differences between them may make the invocation (which is not yet a comparison) appear specious, but the structural affinity between the mythotext of the Old Testament/Tanakh and Marx's chapter is revealing. What the juxtaposition casts into relief is neither an ideology that makes of labor a virtue (though that is implicit) nor secular nihilism in a pre-Nietzschean form, but the characterological dimension of Marx's textual practice. It takes over the device of the speaker-cum-pedagogue (son of David in Ecclesiastes, The Worker in *Capital*) and places the capitalist in the position of the auditing divinity. It is in this context that the question of voice acquires its significance and its force. Let me then quote the oft-cited passage from "The Working Day" in which The Worker appears, or rather is heard, to speak. This event rends the text, interrupting both the discourse of capital and the analytic to which it is being subject: "Suddenly, however, there arises the voice of the worker, which had previously been stifled in the sound and fury of the production process" (*C*, 342; *MEGA*, 240).[8]

7. William Shakespeare, *Macbeth*, ed. A. R. Braunmuller (New York: Cambridge University Press, 1984), 5.5.17–19.
8. The German original reads as follows: "Plötzlich aber erebt sich die Stimme des Arbeiters, die im Sturm und Drang des Producktionsprocesses verstummt war."

The Worker speaks in a mellifluous prose and engages in a kind of disputation that presumes his equality with the capitalist, whom he greets in the market as a seller meets a buyer. He explains that "the commodity that I have sold you differs from the ordinary crowd of commodities in that its use creates value, a greater value than it costs" (*C*, 342; *MEGA*, 240). But this apparently indisputable fact, to which the capitalist is expected to accede, opens onto a point of difference that can only be gasped as the function of the different perspectives of capital and labor, which is to say the different placement of the auditors in the field of interest. Class is presented here not merely as a structure of interests determined by a relation to the means of production; it is an epistemic situation. "What appears on your side as the valorization of the capital is on my side an excess expenditure of labour-power" (*C*, 342; *MEGA*, 240).

What follows is a careful exposition, a veritable pedagogical set piece, which assumes the presence of a third party eavesdropping on the exchange. That third party is the individual laborer-cum-reader who will identify with The Worker that speaks. But The Worker, as the fictive figure in the impossible dialogue between false equals, speaks in the second person, mobilizing the structure of the "I-Thou" relation, only to mock it with an analytic of inequality: "The consumption of the commodity belongs not to the seller who parts with it, but to the buyer who acquires it. The use of my daily labour-power therefore belongs to you" (*C*, 343; *MEGA*, 240). The Worker continues to explain that "by means of the price" paid for it, he must reproduce that power every day, because he must "be able to work tomorrow" (*C*, 343; *MEGA*, 240). Thus creeps in this petty pace; the reference to Shakespeare, and thus to Ecclesiastes, continues in this barely legible form. But the capitalist's desire to extend the working day threatens even the possibility of eternal return: "By an unlimited extension of the working day, you may in one day use up a quantity of labour-power greater than I can restore in three. What you gain in labour, I lose in the substance of labour" (*C*, 343; *MEGA*, 240). Not only is there an irreducible difference between labor value and the substance of labor, between representation and the real, but the two are subject to different temporalities of both reproduction and amortization (the deathly signification of the term *amortization* should be heard clanging in this phrase).

The phantasmatic exchange between The Capitalist and The Worker continues apace here, moving into the mathematical calculation of rates of expropriation across a working life span of thirty years. Finally, the scene closes in a crescendo of indignation:

I therefore demand a working day of normal length, and I demand it without any appeal to your heart, for in money matters, sentiment is out of place. You may be a model citizen, perhaps a member of the R.S.P.C.A., and you may be in the odour of sanctity as well; but the thing you represent when you come face to face with me has no heart in its breast. What seems to throb there is my own heartbeat. I demand a normal working day because, like every other seller, I demand the value of my commodity. (*C*, 343; *MEGA*, 241)

Self-consciously claiming to inhabit the discourse of reason, The Worker delivers his own rationale for a demand that, despite its vehemence, remains trapped within the conventions of the "normal." Such is the "modest Magna Carta" with which Marx bitterly closes the chapter. Not incidentally, the form of this last declaration is purely performative; like the promise, the assertion of a demand recoils upon itself. The truth of the statement (that a demand is indeed being made) cannot guarantee the outcome demanded. In this sense, then, the imaginary lecture dissolves into the fictive space of its appearance, when it first sounded forth as an interruption of the capitalist's discourse.

Recall that the capitalist is in the midst of his own thought, ventriloquized by Marx in a form of indirect third-person narration. Having been described as a mere personification of capital, whose "soul is the soul of capital," and whose "sole driving force" is to "valorize itself," the capitalist "*takes his stand* on the law of commodity exchange" (*C*, 342; *MEGA*, 239, emphasis added). Here, English benefits from the homonymic play that renders the *soul* of capital as one possessed by a *sole* driving force (*Trieb*), but only insofar as the language is sounded. If it is permitted to resonate in the ear, the monomaniacal and the vampiric rhetoric gives way to a kind of possession. But if the aura of the séance suffuses this linguistically overdetermined passage (in the translation Marx did not see), the implied scene is that of a courtroom. The capitalist takes his stand. He is answered by a prosecutorial would-be dictator of proletarian interest.

Insofar as the law is repeatedly posited by Marx as a fiction, the first juridical fiction being that society is founded upon law rather than law upon society, the scenario in which the capitalist takes the stand and is interrupted by The Worker is thus fictive.[9] Or rather, insofar as The Worker

---

9. Marx makes this argument in several contexts, perhaps most bluntly in the article "The Trial of the Rhenish District Committee of Democrats," *Neue Rheinische Zeitung*, nos. 231 and 232, in *Karl Marx, Frederick Engels: Collected Works*, vol. 8, trans. Dutt Clemens et al. (New York: International Publishers, 1977), 323–29.

speaks as the bearer of class interest, addressing the capitalist who is, himself, the personification of capital, it does so as a fiction, and more specifically a characterological fiction. Only as such a fiction can The Worker master capital's discourse and deliver a speech unmarked by social exclusion. And only in this unmarked form can such speech be imagined capable of reaching its target and achieving that transparency and communicative efficacy that leaves nothing unsaid and that says nothing unintended. Nonetheless, it is not merely The Worker who arises here in the form of a fiction. For the capitalist, too, is a figure of fiction, albeit of a different order. The difference is that between the existent fiction and the fiction that marks the place of the inexistent, as well as the not yet existent.

As already stated, the capitalist is a mere personification of that which constitutes the only Subject of history, namely capital. He is thus analogous to the sovereign: a fiction, but one that exists. Marx adduces the existent fiction in his *Notes for a Critique of Hegel's Philosophy of Right* in a discussion of two kinds of sovereignty: that which ostensibly comes into being in the form of a monarch and that which arises within a people. The former is, for Marx, a mere fiction, albeit one that exists. The nature of this fiction is related to the nature of the dialectic, for monarchy is "democracy in contradiction with itself."[10] Because monarchy subsumes beneath itself a whole society, it makes a single mode of existence (the political constitution) stand for the totality, whereas in Marx's analysis, the political constitution ought to comprise only one instance of a society's self-determination. The political structure of sovereignty relates to the economic logic by analogy. Under capitalism, the capitalist appropriates for himself what is the product not of the people per se but of the people as the bearers of labor-power. It is in this capacity that The Worker addresses him. And it is as the bearer of labor-power that he speaks. But, insofar as The Worker is the being in which the difference between *average socially necessary* labor-power and surplus labor-power is marked and manipulated, The Worker

10. Karl Marx, *Critique of Hegel's Philosophy of Right*, trans. Annette Jolin and Joseph O'Malley (Cambridge: Cambridge University Press, [1843] 1977), 25. The translation of this work is notoriously various, including the title *Zur Kritik der Hegelschen Rechtsphilosophie*, which is represented as either Hegel's Philosophy of "Right" or of "Law." The edition included in the *Collected Works*, for example, renders the phrase quoted above as follows: "Monarchy is necessarily democracy inconsistent with itself" (*Karl Marx, Frederick Engels: Collected Works*, vol. 3, trans. Jack Cohen et al. [New York: International Publishers, 2005], 29). The German text reads: "Die Monarchie ist notwendig Demokratie als Inkonsequenz gegen sich selbst." In *Karl Marx/Friedrich Engels – Werke* (Berlin: Dietz Verlag, 1976), 1:203–333, esp. 230.

can speak as the bearer of labor-power only in generalized terms. In other words, The Worker that might be capable of dictating the interests of the proletariat is an inexistent but possible fiction, speaking on the basis of a process of abstraction. It is for this reason that I continue, with such stubborn obviousness, to indicate the word with the upper case letters to mark its status as exception and to mark it as a categorical noun rather than a particular descriptor. These typographical conventions permit the word to signify itself as a nonreferential term, a concept, properly speaking. The question that arises in this context concerns the possibility that this inexistent figure might be realized and what its relationship to "actually existing workers" could be. That question is not theorized in "The Working Day." But it is sounded.

Time and Time Again, in a Manner of Speaking

According to certain conventions of Marxism, one should read "The Working Day" chapter as an excursus upon labor-time and as an analysis of the ways in which it is made the medium of surplus value extraction. The chapter commences with an assertion that the previously operative assumption, namely that labor-power is "bought and sold at its value" is an illusory scenario in which two equal values are exchanged in the market. To the contrary, Marx will demonstrate how capital operates on the basis of the divisibility of time, and on the particular manipulation of the difference between (average socially) necessary labor-time and surplus labor-time, where the former is determined by the function of reproducing labor-power. He will argue that the working day is far from self-evident as an object of quantification, a duration to be measured. It is a mysterious concept, one that is "capable of being determined, but in and for itself indeterminate" (*C*, 341; *MEGA*, 238).[11]

At the most obvious level, the relation between the determined and the indeterminate has to do with the strange nature of human labor-power, which can be intensified and multiplied by social division and technological supplementation but which nonetheless has limits. However, determination is not merely a question of physical limits or even of moral sentiment. It is also a question of law—of the juridical system within which labor-power becomes a commodity subject to contract and of the legislated limits to the working day itself. This is why the establishment of the dialogue

11. "Der Arbeitstag ist daher bestimmbar, aber an und für sich unbestimmt."

between capital and The Worker takes place within the idiomaticity of the courtroom. Now, insofar as law is dictation—whether of the sovereign, the people, or the interests of capital—the question of determination with which Marx opens "The Working Day" is posed from the outset as a question of the relation between the saying and the said.[12] The German-language version of the text opens this question in a relatively overt manner. In German, the resonance between determined and indeterminate, *bestimmbar* and *unbestimmt*, contains within it the echo of a voice, *Stimme*, otherwise absent in the English. According to a certain residual signification, that which is determined/*bestimmt* is that given by divine commandment, and which therefore appears fated. *Bestimmt* is the word made flesh, the said as the congelation and permanent presence of absolute performativity.

We can excavate this metaphorical affinity between the concept of voice (the medium of the said and the saying) and the question of determinateness from within the German and transfer it to the English context. But not because etymology guarantees (determines) the meaning of the word. Rather, to borrow from Maurice Blanchot, the indeterminateness of the word *determined* (*bestimmt*) draws it into a space in which the question of voicing can be heard to resonate at the center of the dialectical method.[13] To understand this, we must attend to the speaking of the workers, and specifically those workers who appear to fall beneath the threshold of possible representation. They are the children of the factories, as well as the women and the girls: in a word, the subalterns. More importantly, the male children are permitted to stand for the subalterns in general. These are the

---

12. There is, of course, a long tradition that insists upon the irreducibility of the saying to the said. If proper names may be permitted to stand in for these traditions, we would want to invoke the names of Jacques Lacan, Paul Ricoeur, Emmanuel Levinas, and Jacques Derrida, though many others might as easily be adduced: Tzvetan Todorov, Clifford Geertz, Edward Said, among them. Lacan's insistence on the distinction between the *énoncé* and the *énonciation* (the latter better translated as "the enunciating" than "enunciation," as is common) is here foundational, though his own position on the matter shifted over the course of his writings. I do not mean to imply that the saying is in any way autonomous vis-à-vis the said. To the contrary, I assume that the latter cannot be accessed except through the saying and, moreover, that the relation between these two levels is not one of isomorphism or homology. Hence, what is accessed is not to be thought of as a mere referent. Nonetheless, there is a relation between these levels, and the mere valorization of the saying is insufficient to the task at hand. It is indeed here that the task of dialectics must be pursued most rigorously.

13. Maurice Blanchot, *The Writing of the Disaster*, trans. Ann Smock (Lincoln: University of Nebraska Press, [1980] 1986), 116–17.

figures whose mediated and redacted speech is given back to English by Eleanor Marx.

Marx indicates that he believes the "depositions of the exploited children" permit him to "deduce the situation of the adults, especially the girls and women" in those branches of industry that lack regulation (*C*, 354; *MEGA*, 250). The question of gender appears and disappears here. Marx recognizes the specific deployment of women in highly mechanized industries. He attends to the risks and consequences that such work has for their status as women. But insofar as their speech, already inaudible, is said to be representable by the otherwise muted discourse of the boys, the girls and women are, as Gayatri Spivak says, "doubly in shadow."[14] It is because of this metonymic capacity—enabled by a sexual difference that is effaced in the same breath that it is acknowledged—that the boys' depositions can function as such fecund sources of evidence. And for this reason, Marx quotes them at length, so that the repetition of similar testimony about long hours, poor wages, and extreme exposure to physical risk comes to appear as the norm. The first task of the marked speech is to generalize itself, even across the divide of sexual difference; the second will be to make visible the limits to such generalizability. Nonetheless, and despite this double function of the male children's speech, the early citations of the reports are weighted in favor of the corporate owners and managers of the enterprises, and only gradually do the testimonials of the children acquire their contrapuntal force.

The key moment in the argument by quotation occurs almost exactly halfway through "The Working Day." It culminates in a description of circumstances in an industry "where the proper hours were from 6 a.m. to 5:30 p.m." There, boys are seen regularly to work outside of the prescribed hours, giving new meaning to the term "adulterated," to which Marx has just devoted several pages. The quotations are from the *Children's Employment Commission*, of 1864 and 1865. But it is the report and not merely the speech that is quoted, and, as a result, it is not always easy to attribute a speaking subject. The report's sociological descriptors of the children are followed by what appear to be direct citations, but they are irregular and unmarked:

> George Allinsworth, age 9, came here as a cellar-boy last Friday; next morning we had to begin at 3, so I stopped here all night. Live

14. Gayatri Chakravorty Spivak, "Can the Subaltern Speak?," in *Can the Subaltern Speak? Reflections on the History of an Idea*, ed. Rosalind C. Morris (New York: Columbia University Press, 2010), 21–78.

five miles off. Slept on the floor of the furnace, over head, with an apron under me, and a bit of a jacket over me. The two other days I have been here at 6 a.m. Aye! It *is* hot in here. Before I came here I was nearly a year at the same work at some works in the country. Began there, too, at 3 on Saturday morning—always did, but was very gain (near) home, and could sleep at home. Other days I began at 6 in the morning, and gi'en over at 6 or 7 in the evening. (*C*, 369–70; *MEGA*, 263)

It would be wrong to say that the report's recorders have transcribed the speech of the boys phonetically, or in dialect, but pronunciation is simulated with the dropped consonant in the last "gi'en," for example. What is more directly intimated is the cadence of delivery, achieved in the punctuation that underlines the clipped syntax of the sentences and the interruption of the exclamatory "Aye!" as well as the emphasis in "It *is* hot in here." The directness and transitivity of the speech is all the more apparent in contrast to the quotations in which we hear its opposite, a baroque evasion, such as that spoken by Mr. Otley, manager of a wallpaper factory, who declares, "I can understand the loss of time not being liked." Even Commissioner White, who, in the *Children's Employment Commission Fourth Report*, expresses his suspicion of the glass manufacturers' rationale for denying regular mealtimes, uses a form of discourse so laboriously indirect that Marx appears as exasperated with it as with the abuse it reports. Mr. White's text reads as follows: "A certain amount of heat beyond what is usual at present might be going to waste, if meal-times were secured in these cases, but it seems likely not equal in money-value to the waste of animal power now going on in glass-houses throughout the kingdom from growing boys not having enough quiet time to eat their meals at ease, with a little rest afterwards for digestion" (*C*, 374; *MEGA*, 267).

Where Marx is most vituperative, however, is when the factory owner or manager uses a pronominal form that simulates an identity of interests between the workers and him. The use of *we, us,* and *our* to describe the experience of workers leads Marx to a paroxysm of parentheticalizing outrage. Smith, "the managing partner of a Manchester factory," is quoted and derided as follows:

"We" (he means his "hands" who work for "us") "work on, with no stoppage for meals, so that the day's work of 10½ hours is finished by 4:30 p.m., and all after that is overtime." (Does Mr. Smith take no meals himself during 10½ hours?) "We" (this same Smith) "sel-

dom leave off working before 6 p.m." (he means leave off from con-
suming "our" labour-power machines), "so that we" (the same man
again) "are really working overtime the whole year round." (*C*, 357;
MEGA, 252)

Marx has urged his reader to "listen for a moment to the factory
inspectors," who have drawn attention to the unscrupulousness of the
managers, but when the speech of the managers themselves is quoted,
it is made the object of a critical commentary—not only at the level of the
said but at the level of the saying. This is because the ideological ruse is
not achieved in the mere statement of a falsehood; it is dependent on the
uttering itself. So Smith can be derided for being "so fond of the plural of
majesty," and the debate about the possibility that children's bodies suffer the same deleterious effects when deprived of light as do animals is
wryly adduced as proof that the mental functions of capitalists have been
adversely affected by capitalist production (*C*, 368; *MEGA*, 263).

The linguistic decrepitude of the working children is, however, seen
to be a function of the poor or nonexistent education that they receive. The
remarkable passage in which George Allinsworth narrates his sleepless
nights under the hot furnace is followed by a lengthy footnote (in both the
English and German editions), in which several children are quoted, speaking what they believe to be mathematical and historical truths. Arrayed on
the page as a kind of subterranean support for the architecture of argumen-
tation that stands upon it, the footnote deserves quotation at length—but
also reading aloud:

> Jeremiah Haynes, age 12—"Four times four is eight; four fours are
> sixteen. A king is him that has all the money and gold. We have a
> King (told it is a Queen), they call her the Princess Alexandra. Told
> that she married the Queen's son. The Queen's son is the Princess
> Alexandra. A Princess is a man." William Turner, age 12—"Don't live
> in England. Think it *is* a country, but didn't know before." John Morris,
> age 14—"Have heard say that God made the world, and that all the
> people was drowned but one; heard say that one was a little bird."
> William Smith, age 15—"God made man, man made woman." . . .
> "The devil is a good person. I don't know where he lives." "Christ was
> a wicked man." (*C*, 370; *MEGA*, 263)

Marx notes the commissioner's own remark that the girl who uttered
the last phrase "spelt God as dog," indicating that at least some of the
inquiry had taken the form of written depositions.

The footnote, one of the longest in Volume 1 of *Capital*, seems mesmerized by this speech, at once repelled by and attracted to the litany of absurdities. Ostensibly, they have nothing to do with the question of the working day, except insofar as the absence of time for education is testified to by the ignorance expressed. But if we bear in mind Marx's own sarcasm about the mental deficiency of the capitalists, the ignorance of the children performs a different and important function—at once mimetic and alienating. The fact that "boys and girls very often work overtime, which not infrequently extends to 24 or even 36 hours of uninterrupted toil," can have no other consequence than the maddened speech cited above. The children, one might say, live as real what is foreclosed in the capitalists' discourse. According to its psychoanalytic formulation, that which is foreclosed in the symbolic returns in the real. What is foreclosed, according to the text of "The Working Day," is the irrationality of capitalism, which nonetheless functions according to reason.

The footnote in which the children are heard to speak comes at the end of George Allinsworth's reported speech. It is at once a dilation and a splitting of the text, with the verbally materialized irrationality produced by the rationalization of production constituting an echo of the chapter's thematized argument to the same effect. Why does Marx insist that this argument be heard and not merely read? If I am correct, the saying is as important as the said of this argument. Recall that we have been asked to "listen for a moment to the factory inspectors" (*C*, 349; *MEGA*, 246). In German, this phrase couples the auditory and the visual senses in a particularly evocative manner: "Hören wir einen Augenblick die Fabrikinspektorien." What Fowkes translates as "a moment" might have been more "literally" rendered as the "blink of an eye" (*Augenblick*). Listen, for the blink of an eye.[15] The brevity of the moment is relative, of course, to be calibrated in relation to the endless prattle of the apologists for child labor and an extended working day. The internal sensory heterogeneity of Marx's German rhetoric is sometimes lost in the English, and the latter tends to privilege the visual sense. Nonetheless, Marx will ask his readers to "hear how capital itself regards this 24-hour system" (*C*, 370; *MEGA*, 264). And he

15. I am reminded by Jairo Moreno of the degree to which this term has been mobilized and amplified in the writings of Theodor Adorno, for whom the *Augenblick* is linked to the experience of a breakthrough, at once emancipatory and destructive, for the work of music. It is also redolent in Walter Benjamin's concept of the flashing, particularly in moments of historical crisis when a dialectical image arises from the inertia of second nature.

will reflect on the discourse of the inspectors by saying we have "heard" (*hörten*) them (*C*, 378; *MEGA*, 270). Repeatedly, if sparingly, he makes recourse to the rhetoric of audibility. Even so, the materiality of the text makes this dimension far more important than might otherwise appear to be the case if the mere frequency of that rhetoric provided us with the only guidance for how to read.

This importance is made abundantly clear when one compares the text of "The Working Day" to Marx's other major expositions on the topic. Even elsewhere within *Capital*, where machinic life is discussed and the predicament of women and children addressed in particular (as in chapter 15), the phenomenological dimension of "The Working Day" is absent, and the inscription of auditory detail is entirely absent. In "Value, Price and Profit," where much of the argument resembles the one presented in "The Working Day," there are no citations of reported speech from Commissions of Inquiry, nor any invocation to the reader to "listen," "hear," or otherwise lend an ear. In "Value, Price and Profit," the matter is one of "seeing": "We have *seen* that the *value of the labouring power*, or in more popular parlance, the *value of labour*, is determined by the value of necessaries, or the quantity of labour required to produce them."[16] The same is true for Marx's earlier, barbed critique of Proudhon, *The Poverty of Philosophy*, wherein he accuses the French anarchist of misunderstanding the nature of surplus labor by reducing the working day to a purely formal concept. There, Marx invariably introduces his citations of Proudhon with the phrase "Let us see," and what he sees is that Proudhon treats the working day as equivalent for all persons, who are then imagined to be individually capable of generating a comparable surplus each day.[17] Instead, Marx argues, the concept of labor-time must be grasped in its sociality. And, because Proudhon wrongly conceptualizes Society as a principle of generality—as the sum of relations between individuals rather than as a stratified set of antagonistic relations—he confuses surplus achieved through rationalized production with the mere surfeit of individual labor (in other words, he confuses absolute and relative surplus value). Indeed, Marx accuses him of failing

16. Karl Marx, "Value, Price and Profit," in *Karl Marx, Frederick Engels: Collected Works*, vol. 20, trans. Cynthia Carlile et al. (New York: International Publishers, [1864–68] 1985), 100–49, esp. 138–39, emphasis added.
17. Karl Marx, *The Poverty of Philosophy*, in *Karl Marx, Frederick Engels: Collected Works*, vol. 6 (New York: International Publishers, 1976), 105–212, esp. 125–30. Although the text was originally published in 1847, the English translation is based on revisions of 1885 (German) and 1896 (French).

to "see" that Ricardo had already "unmasked" the "mysteries of bourgeois economics."[18]

If the analysis of the working day can be undertaken without recourse to the reported speech of workers, what then does Marx gain from its inclusion? How does that addition, and the question of voicing that it enables, change the nature of the argument—in either its substantive or performative dimensions? It is at this point that we must theorize the relationship between dialect and dialectical method. And we may begin doing so by remembering a statement, made in yet another footnote, late in "The Working Day," that describes the successful strike by Scottish dye workers who are nonetheless finally vanquished with the violence that can be written into law by virtue of linguistic ambiguities and loopholes: "Defeated in this way by the very workers in whose name it pretended to speak, capital discovered, with the help of the judicial magnifying-glass, that the Act of 1860, drawn up in equivocal phrases like all Acts of Parliament for the 'protection of labour,' provided them with a pretext for excluding from its operation the 'calenderers' and the 'finishers'" (*C*, 409; *MEGA*, 297). As in the case of Mr. Smith, who claimed to speak as one with the workers, the law speaks in their name but acts in capital's interests. Precisely to the extent that it speaks in the workers' name—in the name of The Worker—however, it cannot speak in their voices.

Voice names the quality of a saying that cannot be reduced to the said but also of a real that contradicts (speaks against) the concept. The Worker whose discourse is heard arising above the sound and fury of the production process speaks in no one's voice. Every time we hear an actual worker speak in "The Working Day" (if via redaction), the speech is dialectically marked by its incapacity to conform—grammatically, syntactically, phonetically—to Standard English. This is what makes it audible *as such*, as the speech of a worker. Moreover, that exteriority to the norm stands in stark contrast to the normativity of capital: "Capital only speaks of the system in its 'normal' form" (*C*, 371; *MEGA*, 264). The normal form does not exist, however (this is partly the basis of Marx's argument with Proudhon). It is an inexistent fiction. Now, the inexistence of "normality" is different from that of The Worker, whose transparent speech and concomitant access to universality marks its status as unreal. The Worker's discourse exceeds the cacophonous voicings of the workers in whose collective names it, too, speaks, if relatively legitimately. The Worker, we might say, is the figure of a

18. Marx, *The Poverty of Philosophy*, 124.

possibly existent fiction. In other words, The Worker must be fabricated, and fabrication is, of course, a primary signification of the very word *fiction*.[19] If we take this seriously, if we listen to the text, we have to take on its radically historicizing implications, as well as the repudiation that it offers to every form of spontaneist politics, whether in the form of a now outmoded worker-ism or in a discourse of the multitude. For if The Worker doesn't exist, it cannot be the agent or the ground of self-representation. To the contrary, the labor of self-representation must precede its existence.

Discourse, Dialect, Dialectic

Thus far, I have sketched an opposition between the voicing of The Worker and the voicings of the workers, mainly children, whose redacted speech is embedded in "The Working Day." I have suggested that the poetic strategy of the chapter inscribes this difference by letting the "visualized sound" of a broken, grammatically marred English signify the heterogeneity not only of society but of the working class itself, that class which is otherwise imagined as the bearer of universality's future realization. And I have argued that Marx's privileging of the auditory register and his attention to the *form* of saying in this text, which distinguishes it from other of his writings on the topic, have implications for the theory and practice of dialectics. Together, these arguments may give the impression that the voicings of the workers stand in relation to The Worker's discourse as the empirical to the conceptual. I need, then, to be clear that I am not making this argument. The point may be easiest to grasp through contrast.

To make that contrast, I have in mind James Agee's famously limpid introduction to *Let Us Now Praise Famous Men*, which declares one of the most impassioned, if self-constraining, aspirations to overcome the limits of textuality in the history of literature about poverty. Agee, it will be remembered, would have relinquished writing altogether had it been possible to insert between the covers of his book "fragments of cloth, bits of cotton, lumps of earth, records of speech, pieces of wood and iron, phials of odors, plates of food and excrement."[20] Walker Evans's photographs are as close to that trace of the real as the book can get, and for this reason, they, too,

19. In the case of the reference to the *Critique of Hegel's Philosophy of Right*, the term translated as "fiction" is *Unwahrheit*. This would not have the implications of material fabrication, particularly in the literary sense, that accrues to the English term.
20. James Agee, *Let Us Now Praise Famous Men* (Boston: Houghton Mifflin, [1941] 2001), 10.

are placed at the beginning, before the text, and thereby saved from the status of illustration. Agee writes nonetheless — with more loquacity than his fantasy might have suggested — but only because of the putative onto-logical difference between the empirical and the conceptual, or, as Edward Said would have it, the world and the text. He is correct in presuming the opposition between these two. But Agee grants to "records of speech" the status of the real (whether as substantial as excrement or as ephemeral as odors). This would not be so grave a problem if it did not at the same time entail an idealization of the concept and a reification of its unity. In this respect, Adorno's "negative dialectics" offers us a more satisfying analysis, one whose proximity and seemingly direct address to Agee's phenomeno-logical naïveté makes it all the more instructive as a result.[21]

As if echoing Agee, Adorno writes that "no philosophy, not even extreme empiricism, can drag in the *facta bruta* and present them like cases in anatomy or experiments in physics; no philosophy can paste the particulars into the text, as seductive paintings would hoodwink us into believing."[22] But it is not the fetishism of the empirical that worries Adorno; it is rather a fetishism of the concept. "In truth," he continues, "all concepts, even the philosophical ones, refer to nonconceptualities, because concepts on their part are moments of the reality that requires their formation" (*ND*, 11). He advocates an "infinite" philosophy, the substance of which "would lie in the diversity of objects that impinge upon it and of the objects it seeks, a diversity not wrought by any schema; to those objects, philosophy would truly give itself rather than use them as a mirror in which to reread itself, mistaking its own image for concretion." Above all, such a philosophy would avoid the errors of the "science of empirical consciousness," which reduces "the contents of such experience to cases of categories" (*ND*, 13).

To follow Adorno's analysis requires that we read the workers as something other than a case of the category Worker.[23] The discontinuity between the characterological figure (The Worker) and any actual workers is, in fact, signified in and by the distance between their utterances, *as they appear to have been sounded* in "The Working Day," as well as in their generic structure and semantic content. This imaged (and imagined) sound signifies the remainder, that which "indicates the untruth of identity,

21. Adorno is actually referring to Husserl's phenomenology and not Agee's.
22. Theodor Adorno, *Negative Dialectics*, trans. E. B. Ashton (New York: Continuum, [1966] 1994), 11. Hereafter, this work is cited parenthetically as *ND*.
23. The linguists, who substitute the "type/token" distinction for that of case/category, merely reproduce this failure of dialectical thought.

the fact that the concept does not exhaust the thing conceived" (*ND*, 5). On one level, the text works by making audible both the aspiration to unity and the fact of heteroglossia in the language of the English working classes. It gives form to the stratification of the linguistic field that is, as Mikhail Bakhtin says, an artifact of industrial modernity.[24] If "The Working Day" were a novel and not merely a characterological fiction, then, according to Bakhtin's analysis, the multiplicity of speech genres and social languages would be completely internalized, and the movement between perspectives would be implicit. But, in fact, as we have seen, the various strata are managed, the speech forms isolated through punctuation (especially parentheses), and the spatial distribution afforded by the textual practice of footnoting. It is not doubled-voicedness that inhabits the utterances of The Worker and the workers, or even the capitalist, in "The Working Day." Marx's analytic position is always marked by its exteriority to the cited discourse, with the result being an impression of coherence within the figures—Worker and Capitalist—in relation to which the workers (appearing here in the echo of their speaking) constitute both a limit to be overcome and a residue exceeding what can be posited.

In this sense, The Worker functions like the "speaking person" of the novel, who is "to one degree or another, an *ideologue*, one who "is not a man in his own right, but a man who is precisely the *image of a language*" (DN, 333, 336). This remarkable phrase appears in Bakhtin's account of novelistic discourse, that discourse which has discourse as its object, and it is followed by an equally provocative assertion that "in order that language become an artistic image, it must become speech from speaking lips, conjoined with the image of a speaking person" (DN, 336). The Worker's disputation of the Capitalist conforms perfectly to this description, even as it plays out the pure form of the Aristotelian dialectic. The Worker is "able to syllogize about every posed problem on the basis of generally accepted opinions [*endoxa*]" and to "say nothing self-contradictory."[25] What makes the syllogism dialectical for Aristotle is that it commences from generally accepted principles rather than self-evident truths; Marx would refer to these principles (this doxa) as ideological. But what does this mean for the sayings of the workers? Perhaps that they are the image not of language

---

24. Mikhael Bakhtin, "Discourse in the Novel," in *The Dialogic Imagination: Four Essays*, ed. Michael Holquist, trans. Caryl Emerson and Michael Holquist (Austin: University of Texas Press, 1981), 259–422. Hereafter, this work is cited parenthetically as DN.
25. Aristotle, "Introduction to Dialectic," in *On Rhetoric: Theory of Civic Discourse*, 2nd ed., trans. George A. Kennedy (New York and London: Oxford, 2007), 263–66, esp. 264.

and not of the voice of The Worker as it arises but of dialect arising. What Marx's voluminous quotation makes clear, even if consigned to the nether regions of the page, is that the form of these sayings contains within itself a meta-signification. It indicates what Bakhtin would call a "potential dialect" (DN, 356). Full dialecticization would require the norming of pronunciation and speech in relation to a community of speakers' historical unification but also the sedimentation of their marginality, their nonnormativity. Transcribed as it is, the speech of the workers is thus only a potential dialect. Whether Marx "intended" for this to be the reading of "The Working Day" is here irrelevant. It gives itself to be read insofar as it makes audible the difference between the image of language as transparency and of dialect *as audibility*.

Again, a novel would have internalized this heterogeneity, importing it into the text's narration—as in the novels cited by Bakhtin and included by Marx in the category of "splendid fiction." Nonetheless, *Capital* shares this capacity to "talk about it [i.e., a language] and at the same time to talk in and with it" (DN, 358). It is therefore interesting that the moment in which "The Working Day" appears to approach most closely the generic form of novelistic fiction—when the voice of The Worker suddenly arises and a pseudodialogue occurs—is that in which "authoritative discourse" is given free rein. Authoritative discourse can be transmitted, according to Bakhtin, but not represented (DN, 344). It is defined by inertia, semantic finitude, and antipathy to stylistic innovation. But if authoritative discourse would be unconvincing as a mode of fictive speech, this very attribute enables it to function as the self-reflexive signifier of its own fictiveness in "The Working Day." Its formality and hyperbolic appeal to reason mark it as untrue, because it is overly and fetishistically conceptual. Why? Because it lacks that very heteroglossic sociality that is testified to by the reported speech of the workers.

The realism of "The Working Day" thus consists in making the speech of the workers signify the real, which, heterogeneous by definition, then provides the point of departure for The Worker's drive to universality and thus unity. Indeed, if The Worker, as figure, is the image of a language, it is the image of a language aspiring to universality, one shorn of its accent, its dialectic specificity. The tragedy of "The Working Day" is that this aspiration takes place within the terms of liberal contract, without disputing the legitimacy of the wage system.[26] So, if The Worker speaks in an authorita-

---

26. Marx, "Value, Price and Profit," 149.

tive discourse and achieves the image of universality when engaging the capitalist *by speaking in his language*, it is not truth but the *endoxa* of capitalism that he inhabits and articulates. That position has no real ground outside of history, of course; it is governed by the epistemic and material conditions of the context in which capitalism dominates (where economy functions as the determining instance of social life).

What can it mean for dialectics (as a philosophy and a method) that the workers appear as the signifiers of the real? What can it mean that their speech *contra-dicts* The Worker and only becomes audible, if not intelligible, in so doing? Among other things, that dialectic cannot be confined to the problematic of class contradiction. Contradiction, speaking against, speaking otherwise: this is the truth of dialectics and what makes it available for a history without teleology, despite the fact that, since Hegel, it has been the very medium of all teleological thought.

When Marx wrote the "postface" to the second edition of *Capital*, he had to underline his own difference with Hegel but also distance himself from those who would merely dismiss him as a "dead dog." The famously sharp distinction was one between idealism and materialism:

> My dialectical method is, in its foundations, not only different from the Hegelian, but exactly its opposite. For Hegel, the process of thinking, which he even transforms into an independent subject, under the name of "the Idea" is the creator of the real world, and the real world is only an external appearance of the idea. With me the reverse is true: the ideal is nothing but the material world reflected in the mind of man, and translated into forms of thought.[27]

This is Marx at his most reductionist, when rhetorical formula has overwhelmed critique, so it is not surprising that he must quickly add a qualifier, emphasizing the revolutionary threat and potential of the dialectic as a mode of thought characterized by negativity: "In its mystified form, the dialectic became the fashion in Germany, because it seemed to transfigure and glorify what exists. In its rational form it is a scandal and an abomination to the bourgeoisie, because it includes in its positive understanding of what exists a simultaneous recognition of its negation" (*C*, 103; *MEGA*, 709).

In 1873, the time of the "postface," Marx could reflect that his contempt for the easy dismissal of Hegel had led him to stylistic mimicry, admitting that he had "coquetted with the mode of expression peculiar to him" in the chapter on value (*C*, 103; *MEGA*, 709). But if his late critique of Hegel reiterated

27. Karl Marx, "Postface to the Second Edition," in *C*, 94–103, esp. 102; *MEGA*, 709.

the repudiation of his idealism, Marx's early engagement was motivated by his recognition of Hegel's concern with labor: "The outstanding achievement of Hegel's *Phenomenology*—the dialectic of negativity as the moving and creating principles—is . . . that he grasps the nature of labour, and conceives objective man (true, because real man) as the result of his own labor."[28] The problem, to begin, is that Hegel can only conceive of "abstract mental labor."[29] From the point of view of Hegel's idealism, which makes mental labor the measure of all labor, the verbally stunted unreason of the worker children quoted in "The Working Day" would be mere evidence that manual labor renders individuals incapable of functioning as the incarnation of spirit.

In the early writings, Marx displaces spirit with human species-being and puts society in the place of the universal: "The *real, active* orientation of man to himself as a species-being, or his manifestation as a real species-being (i.e., as a human being), is only possible if he really brings out all his *species-powers*—something which in turn is only possible through the co-operative action of all of mankind, only as the result of history—and treats these powers as objects: and this, to begin with, is again only possible in the form of estrangement."[30] Adorno pays particular attention to this early moment of Marx's response to Hegel, implying that it is the point of greatest convergence in their thought but also the point of most radical departure. He clarifies the import of the materialist rereading, however, insisting that it is not a matter of displacing the conceptual (The Worker) with the empirical (actual workers):

> The moment of universality in the active, transcendental subject as opposed to the merely empirical, isolated, contingent subject, is no more a fantasy than is the validity of logical propositions as opposed to the empirical course of individual acts of thought. Rather, this universality is an expression of the social nature of labor, an expression both precise and concealed from itself for the sake of the general idealist thesis; labor only because labor as something for something else, something commensurable with other things, something that transcends the contingency of the individual subject.[31]

28. Karl Marx, "Economic and Philosophic Manuscripts of 1844," in *Karl Marx, Frederick Engels: Collected Works*, 3:229–346, esp. 332.

29. Marx, "Economic and Philosophic Manuscripts of 1844," 333.

30. Marx, "Economic and Philosophic Manuscripts of 1844," 333.

31. Theodor Adorno, "Aspects of Hegel's Philosophy," in *Hegel: Three Studies*, trans. Sherry Weber Nicholsen (Cambridge, MA: MIT Press, [1963] 1999), 1–51, esp. 18. Hereafter, this work is cited parenthetically as AHP.

In his own rebuttal of Hegel's idealism, which follows Marx in approving the dialectic as a method beyond method and a philosophy beyond philosophy, Adorno credits Hegel with overcoming the opposition between subject and object, form and content, and thereby, of escaping Kant's melancholically modest conclusion that humans are confined to the world of phenomena, incapable of knowing the absolute. For if Hegel acknowledges the oppositions, he also claims that in grasping the limit of human subjectivity, "in understanding subjectivity as 'mere' subjectivity, we have already passed beyond the limit" (AHP, 6). But this is precisely the moment of idealism that gives to Spirit the appearance of a process of negation and reconciliation with itself toward the end of pure identity. Adorno rebukes Hegel in this context for not being sufficiently inconsistent in a manner consistent with dialectics. In other words, he accuses Hegel's system of failing on its own account, because it effaces the moment of nonidentity. And he calls for the dialecticization of the dialectic. That process receives its poetic form in "The Working Day," where the sonic staging of the inadequation between The Worker and the workers allows Marx to demonstrate not only that the concept exceeds the facticity of which it nonetheless partakes but also that the idealist absolutization of labor is itself both a material and an ideological process that short-circuits the task of politics.

If Marx is able to realize the potential of the Hegelian dialectic, it is by making contradiction work, of holding open the nonidentity of concept and empiricity as a source of invention and self-transformation. Even with the "I," which Kant, Fichte, and Hegel all attempted to abstract from the empirical "I," abstraction remains incomplete (AHP, 16–17). Shorn of any reference to a spatiotemporally bound, individuated consciousness, "I" can mean nothing, even when its functional vacuity is held open (anyone can say "I," but in saying "I," the one speaking becomes something other than "not-I"). The same is true of the term *society*, which Hegel uses to refer to a "functional complex of empirical persons" as well as the concept of labor. However, if it is true that Hegel's own rhetoric, inherited from earlier idealisms, is one that conceived spirit as original production, this conception is far from Marx's notion of labor, though both assume an initial division between mental and manual labor. The Worker is, of course, the agent of manual labor, but the manual comes to stand in for both materiality and particularity in the set of oppositions that unfold from the first division, indicating the slippage between the concept and the empirical that Adorno had diagnosed in Hegel's concept of society and that Marx had felt it necessary to theatricalize in "The Working Day." As Adorno argues, the distinction between mental and manual labor is the means by which one class reserves for itself the easier part, while making mental labor appear to be the mediation of merely physical activity, of matter itself. But by absolutizing labor, by rendering every action of spirit as labor, in order to escape its painful demands, Hegel recapitulated the ideology of his own moment and ontologized it. In "The Working Day," the characterological fiction and the staging of empirical voices as the limit of The Worker's capacity to achieve identity in self-representation stage the process by which class actually effects the absolutization of labor. The chapter assumes that "a humankind free of labor would be free of domination. Spirit knows that without being permitted to know it; this is the poverty of philosophy" (AHP, 26).

Hegel's moment is not ours. But ours, or at least that of the mid-twentieth century, had, for Adorno, become what Hegelian philosophy asserted and Marx's *Capital* critiqued: a "societalized society," in which subject and object have become one, in which everything is produced for something else, and where contradiction goes unrestrained such that pauperism increases with wealth. A philosophy that makes production into an essence is a philosophy that worships production and, implicitly, the fact that it is organized by domination. Hegel's mistake, then, is to insist that society is a concept. But it is not not concept, either. If there is no identity between the concept and its referent, the thing-in-itself, merely asserting this nonidentity only fetishizes the concept. It is as jejune to say that there is no "society in general" as to say there is no individual who is not also social. The contradiction between every real and every concept is at once an excess in the real and a negativity in relation to the concept. If this relation is confined to a narrow conception of negativity, however, the possibility for political invention is nullified. The Worker is the figure of universality for Marx, one that does not nullify the individual workers, and especially the doubly shadowed subalterns, so much as subsume them in a transcendent movement toward a value from which they have been constitutively excluded. This negation is not destructive but productive, in a manner that must remain infinitely open to a future which is, by definition, the realm of the inexistent empirical.

One must acknowledge here the degree to which the value of universality has been eviscerated in political and social movements that have arisen since the fall of the party-state, a process that commenced in the 1960s and continues to this day. And social movements organized by identitarianism (as are many rights-based movements) do not escape the charge of such universalism to the extent that they aspire to a representation identical to the interests of existing constituents. Adorno's project, aimed, it must be admitted, at the critique of totalitarianism, would force us to recognize that every aspiration to forge an adequation between concept and facticity is guilty in this respect. But the dialecticization proposed here is not, either, a mere invocation of the "to-come." If Marx shows up the fictiveness of The Worker, it is in order to make clear that this figure cannot close the gap between a concept's universality and a concept of the universal, on one hand, and between a concept of universality and the actuality of a violently divided world, on the other hand. The concept born of the communist hypothesis is one of radical equality. The Worker is the voice of that concept. The workers sound forth its inexistence, but in so doing they open the horizon in which the negative is, as already stated, a source of more.

Capital is not primarily a philosophical text, of course. It cannot be satisfied with emphasizing the mere opposition between mental and manual labor, as was the young Marx. Its analysis is relentlessly specific. "The Working Day" traverses the industries of potting and spinning, glass making and dye making. Yet, reading from within Adorno's nonschematic schema permits us to grasp the significance of those utterances that are so strikingly absent in Marx's other writings on labor-time. Alongside the duel within each concept, in the exchange between the Capitalist and The Worker, there is something like a duel between concepts. The Worker who speaks in the name of workers claims for himself the capacity to point out the inadequacy of the Capitalist's argument, but only insofar as it is not true to itself. Here, nonidentity serves the purpose of identity. What can be gained from making capitalism true to itself? In this case, merely gaining a limited working day. But such limits will have no capacity to address the fact that time itself is the medium of an extraction, of surplus value's production via the division of socially necessary and surplus labor. The Worker stands against the Capitalist as a mirroring identity, a reciprocal unity, the image of Capital's concretion, as Adorno says.

If the text hosted no other voices in the sound-image of a potential dialect, signifying the inadequacy between the concept and the thing, the "modest Magna Carta" might appear as an adequate solution, or, more precisely, a moment of true reconciliation, rather than what Marx elsewhere declares it to be, namely a deferral of more radical contradiction and, on that basis, the end of contradiction in a laborless world (let us not forget the literal signification of contradiction: of speaking against and otherwise). The Worker might thereby appear to be an already existent fiction, one in whom the workers find their voice and the means to be heard saying what they wish to say. Their desires and their interests would converge in a perfect identity. But only a pious nostalgia or a blind messianism can imagine that the end of contradiction is a historical possibility rather than the end of history—if the end of history means not capitalism's victory but its overthrow. "The Working Day" makes it possible to think beyond this nostalgia and otherwise than messianism. That Marx did not sustain this suspicion throughout *Capital*, or that he may not even have intended it, does not change the fact that the text holds open this possibility, if not in theory, as Adorno said of Hegel, then in word, or, more precisely, the saying of the words of the workers.

Concluding Contra-Dictions;
or, Speaking Otherwise than Capitalism

It has been a long time since the systematic critiques of workerism were first proffered and the last nostalgias for proletarian internationalism relinquished in the name of either critical philosophy or historical realism. Those critiques came from various quarters and made different claims. Jean-François Lyotard's late lament for the tragedy of politics expresses the disappointment of the European left in the aftermath of post-Stalinism: "The Solidarity movement, which was Marx's criterion for the existence of the proletariat, never developed. Today, such an alternative no longer exists, especially after the collapse of Stalinism and post-Stalinism, the proletariat's official representative, which, after all, in the 1960s we of *Socialisme ou Barbarie* always criticized as just another fraud. Today . . . we are now dealing with an enormous System, once called capitalism, which today has no 'challenger.'"[32] Addressing the same historical moment, this time with China as his referent, Alessandro Russo rereads the crisis in the discourse of the Proletariat in terms of its collapse under the pressures of a technologically mediated governmentality driven by the confusion of governance with control:

> In Shanghai's January Storm of 1967, the clash between millions of "red" workers and millions of "scarlet" workers led to a subjective breakdown within the very category of "working class" and therefore within the entire conceptual chain "worker-factory-class-party-

32. Jean-François Lyotard, "Resistances: A Conversation of Sergio Benvenuto with Jean-François Lyotard," *JEP: European Journal of Psychoanalysis*, no. 2 (Fall 1995–Winter 1996), www.psychomedia.it/jep/number2/lyotard.htm.

state" that constituted the ideological and organizational pillar of the socialist state. The first result was in fact the collapse of the entire institutional machine of Shanghai's party-state. . . . The promise, essential to the existence of the socialist state, of a full political recognition of workers was reduced to forms of productive and social control, disguised with loyalty to a historical-political ideal.[33]

And to provide one last example, Gayatri Spivak chastised both European philosophy and subaltern studies for their secret recourse to a metaphysics of presence, on which basis the working class could be imagined as spontaneously capable of self-representation. Effaced in this verily primitivist adoration of the working class as bearer of true self-knowledge were not only the tasks of ideological counterproduction (education) but also the fundamental and structuring differences encoded in gender and sexual difference, which vanished in the positing of an identity between The Worker and the workers.

As we have seen, Marx himself raised and nullified the question of gender and sexual difference in his claim that the words of the boy children could suffice, in their representative subalternity, to express the dilemmas of the women workers in the factories. Despite this failure, he did not thereby negate the task of transformative education. The voices of "The Working Day" are adduced as testimony to the failure of education, if partially reduced to a question of time for study. We cannot indulge the errors of a generation that reduced the question of education and ideological counterproduction to a matter of "consciousness raising" nor defer to the new antidialectical materialists, who claim that biopolitics negates the problem of subject formation. With the *Eighteenth Brumaire of Louis Napoleon*, Marx made clear that ideology is never reducible to ideas and consciousness. Epistemic transformation (education, rather than ideology) is, dialectically speaking, only possible in and through material intervention and structural change.

It is not my intention to repeat or debate the sometimes different, sometimes converging arguments cited above about the limits of The Worker as a figure around which to organize struggles for economic jus-

33. Alessandro Russo, "The Conclusive Scene: Mao and the Red Guards in July 1968," *positions* 13, no. 3 (Winter 2005): 533–74, esp. 564. Russo is here writing in conversation with Alain Badiou, with whom he shares an understanding of Maoism as a global signifier of political inventiveness betrayed. See Badiou, "The Cultural Revolution: The Last Revolution?," trans. Bruno Bosteels, *positions* 13, no. 3 (Winter 2005): 481–514.

tice, let alone opposition to capitalist exploitation. Nor do I aim to augment those critiques with an expanded theorization of exploitation in an era that no longer makes wage labor the exclusive medium and goal of "originary accumulation" or surplus value production. I have explored that issue elsewhere, as have many other scholars.[34] My aims here are more modest: to reread "The Working Day" in a manner that makes it legible as an exemplary experiment in dialectical writing—a writing that grasps dialectics as a method beyond method, and a philosophy beyond philosophy. In that project, which attempts to address the political problem of acquiring a voice in the field of representation, Marx makes the auditory register the vehicle of a performative textuality. The Worker, a concept in the mode of a character, a person in the image of a language, can be thought of dialectically not because he addresses The Capitalist but because, in his shadow, workers can be heard speaking otherwise, contradicting the transparency of his discourse, and revealing, therefore, the limits within which the concept appears to speak in their name while holding open an ideal of having a voice. We should listen, carefully.

What Adorno wrote in 1963 is all the more valid today: dialectical thought "is subject to the paradox that it has been rendered obsolete by science and scholarship while being at the same time more timely than ever in its opposition to them."[35] Around the world, the clamor to be heard resounds among those excluded from the surplus generated by the organization of a globalized, and not merely internationalized, economy, with a division of labor that extends across nations and that often uses gender as its alibi and medium. Often enough, these vociferous individuals imagine that they can bypass the labor of representation thanks to technologies that promise immediate expressivity. And they are abetted by those who insist on the need to avoid any and every mediating structure. (The protestors of "Occupy Wall Street" and in squares around the world assertively eschewed spokespeople.) Not incidentally, the medium for this aspiration to immediacy is termed *social media*, a word that implies that the task of socialization can adequately be assumed by technomedia rather than the exchange relations of a system governed by production. In substituting social media for a restructured sociality, they disavow representation

34. Rosalind Morris, "*Ursprüngliche Akkumulation*: The Secret of an Originary Mistranslation," forthcoming in a special issue of *boundary 2* edited by Nergis Ertürk and Özge Serin.
35. Theodor Adorno, "The Experiential Content of Hegel's Philosophy," in *Hegel: Three Studies*, 53–88, esp. 55.

but only because they assume that life can be contained within the field of representation. History has shown that spring quickly becomes autumnal. These social movements, depoliticized because totally politicized, become ephemeral in the moment that they collapse the difference between the real and the immediate. Their failure is thus the inverse of Hegel's, a fetishism not of Spirit but of concreteness; they do not grasp that what they lack vis-à-vis the concept (whether that concept is The Worker or the Citizen-Subject) is also a source of more, of what they might become if the universal is truly to be read as the social, and thus as that whose material incompleteness—its openness to the future of generations yet to come—is the form of its existence. Replacing The Worker with another more capacious concept, which would be more "adequate" to the real, is not a sufficient solution. Nor is dialectics itself a political solution. But as the name of a movement irreducible to "social movements," it speaks otherwise than in the name of power without collapsing into the mere sum of speakers who have already spoken.

Books Received

Buffington, Robert M. *A Sentimental Education for the Working Man: The Mexico City Penny Press, 1900–1910.* Durham, NC: Duke University Press, 2015.

Cohen, Jeffrey Jerome. *Stone: An Ecology of the Inhuman.* Minneapolis: University of Minnesota Press, 2015.

Dreyfus, Hubert, and Charles Taylor. *Retrieving Realism.* Cambridge, MA: Harvard University Press, 2015.

Dubrofsky, Rachel E., and Shoshana Amielle Magnet, eds. *Feminist Surveillance Studies.* Durham, NC: Duke University Press, 2015.

Engels, Jeremy. *The Politics of Resentment: A Genealogy.* University Park: Pennsylvania State University Press, 2015.

Erjavec, Aleš, ed. *Aesthetic Revolutions and Twentieth-Century Avant-Garde Movements.* Durham, NC: Duke University Press, 2015.

Field, Allyson Nadia. *Uplift Cinema: The Emergence of African American Film and the Possibility of Black Modernity.* Durham, NC: Duke University Press, 2015.

Kwon, Nayoung Aimee. *Intimate Empire.* Durham, NC: Duke University Press, 2015.

Lowe, Lisa. *The Intimacies of Four Continents.* Durham, NC: Duke University Press, 2015.

Luisetti, Federico, John Pickles, and Wilson Kaiser, eds. *The Anomie of the Earth.* Durham, NC: Duke University Press, 2015.

Madera, Judith. *Geography and Flow in Nineteenth-Century African American Literature.* Durham, NC: Duke University Press, 2015.

O'Gorman, Marcel. *Necromedia.* Minneapolis: University of Minnesota Press, 2015.

boundary 2 43:1 (2016)   DOI 10.1215/01903659-3340865   © 2016 by Duke University Press

Schreier, Benjamin. *The Impossible Jew: Identity and the Reconstruction of Jewish American Literary History.* New York: New York University Press, 2015.

Svensson, Patrik, and David Theo Goldberg, eds. *Between Humanities and the Digital.* Cambridge, MA: MIT Press, 2015.

Vinken, Barbara. *Flaubert Postsecular: Modernity Crossed Out.* Stanford, CA: Stanford University Press, 2015.

Watkins, Evan. *Literacy Work in the Reign of Human Capital.* New York: Fordham University Press, 2015.

Contributors

Amy Cimini is currently assistant professor of music at UC San Diego. Her research engages twentieth-century philosophy and political thought, with an emphasis on theories of the body and the ethics of experimental practice. She has published work drawn from this research in *Contemporary Music Review*, *Gamut*, and a number of edited volumes, and remains an active violist, in contemporary classical, noise, and rock idioms. She is currently writing a book about the twentieth-century listening practice, entitled "Listening in the Future Tense."

Bill Dietz is a composer and, since 2007, the artistic director of the Berlin-based Ensemble Zwischentöne. He is currently the co-chair of music/sound in Bard College's Milton Avery Graduate School of the Arts. Dietz's work examines the genealogy of the concert and the performance of listening. In 2011 he was the recipient of a working fellowship at the Künstlerhaus Lukas in Ahrenshoop and a residency fellowship from the Goethe Institute in New York, from 2012 to 2013 he was a resident fellow of the Akademie Schloss Solitude in Stuttgart, and in 2013 he was artist-in-residence of the Cité radieuse in Marseille, as well as gmem-centre national de la création musicale.

Jairo Moreno is associate professor of music and graduate chair at the University of Pennsylvania. He is the author of *Musical Representations, Subjects, and Objects* (2004). His work engages the production of knowledge with sound and aurality as its basis and materiality and technics as central concerns, and on the political wagers on such knowledge in European modernity and in the contemporary Americas. He is currently finishing "Syncopated Modernities: Musical Latin Americanisms in the United States, 1978–2008."

Rosalind C. Morris is professor of anthropology at Columbia University. She has worked extensively in South Africa and Southeast Asia, and is the author of numer-

boundary 2 43:1 (2016)   DOI 10.1215/01903659-3340877   © 2016 by Duke University Press

ous essays and books that traverse the disciplines of anthropology, literary criticism, media studies, and art history. Her most recent books include *Drawings and Accounts from Underground* (with William Kentridge, 2014), *That Which Is Not Drawn: Conversations* (also with William Kentridge, 2013), *Can the Subaltern Think? Reflections on the History of an Idea* (2010), and *In the Place of Origins: Modernity and Its Mediums in Northern Thailand* (1994). She is at work on a major monograph, entitled "Unstable Ground: Conditions of Change in South Africa."

Ana María Ochoa Gautier is a professor in the Department of Music at Columbia University. She has worked on the global politics of music circulation and histories and anthropologies of aurality in Latin America and the Caribbean.

Ronald Radano is professor of music and a senior fellow at the Institute for Research in the Humanities at the University of Wisconsin–Madison. He is currently completing a historical analysis of black musical value, tentatively titled "The Secret Animation of Black Music." His coedited volume, *Audible Empire: Music, Global Politics, Critique*, will be published by Duke University Press in 2016. He coedits the book series Refiguring American Music (Duke) and Chicago Studies in Ethnomusicology.

Gavin Steingo is assistant professor of music at the University of Pittsburgh. He completed his PhD in the anthropology of music at the University of Pennsylvania in 2010, and from 2010–2012 was a Mellon postdoctoral fellow at Columbia University. He has published numerous articles in journals and edited collections, and his book *Kwaito's Promise: Freedom and Aesthetic Experience in South African Music* is forthcoming from the University of Chicago Press.

Peter Szendy is professor of philosophy at the University of Paris Ouest Nanterre and musicological advisor for the concert programs at the Cité de la musique. He has been the senior editor of the journal and book series published by Ircam. He is the author of *A Coups de points: La ponctuation comme experience* (2013), *Hits: Philosophy in the Jukebox* (translated by Will Bishop, 2012), *Prophecies of Leviathan: Reading Past Melville* (translated by Gil Anidjar, 2009), and *Listen: A History of Our Ears* (translated by Charlotte Mandell, foreword by Jean-Luc Nancy, 2007).

Gary Tomlinson is the John Hay Whitney Professor of Music and Humanities at Yale University and director of the Whitney Humanities Center there. He is a musicologist and cultural theorist whose work ranges from the singing of the Aztecs to Wagner, from critical historiography to early-modern musical magic. His latest book concerns music and human evolution and is entitled *A Million Years of Music: The Emergence of Human Modernity* (2015). Tomlinson numbers a MacArthur Fellowship and election to the American Academy of Arts and Sciences among many awards.

Naomi Waltham-Smith is assistant professor in music at the University of Pennsylvania. Her research interests sit at the intersection of music theory and recent Continental philosophy, and she is currently writing a book on the relation between notions of political community and the way in which communities of listeners are created through the formal and stylistic characteristics of late eighteenth-century and early nineteenth-century music. She is also embarking upon a project on urban street sound, which investigates how the sonic participates in the logics and econo-mies of precarity, immunity, and biopolitics in the everyday life of the city.

Printed and bound by CPI Group (UK) Ltd, Croydon, CR0 4YY

18/12/2025

14796111-0001